Diary of a Welsh Swagman
1869-1894

ROBERTS PHOTO BALLARAT

Diary of a
WELSH SWAGMAN
1869-1894

Abridged and notated by
WILLIAM EVANS

SUN
AUSTRALIA

First published 1975 by The Macmillan Company of Australia Pty Ltd
This edition published 1992 by Pan Macmillan Publishers Australia
a division of Pan Macmillan Australia Pty Limited
63-71 Balfour Street, Chippendale, Sydney

Reprinted 1977, 1982, 1984, 1987, 1990, 1993

Copyright © William Evans 1975

All rights reserved. No part of this book may be reproduced or transmitted in any form or by any means, electronic or mechanical, including photocopying, recording or by any information storage and retrieval system, without prior permission in writing from the publisher.

National Library of Australia
cataloguing-in-publication data:

Jenkins, Joseph, 1818-1898.
Diary of a Welsh swagman, 1869-1894.

ISBN 0 7251 0246 2

1. Tramps – Australia. 2. Australia – Rural conditions. 3. Australia – Social conditions – 1869-1894. I. Evans William, ed. II. Title.

301.44940994

The line drawings appearing in this book are taken from *The Picturesque Atlas of Australasia*, Volumes I and II, ed. by Hon, Andrew Garran and published in 1886 by Picturesque Atlas Publishing Company, Limited, (U.K.)

Set in Melior by P.P. Typesetting, Melbourne
Printed in China

Contents

	Page
The diarist, Joseph Jenkins	frontispiece
Acknowledgements	vi
Dedication	vii
Introduction	ix
Extracts from diaries	xvi
Publisher's note	xvii
The diary of Joseph Jenkins 1869–1894	1

Acknowledgements

During a visit to Wales, Dr Thomas Paxon of Adelaide encouraged me to extract my grandfather's diaries, and offer them for publication in Australia. He showed me further kindness through enlisting the ready and valuable help of Dr Earle Hackett, deputy director of the Adelaide Institute of Medical and Veterinary Science, Chairman of the Art Gallery of South Australia and Vice-Chairman of the Australian Broadcasting Commission, and Mr Geoffrey Dutton, poet, author and editorial director of Sun Books. In respect of these services I wish to tender my sincere thanks to Dr Paxon.

William Evans

To Frances Evans,
the diarist's great-granddaughter.

Introduction

My grandfather, Joseph Jenkins, was born in 1818 at Blaenplwyf in the parish of Llanfihangel-Ystrad, Cardiganshire, West Wales. He was 1 of 12 children, having 5 sisters and 6 brothers. He farmed at home until his marriage at the age of 28, when he moved to farm Trecefel, Tregaron. At the age of 51 he emigrated to Australia, and returned to Trecefel after spending twenty-five years in the Colony. He died at the age of 80 in 1898. He came of a farming stock, many of them being poets of repute.

His uncle, David Davies (1745-1827) of Castell Hywel, was a farmer, preacher, scholar, and distinguished bard who composed several noteworthy poems, among them a Welsh translation of Gray's Elegy which has been judged by many as having greater merit than the English version.

His brother Jenkin (1835-1907), after a term of schooling in Hereford where he gained the prize for penmanship, returned to manage Blaenplwyf farm, and immediately undertook to improve the breed of Welsh Black Cattle, Cardiganshire Cobs, and Welsh Mountain Sheep. His animal stock won prizes in Wales and England, while he later judged at agricultural shows in both countries. Among his many prized animals, he bred a wonderful little mare, *Nans o'r Glyn* (Nance of the Vale), which took part in 268 races, being placed first in 184, second in 60, third in 16, and was unplaced on only 8 occasions.

Another brother John (1825-94) whose bardic name was *Cerngoch*, was a ready and prolific versifier and composer of englynion. A tithe of his verses and stanzas appears in *Cerddi Cerngoch* (Caxton Press, Lampeter, 1920). His prize-winning englyn to 'The Lost Sailor', is acknowledged to be a masterpiece, and is quoted in my grandfather's diary for March, 1873 (vide). To the complaining Mrs Jones of the Corner Shop in the village, he let loose the immortal phrase, *Dan ei faich mae dyn i fod (man must aye bear his load).*

Joseph Jenkins had nine children. His two eldest sons died at an early age. His daughters, Margaret, Elinor (*my mother*), Mary and Jane, left home when they married. His son Tom remained on the farm, as did his youngest daughter Anne who kept a diary throughout her adult life which is presently in the keep of the National Library of Wales at

Aberystwyth. His youngest son John gained his Doctorate in Medicine at the London University.

In his able hands, Trecefel became an acknowledged pattern of the ideal agricultural unit, which in 1857 was judged to be the best farm in the County. In 1861 he was appointed to adjudicate the same competition. From among nine contestants, an industrious farmer David Thomas gained the prize, and from the judge he received a special commendation in verse:

As David Thomas, Llanfair,
Is such a tenant farmer,
Let him have a lasting lease,
If that should please his Master.

Cattle exhibits from Trecefel won prizes in agricultural shows, and fetched top prices in the market.

Joseph Jenkins favoured the rotation system of growing crops, spoke against deep ploughing, favoured thorough harrowing, and was a strong advocate of the virtue of feeding the soil with farmyard manure. In his writings appearing in farming journals, he emphasised the importance of harvesting young hay, and preparing lucerne and clover crops to provide fodder for cattle during a severe and prolonged frost in Winter and periods of drought in Summer, adverse circumstances which denuded the land of grass. He was a capable practitioner of all farming exercises such as ploughing, scything, hedging, ditching and thatching.

A visionary in the field of farming machinery, he continued to plague manufacturers to produce a combined dung cart and distributor at least sixty years before any became marketable. He advised on the construction of dykes for the purpose of irrigation and as a means of transporting water to places of industry over rugged terrain, and on the siting of bridges when the Manchester and Milford Railway was under construction.

He was a keen educationalist. In the *History of Tregaron* (Gomerian Press, 1936), the author, the Rev. D. C. Rees, had this to say: 'The most famous person to live at Trecefel was Joseph Jenkins, a poet, and a leader of the people in the fight on behalf of elementary education.' On the 9th of September 1857, he convened and chaired a public meeting at which twelve resolutions were proposed and carried unanimously. Pursuant to this meeting a substantial school was erected and it stood monument to the energies of those who had worked so hard to bring the project to a successful conclusion.

He also founded a Cultural Society in the town and he organized its weekly meetings. Some of these were competitive and concerned with literature and poetry, items which he adjudicated. Other sessions were devoted to debates on contemporary topics and events. Among the ones handled, three might be mentioned: 'Which is the most injurious to Society, the miser or the drunkard?'; 'Which is the greater benefactor to man, the sheep or the cow?'; 'Is the perpetuation of the Welsh language, a benefit or hindrance to Wales?' (Echoes of this last debate have been heard in the land a century later.)

He was in demand in the County as counsellor on diverse matters, drawing out wills and agreements for the common man, and advising landowners on land-reclamation and drainage, and on animal husbandry. Those that sought his advice on estate management included Powell of Nanteos, Davies of Llandinam and Lord Lisburne.

Acknowledged as a poet of distinction, he composed under the bardic name of *Amnon II*, and exercised strict discipline in regard to metre and rhyme, and the special rules governing the englyn. Some eighty of his poems have been published in *Cerddi Cerngoch*, and many more remain unpublished. Englynion appear frequently in his diary, but only a few of them have been included in the text. At Ballarat (Australia) an eisteddfod was held each St David's Day. He competed at these meetings on thirteen consecutive occasions while in the neighbourhood, capturing the premier prize for an englyn each time. In 1882 his three stanzas of welcome to Queen Victoria's two grandsons, the Duke of Clarence and the Duke of York, to the Colony, were proclaimed the best in the competition, and awarded the prize. On Good Friday in 1870, he embodied 'Advice to his son Tom' in a Welsh poem of twenty-six verses (*Cerddi Cerngoch*, pp. 140-4). Its inordinate merit deserves its translation to other languages, for presently when specific instruction in citizenship is either neglected or even goes unheeded in so many homes and schools, every parent and teacher should seize upon this model directive to place before their incumbents of either offspring or pupil.

Both he and his brother John, when walking in each other's company, would compose alternate verses on some topic, and he mentions casually that he could compose poems as quickly as he could write them down. Indeed, many examples of such instant compositions appear in his diaries.

He was a Unitarian, but since that denomination had no place of worship near his home at Trecefel, he frequented St Caron's Church where he was churchwarden for many years. One Sunday he confesses to absenteeism from divine service in a verse:

A'i cloch y llan a glywa'	'Tis Sabbath day, I hear the church bell's distant call
Ai thôn yn galw arna?	To wicked folk to bend their knees in earnest prayer.
Ond mae'r churchwarden yn ei chwant	They pledge, to sin they never more will yield or fall,
Yn dysgu'i blant i gneua.	While I a-nutting go, and fail to join them there.

He believed in the Bible, which he had read more than once from cover to cover, and especially in the teachings of Christ. He adhered particularly to the tenets enunciated in the Sermon on the Mount, and the Ten Commandments. Equally, he worshipped God as manifested in Nature.

This combination of beliefs he often repeats in his diary. Nowhere does he mention Sir Thomas Browne, but his belief tallies precisely with that held by this great thinker, and which he unfolds in his treatise, *Religio Medici*, 'There are two books whence I collect my divinity, the one written of God (the Bible), the other written in His servant, Nature, that universal manuscript which is spread before the eyes of all. Those who have not seen Him in the one, have discovered Him in the other.'

The epitaph which my grandfather composed for himself and which is recorded in his diary for April 1890, is the embodiment of his faith in the impartiality of the Creator (p. 182).

At the age of 51, he decided to leave his wife and family at Trecefel and emigrate to Australia. He arrived in Melbourne harbour on the 12th of March, 1869. The reader will want to know the *reason* for this exodus at his late age. It would appear that it was intended to be a prolonged stay and not a mere visit. No relative or close friend had preceded him to the antipodes, and although he found on arrival in the Colony that a number of his countrymen had already settled there, many of them prospecting for gold, there is no record that he was lured to make the voyage in response to any such call. Again, although wealthily imbued with curiosity and an avid explorer into all things hidden from his understanding, he had nowhere disclosed that it was a burning desire to see how a young country was taking shape, which brought him to her shores. One reason can be rejected out of hand, namely that it was financial stringency that caused him to abscond from his responsibilities, because he was a successful farmer, leaving behind him a thriving agricultural unit. He was not a total abstainer from alcohol, and this he admits in a poem (*Cerddi Cerngoch*, p. 150) written on the occasion of his son John sustaining a fractured arm when he fell when riding a moke. He was not, however, addicted to alcohol. Thus, during his sojourn of twenty-five years in Australia, he seldom tasted alcohol even on festive occasions, while he was loud in his condemnation of its effects as he saw them in the Colony. The reason he left home is laid at the door of his spouse, my grandmother. She had been 19 when they were married, and he was 28. Their married life had often been marked by discord and disaffection. Even when he returned home from Australia, weakened through age and ill-health, she showed him little compassion, while his married daughters who had corresponded with him regularly throughout twenty-five years of estrangement, welcomed him on his return, and presented to him his grandchildren whom he had pined to see, and whose affection had lured him home.

My grandfather kept a diary continuously for fifty-eight years, commencing when he was 21. The first twenty-nine or thirty were written in Wales, and subsequently twenty-five in Australia, and the last three after he returned home until his death. Only one parcel of my grandfather's diaries are presented here, namely those covering the years 1869 to 1894 during his stay in Australia. These twenty-five volumes he presented to my mother on his return to Wales, and are now in the possession of my niece and his great-granddaughter, Miss Frances Evans of Tyndomen, Tregaron.

Admittedly, it is difficult to discontinue any habit which has been adopted continuously for a decade or so, but it is more difficult to determine how the stimulus to form a particular habit is first born, and in this context to decide what prompted my grandfather at the age of 21 to embark on the task of keeping a diary. It is obvious in his case that it was not at the instigation of either parent or teacher, nor at the behest of prevailing social custom, because it was rare practice. He supplies the explanation in his entry for January 1876, being his thirty-seventh consecutive diary, and the seventh in Australia.

I undertook to keep a diary to enable me eventually to correspond with others in the English language (Welsh had been the language of the hearth). I only received two 'quarters' of schooling, and that at a time when I was very young, and indifferent to learning anything beyond work on my father's farm. My first diary in 1839 gives proof of my inability to write a single line in legible form, but with persistent practice in writing a diary and letters, along with reading newspapers and books, I became able to correspond with my friends and relations in both Welsh and English.

His early Australian diaries appear in books arranged for that purpose, but sometimes when unable to procure these, he wrote on notepaper 8 ins x 5 ins which he bound together by means of thick brown twine and covered each volume in thick brown paper or linen, the final product bearing the stamp of ingenuity. The fact that they have resided in the attic of a farmhouse for over seventy years, and are presently in a good state of preservation, is proof of the durability of the initial creation.

He wrote in ink with a quill pen and never in pencil, for he intended that his writings should be read by a future generation. In places the diary exhibits examples of fine penmanship. Latterly, with the passage of years, on account of ageing, and when the fingers of his right hand became deformed by an accident with the addition of rheumatism, his writing naturally deteriorated (see specimen pages). Even the ink has only paled slightly. Three examples of the writing are shown, each drawn from separate periods. Allowing for the circumstances under which he wrote, and the difficulty under which his diaries were transported from place to place, it is remarkable that they should be so well preserved. At times the events of the day would be recorded during his trek through trackless Australian Bush, or along unmade roads, carrying his heavy swag, when his improvised writing table took a variety of forms, sometimes resting his book on bent knees, on the trunk of a fallen tree or a boulder of rock, or while reclining under a hedge when he would arrange his swag of fifty pounds or more in front of him to serve as his writing-desk. Once when a rick of straw served as his bedchamber, portions of the stalks still lay between the pages which recorded the events of the day. Falling rain had sometimes smudged his writing, but considering how often it would be exposed to the elements, such blemishes are surprisingly few. Moreover, his persistence in recording the happenings of each day which had ended at 10 p.m. and found him tired after seventeen hours of hard physical labour, is truly amazing. Indeed, he recounts that during the ploughing season he rises consistently at 4 a.m. sometimes at 3.30 a.m. when his own shadow and that of his team of horses, would be cast not by the rising sun, but the waning light of the moon.

I am given to question whether anyone, anywhere, and at anytime, has succeeded in keeping a diary through a quarter of a century, under circumstances so disadvantageous to its writing and preservation.

Naturally, the narrative which follows, and which is a précis of twenty-five years of composition cannot thrill the reader as it has done his grandson, who through the medium of the diary, has accompanied his grandfather day by day on his adventurous journey. Naturally too, the reader can only be treated to small parcels of the journey, while he is invited to bear in mind that between the incidents which are recorded, there took place many others of less interest. Thus, every single day he mentions the time of rising, the preparation and time of breakfasting, the state of his health, sometimes far from well, the nature of his day's work, the state of the weather, the exact direction of the wind, the people he worked for and their activities, and the time he retired for the night. He discusses the books he read, and the news which appeared in the Australian papers and in the *Cambrian News* or letters which had come from relations or from friends either in Wales or in Australia.

I have kept such close company with him that I have entered into, and shared in, his diverse moods. Whenever he has tendered for a job and has been accepted, or won a prize for poetry, I have been gladdened even more than he, for he might not have confessed to feeling elated. When he suffers from an illness, I have been at pains to diagnose the complaint, and suffered with him. When he has toothache, I have willed that he should have his molesting molar extracted. When he has indigestion, I am filled with an urge to advise him what to do to be rid of it. When he builds a chimney for his dwellings, which he did on four occasions, I have been anxious to turn over a few pages to learn whether it draws smoke, but I have refrained from doing so, having foresworn that I shall walk deliberately at his side, day by day.

What has drawn my admiration is his abiding philosophy under adverse circumstances, his unyielding cheerfulness in the face of cruel disappointments, his benevolent compassion for his fellow-man freely lending them (never to be repaid) monies from his puny wages, his unfailing optimism when dogged by recurring ill fortune, his implicit faith in the permanence of Nature, and his resolve to keep in unison with her laws, while labouring for long hours in return for food, and while facing the handicap of declining health and old age.

Such, therefore, is the pen-picture of my grandfather whose diaries I mean to present to the reader. The task is not easy. My purpose to share his diaries with others is twofold, obligatory and substantive. Obligatory, in that it was clearly my grandfather's wish that the thoughts he had propounded day by day should be offered for the enjoyment of others, and perhaps profit to some. Substantive, in that they record the shortcomings and successes of those years in the life of a young Colony, portraying especially the inevitable difficulties that faced a Nation emerging from its cradle, and situated so far afield from the mother-hand that tenderly rocked it. A Colony which has long since grown to the full stature of nationhood and independence.

The diaries have been severely abridged, chronologically year by year, and month by month. I have allowed my grandfather to tell his own story. Should I add remarks of my own, they appear in italics when the diarist is referred to in the third person. The headings for each month are also my own, and are meant to emphasise some event. Otherwise, the complete script is in my grandfather's own words and his telling, for this surely is the form which should be assumed for any record of a personal diary.

William Evans

Extracts from diaries.

25 April 1871

18 April 1877

2 May 1894

Publisher's note

When Joseph Jenkins arrived in Australia in 1869, Victoria was still struggling to absorb the large number of workers who had arrived during the gold rushes of the preceding decade. Politicians found the problem of providing secure employment for ex-diggers to be one of pressing importance and the 1860s was an era of fierce political debate which usually centred round the question of land control, cultivation and the development of industry through protection. Colonial fervour and reforming zeal ran high, and there was an emerging awareness of the vigour and future of Victoria.

Cultural, business and social activity were beginning to adapt to the new-found importance of Victoria. Parliament had flexed its muscles and found strength in the protectionist and land bill issues and Victorians were becoming increasingly aware that the reins of power were not necessarily linked with those of New South Wales, nor indeed, to the mother country. The bustle, independence and growing prosperity of the colony was an intimation of the bigger and better times to come — 'the lush 1880s'.

Throughout this period of optimism and growth, Joseph Jenkins recorded the events and impressions of the age from his chosen position of a rural worker. His diary distils the weaker brew of history books, giving events a sharp and immediate flavour. His concerns lie with the day-to-day struggle for existence: the cost of bread, the success of the harvest, the wages for hired labour. The raging issue of republicanism receives only passing notice, ('I consider her [Australia] too young to risk this chance'), and the capture of the Ned Kelly gang is briefly mentioned, but the treatment of the Aboriginals receives harsh though rapid comment and the reader is left in little doubt of the diarist's opinion of the 'white man's benevolence'.

Yet on the local scene Jenkins proves himself to be a valued and acute observer. His diary shows him to have been a man of firm judgment, trusting, generous, with a great love and knowledge of Nature and a certain dry wit. Perhaps not an easy man to know — there is a degree of pride which may have rubbed roughly against the more easy-going digger type — and his difficulty with the English character may well have operated against a closer intimacy. His literacy may also have prevented closer friendships for it must surely have been an unusual swagman who employed his few spare hours in writing englynion and maintaining his diary.

During the 1870s the ranks of the unemployed were affected intermittently by export earnings and weather conditions. The 1880s saw a period of unbridled extravagance in both public and private expenditure. The increasing wealth of local councils and civic pride may have been instrumental in the appointment of Joseph Jenkins as a street worker for the Maldon council. Such employment was a lucky opportunity as the great prosperity of the time was soon to draw to a close. Prices of all colonial exports fell sharply between 1884 and 1893 resulting in a fall of incomes and employment; the land market collapsed and bank shares and other stocks commenced to slide. Many of the unemployed flocked to the city, and during 1892 there began an exodus to other colonies and countries. The fires and burglaries at the Maldon hut at this time were undoubtedly attributable to the mass unemployment and vagrancy.

The uneasy atmosphere of the collapse of the boom must still have been prevalent when Jenkins sailed for England in 1894. Victoria's economic revival did not really commence for another three years, and Jenkins did not stay to see the long awaited development of Victoria's agricultural industry. Nor did he stay to commend (as he undoubtedly would have done) the first legislative steps to protect the rights of workers and ensure decent wages, or to comment on the gathering support for federation.

As a swagman, Jenkins had taken part in the development of Australia during its prosperous, expansionary era. He had been a small, articulate and, luckily, a literary individual in the vast, vague number of itinerant workers on whom the success of the rural industry depended. This condensed version of his diary provides a fascinating record of Victorian life of the period, the prejudices, the beliefs, social practices and the sheer practicalities of life in rural Victoria.

The diary of Joseph Jenkins
1869~1894

1869

March *The start of a new life*

I entrained at Aberystwyth in Cardiganshire, for Liverpool on the 8th of December 1868. Here I embarked on the ship 'Eurynime', and docked in Port Melbourne on the 22nd of March 1869. The following day I sent home my diary or log-book of the voyage by a man named Richard Jones who was sailing for London by the clipper ship 'Agamemnon'.

I slept last night at the Carnarvonshire boarding house in Queen Street, which is kept by Mrs Eleis Thomas. Two Welshmen, sleeping in the same room, had come from the Bendigo gold mines, and were on their way to the coal mines of New South Wales. I took a walk into the countryside in search of work. The morning was close and hot. Meat only keeps for a day. A few drops of rain failed to keep down the dust. The cattle are in a deplorable state; nothing but red sand and dust to be seen for miles around. The flies are very troublesome both in- and outdoors. The mosquitoes are busy at night and my face is swollen from their poisonous bites. The colony does not look very inviting for emigrants so far. Many of my shipmates are worse off than myself. I enjoy my liberty, and I will continue to keep it so. It appears to me that this splendid and well-formed city was built mostly by the English with foreign capital, for the gold is soon shipped off and only paper money remains. I call at a farm and show my credentials from home with details of my farming experience, but there was no work for me. The land looks more like scorched hearths than green grass fields. Cattle are bellowing for water, and dying by the scores. The stench is unbearable. Goats are numerous. Cartloads of rabbits are brought in for sale at 1s a pair. A single cabbage costs 10d. I walked hard. Very little to eat.

It was Good Friday and a national holiday. People in festive mood were boating in the bay and on the Yarra river. A boat carrying three young men capsized; two swam ashore, the third sank and was drowned. The occupants of other boats sailed by unconcerned. The relations of the victim when found were too drunk to attend the search for the body. I was amazed at the indifference of those at the scene of the accident. The victim of the disaster might have been a cat, so off-hand was everybody. I returned to my lodging house and slept on the sofa in the dining room because the place was full of holiday-makers.

I left my box of clothes at my lodging until such time as I can discharge my debt of 4s 6d, took up my swag and again went in search of work. Scores of swagmen like myself pass on their way to the Bush. No work. Threshing on the farms was finished, and ploughing has not yet started, for the ground is too dry and hard. Farmers are disheartened because of the long and severe drought. It is the seventh consecutive disastrous season. I walked hard in the intense heat and through clouds of dust which rise from the road, towards Castlemaine. Hundreds of vehicles head for the race-course. I turned in to witness the first hurdle race. I placed 1s on a horse and he won. I went to collect my 10s, but the bookie had fled. No more races for Joseph.

Found a bed for 6d, and left in the morning without breakfast. Unbearably hot with the thermometer registering 118°F. I came upon a large park which held some 22,000 half-starved sheep devoid of grass and water, which was carted to them a distance of four miles. Dreadful stench from the carcasses of dead sheep. I had a contest with a large snake on the road, but as I had no stick I retracted. There is no twilight in this country. When the sun goes down it gets dark suddenly. No breakfast in the morning, so I walked on thirsty and hungry. I pawned a pair of gloves which I had bought in Liverpool, for a drink of water. Began to value water for the first time in my life. Calling at farm after farm, but told there was no work.

Making for Taradale. Directed to a shattered shed where I prepared my bed from my swag. Was awakened by a traveller. He had an axe and a dog. He made to steal my bedclothes. We fought and I overcame him, took the axe from him, and sent him and his dog out into the night.

The goats, rams, and cattle around here carry bells so that they can be located in the Bush, and also to frighten away marauding kangaroos.

Presently, he became lost in the Bush, and he describes in a poem of sixteen lines how a Welshman came upon him, addressed him in Welsh, took him into his home, and treated him to food and drink. He was greatly refreshed in mind and body from this spontaneous hospitality.

April *Prospecting for gold*

Up at 5 a.m. and walk through the township of Taradale which is a neat little village. I watch a cottager's wife milking goats. There were about sixty in the flock. I take to the road leading into the Bush. It was a pity to see the half-starved cattle eating all the horses' dung that they could find. Entered another village. Called in turn on a baker, hotel-keeper and butcher asking for a little bread to eat, but was rudely admonished by each. I reached Chewton and entered a hotel and begged for a glass of water. I was given it, and having spotted my Welsh accent they asked me to converse in Welsh, for both the landlord and landlady were Welsh. I was given a hearty meal with ale. My faith in humanity was restored.

After a short rest on a bench, the landlady took me to the residence of John Lewis whom I had known in Cardiganshire. He, along with his son and brother-in-law were out digging for gold, and filling the soil into a cart. I approached him and asked, 'How much do you want for that cartload?' He looked at me awhile and shouted, 'Trecefel, what has brought you out here?' I was never more glad to meet an acquaintance for I had met none since I left Aberystwyth over three months before, and we shook hands warmly.

There are many quartz reef works here, and many of them have been abandoned. Innumerable holes in the ground from which the earth has been taken away and washed, and much of it washed more than once, to separate the precious metal. Taking it all in all it is estimated that the cost to mine each ounce of gold is £4 10s, that is 12s 6d above its real value. Digging commenced in 1850 and an immense quantity of surface soil has been removed since. The gold jobbers and bankers have been the most successful, for in the past they acquired tons of gold below its standard value. The Lewis team of three men and horse and cart when labouring for eighteen hours reckon to get gold equivalent to a wage of 1s 4d an hour. Many Chinamen walk about carrying simple riddles on their shoulders. Castlemaine was a flourishing place when the alluvial gold, up to one ounce, could be picked up each day by every digger. *(He then writes a sonnet of 172 lines on the Gold-Rush. Much of it contains a good deal of wisdom.)*

e.g.
Gold has built the biggest town,
And gold in time will bring it down.

∾

I wish you all to understand
That gold won't stick to every hand.

∾

Let us not covet useless store,
But live with plenty and no more.

I went to the market at Castlemaine and met many Welshmen there. I saw pears there which weighed two pounds. Potatoes sold at 8s a cwt, butter at 1s 6d a lb, beef at 3d a lb, mutton at 2d a lb, and hay at £6 10s a ton. Took up my swag and visited several farms where I received kindness, but not the offer of work.

I'm walking hard from farm to farm,
With heavy bedding on my arm.
I have to carry with the 'Swag',
Some useful things in carpet bag.
The day is cool with southern breeze,
which makes my labour middling ease.
I am directed here and there,
No work for Joseph anywhere.

I pass a sheep station holding 20,000 ewes which are collected into enclosures every night. Each of three shepherds had 6,500 under his care. I received hospitality in the shepherd's hut. Next day, I called with some 'Squatters' as they term the small farmers here. I failed to get anything to eat either gratis or for money. I have been told that I have twenty miles to walk before I reach any farm of renown. The grass begins to grow after the long drought. The Government offers £200 reward for information about the careless use of matches on farms. I have seen many swarms of bees in hollow tree trunks. The ants are numerous and three times bigger than the breed in Wales. The magpies are shorter in the tail than ours, but their morning song is sweeter than our thrush's. I journey towards Smeaton through fine agricultural country. Both sides of the road fenced for a distance of five miles and as straight as a gun's barrel. Better fences than I have ever seen. The posts are strong and three yards apart, with a top timber rail and five tight strands of wire underneath.

I called at a farm which had no name, kept by an Irishman, Morgan Lane. I was engaged to work for 15s a week. The food was good. I took the two horses, 'Tom' and 'Prince' out to plough, and slept with them in the stable at night. It was the best bed since that last night at Aberystwyth. The next day I was up an hour before sunrise, and beheld most wonderful colours in the sky, the likes of which I had never seen before.

How splendid was the view
To see the coloured sky.
Dark and white, red and blue,
I cannot reason why.
All things below, all things above,
Declare the Author's pure love.

Once more, I picked up my swag to leave, but the master called me back and asked me to do some more ploughing at a wage of 18s a week. I was asked to do other jobs, such as salting two pigs which one of the workers, a Chinaman, had killed, but I ploughed a large paddock with the two grand horses moving at a rate of five miles an hour.

May *Cheated of a wage*

I called at other farms, many of them occupied by Welshmen; some were kind to me and some were not, but all of them made no offer of work. The bells around the necks of cows I was told, differed slightly in pitch one from another, and their calves recognized the difference from a distance. Many of the so-called hotels which I passed have farms attached to them, and the hoteliers expect the labourers they employ to spend their wages on drink. The proprietor of one such hotel at Smeaton was a German named Minster. He employed me to plough for a wage of £1 a week. He accused me of not spending any money on drink in his 'house', and dismissed me while he refused to pay me for two weeks of hard ploughing. I dislike these 'Jacks of all trades' who take up two livings. At Smeaton, the Cumberland Hotel was also the post office. I moved to another farm where the master brought a strong yearling calf for 16s from the 'pound'. Most farmers dislike buying their neighbours' straying cattle from the pound-keeper after only a week's custody, but this farmer it appears is fond of doing this. His farm buildings have been set on fire three times, once at a loss of £500.

Thousands of acres of fertile land around Smeaton, but poorly farmed. The farmers consider it too expensive to cart farmyard manure to the land, so they pay 9s per cwt for potatoes which they are unable to grow. No land is properly cultivated around here except the townspeople's gardens. A German named Smith died very suddenly yesterday. They held an inquest on the body today. Nine of the twelve jurors were hotel-keepers, and they brought in a verdict that death was caused by alcohol. He had property, but no relations, so they gave him a decent and hurried burial with a good deal of drinking.

I was up before dawn and again beheld a most colourful pattern in the sky which I was told later meant a severe thunderstorm at sea about 130 miles south.

At wondrous sky I have a peep,
While thousands heedless sluggards sleep.
Some useless creatures cannot find
In Nature, none to please the mind.

I love a little of Bush-life now and then, when the weather is favourable, the magpies singing their sweet song and the parrots' prattle. A group of ladies in their long dresses looked elegant as they galloped by on fine horses. The 'Laughing Jackass' bird swooped down on a snake, threw it up three or four times until it was dead, carted it up a tree, there to eat it.

June *An improvised stable*

I spoke to a Mr George Hepburn about a job. He gave me a letter to his bailiff or overseer at Kangaroo Farm, Smeaton. My first job was chaff-cutting. The cutter had three knives and was worked by two horses which turned it as steadily as steam or water. It cuts forty-three bagfuls in a short time. Engaged with three other men in ploughing, harrowing, and sowing corn. The farm is well run and food is good. The butcher's boy brought 25 lbs of fresh beef to the hut in which we lived. A stream or creek runs past the hut, and this has filled after the recent rain. We enjoy a good fire in the hut because there is plenty of timber to burn. There is a good supply of potatoes grown from virgin and unmanured soil. Very little lime can be got in the Colony. The horses are fed, watered and cleaned before breakfast. Everything is done here in an orderly fashion. Meals are well prepared and served in proper time. We all work very hard from 5 a.m. till dark. Mr Hepburn has another big farm connected with the Sportsman Hotel and we took the four horses and implements over there to plough and sow corn. Rain has been plentiful here since the latter part of May. Some are sowing wheat, and some are sowing barley and oats. They are particular about ploughing and harrowing. On this first frosty morning I find one-fourth of an inch of ice on the surface of the water.

Up about 5 a.m. Drew water for the horses and tended to them as usual. In for breakfast of fresh meat, bread and tea as usual. Good stuff for a working man. Jeremy went to plough, James to sow oats and I went to harrow after him. Next day I went to a ploughing match two miles from Smeaton at a farm owned by a Mr Wright. Forty competed, and a Welshman, David Harries was judged the best. The cook, John Kelly, returned here today, he has been away 'on the booze' for a whole month.

Up at 4.30 a.m. on a very squally morning, and went to the paddock in search of the horse, 'Major'. I could not find him and returned for breakfast. I renewed the search and found him sheltering in the hollow of a big tree nine yards in circumference:

In search of 'Major' I did go,
And walked the forest to and fro.
Then after looking all about,
I did perceive his spotted snout.
It was a curious thing to me
To find him stabled in a tree.
Neck, limbs and body there remain
Warm and dry from wind and rain.
If this will ever get to Wales
They soon will say its Joseph's tales.
But Joseph will not care a pin,
Believe or not he was within.

I went out after work to shoot possums. These are innocent creatures, but bore holes in roofs and disturb one's sleep. They are principally killed for the value of their skins which are made into rugs and cloaks.

July   *A recipe for tree-planting*

I take a cart — or dray-load — of timber to Hepburn's town house. (Smeaton House.) That much firewood is consumed there each day. A regular wood-cutter is kept in the Bush, a nice old man, to provide for this regular supply. The Master prepares a new garden and he then proposes to hire a Chinaman to look after it, because they prove to be the best gardeners in Australia. Brought my bedding back from Smeaton House to the hut at Kangaroo Farm. I take the mare 'Diamond' to a veterinary surgeon at Kingston, some five miles from here. He dosed her. I pass through fine agricultural country, but tilled and not manured well.

Over the hills and muddy roads,
I lead the mare to Kingston,
I met some teams with heavy loads
Which scarcely kept in motion.

Started cutting hay and tying it at a wage of 5s a ton. Possible to do 24 cwts in a day. A stewed hare for supper was delicious. James (the bailiff) and I were cutting firewood in the afternoon. This is plentiful. In a paddock of 134 acres, the dead and fallen trees take up one-fifth of the area. Some of this timber has fallen from the effects of time, some from the woodman's axe, some at the hand of the grubber, and others blown down by strong winds. Many of the trees are barked or ringed in order to wither them, so that the land can be reclaimed for grazing.

I commenced to dig the orchard at Smeaton House, while part of it was ploughed and harrowed. Many of the apple trees are withering. They have been planted too deep in the soil. Big and thriving trees always have their roots near the surface, for heat, air and moisture are their principal nourishment. I have never seen a big tree with very deep roots.

August *Grubbing before the plough*

Heavy snowstorm has left a thick layer, but I am told that it usually melts within two days or so. I now work more at Tea Tree farm near Smeaton House than at Kangaroo Farm. I sleep well and two new blankets keep me warm. We have a good fire in the evening in the saddle room. The food is good, tea, cream and sugar at every meal, and plenty of beef and mutton. I fear that like Adam I shall be sent out of Paradise before long.

In order to get a parcel of the Bush fit for the plough it has to be grubbed out, a process which involves felling the trees, taking up the roots and burning them along with the scrubwood, and removing the stone boulders. One of the men on the farm felled twenty-five trees in five days at 2s a tree, so he is earning 10s a day. It costs £7 an acre to recover such land ready for cultivation. I have just heard the cuckoo; its song resembles the one at home, but I did not see the bird.

Hard frost, but this does not affect the leaves of the native trees. The gum tree sheds its thin shell of bark leaving a white trunk with its red stripes. Digging hard in the orchard and I covered 9 by 22 tailor's yards. The small daughter of 6 has a little garden of her own. They hold frequent balls in the big house. It is a teetotal occasion and they charge 5s for admission. Some of the lady-guests are conveyed by a four-wheel buggy drawn by two fine horses and Mrs Hepburn handles the reins well.

I grease my boots. The natives do not hold with this custom, maintaining that it does more harm than good, in that it keeps open the pores of the leather, and causes the boots to leak. I shall continue with the practice because it makes the leather pliable.

All the squatters (that is those with small farms) complain of the drought. Lambs are killed off to save the ewes. Sheep are customarily washed at this time of the year, but not this year because of the shortage of water. The grass is short and the cattle are lean for want of fodder.

September *On the road again*

It is Sunday and I washed my underclothing in warm water, and then swilled them in the running water at the creek. As soon as I hung them up to dry they became frozen stiff. When I was engaged in these ablutions, a bird in the overhanging branches of a gum tree sang, 'Believe me; believe me,' as plain as ever any lady pronounced the words. I answered back:

No, No, my bird I cannot.
I have believed too many.
Thou mayst be 'nother 'scariot,
And might'st betray me badly.

While walking through the local cemetery, I read the following inscription on a monument raised to the memory of the Hepburn family — 'Sacred to the memory of John Hepburn who departed this life August 7th 1860, aged 60 years,' etc.

A snow storm rages for two days. I am given a cheque for £4 18s in respect of my wages, and there is no more work for me. I make my way into the shearing country. I buy a new jacket and trouser at the local stores. I stopped at the roadside and tried them on. The police came upon me and accused me of stealing them. It reminds me of a man apprehended at Aberystwyth because his trouser appeared to be too big for him.

I sleep successively in a hut, (*which he dubbed Joseph's hut*), on a Mr Bateman's farm, in the Cumberland Hotel at Smeaton, Glengower Hotel, in an empty house, and one night along with a calf in a shed, where the mother-cow in the adjoining building kept bellowing all night. My billy-can was stolen while I slept.

Ultimately, I arrive at the home of my friend John Lewis at Rheola or New Berlin, near Castlemaine. It was very hot.

Light, variable northern breeze,
Was welcomed like a friend.
It came more pleasant by degrees,
And crowned the journey's end.

Mrs Lewis's goat gives two quarts of milk daily. She has a cow too. The goat comes when called, but the cow takes no notice; she comes when her udder is full. Price of flour has risen from 27s a sack to 47s. Potatoes, 7s 6d a cwt. Butter, 2s a lb. Cheese, 1s 3d a lb. Mutton, 1½d a lb. Beef, 3½d a lb. Pork, 6d a lb.

John Lewis and his son, horse and cart, a new puddling machine, with provisions for a week, proceed to dig for gold at a fresh claim at Sandy Creek, Newstead, nine miles from here. I am going with them.

October *Hard labour earns little gold*

Great quantities of alluvial gold were found in this locality some ten years ago. Eight loads of surface soil were puddled and washed, but only one pennyweight (*equal to 24 grains or 1/20th of an ounce Troy*) of gold was extracted from it. Rain has stopped operations temporarily. There would appear to be sufficient for the diggers to wash and puddle for six months. Under a new Act the Government is selling land in order to build more public works and extend the railways. Yields of gold during subsequent days by the Lewis family were 9 pennyweight from 20 loads of soil, 6 p.w. from 27 loads, 4 p.w. from 28 loads, 6 p.w. from 28 loads. It seems poor wage for four people with a horse and cart, and puddling machine, during a period of fourteen days. It would be better to dig and puddle land for cultivation.

I received a letter from home, which took sixty-four days to travel, informing me that my second son Lewis, aged 20, had died after an illness lasting five days. (*He writes an englyn and two verses on this sad occasion.*)

November
A neglected labour force

It is Sunday, the Lewises have gone to chapel. I remain in the house reading Christ's Sermon on the Mount, the Colonial papers, and the Weekly Dispatch. A certain Mrs Beecher has written disparagingly of the late Lord Byron. This is in very bad taste as he is not alive to defend himself.

About 4,000 sheep pass the house daily on the way to Melbourne to be slaughtered and shipped to England. Fat sheep can be bought for 3s. Haymaking has commenced in the Castlemaine district. The hay is mown with a scythe and cocked on the second day and kept for a fortnight when it is carted to a rick. I am told that it is in good condition and green when it is fed to the cattle.

Today (the 9th of November) they are celebrating the Prince of Wales's birthday. The Colony thinks and talks of managing its own affairs without the assistance of Great Britain, the mother-country. I consider her too young to risk this chance. *He writes a forceful and constructive letter to the Editor of the 'Australian', under the title, 'Pity the Swagman', in which he describes their destitute plight and emphasises the need for the Colony to use this potential labour-force to improve agriculture, to promote industries, to construct water-works, to build cities, and extend the railways. He suggests that a tax of 1s should be levied annually on every acre of neglected land which has been fenced by the squatters.*

Finding gold-digging a fruitless adventure, he settles up with his host and employer John Lewis, paying him £1 10s 4d, and has £1 7s 6d left to sustain him on his prospected journey to find work at hay-harvesting. He picks up his swag and leaves.

I stopped one night at the Cumberland Hotel at Smeaton. Could not sleep much because of the rowdyism of the drunkards. I was up early. I visited the show ground. Saw a combined reaper and binder for the first time. Trick cyclists travelling at twenty miles an hour were picking up 4d bits laid on the ground. I witnessed a shearing match, the quickest finished within 9 minutes, but made several bad cuts in the skin. One interesting exhibit showed forty-seven different eggs layed by the Colony's wild birds. It was a great show.

I took up my swag and made towards Ballarat. I passed through fine agricultural country and arrived at Creswick, a small shire town, where

I bought provisions before entering the Bush. Gold-digging, both alluvial and quartz reefs, were much in evidence. I came to a town called 'The Miner's Rest'. It had a store, two churches and a post office.

I was engaged by John Wilson, at Spring Garden Farm, Mount Blow Hard, at 15s a week until hay-harvesting time, and shown into hut. Weeding a paddock growing mangold wurtzel. There were more weeds than mangolds. Wilson has two sons and two farms. He has sixty milch cows and finds cheese-making more profitable than butter. The gardener and I went in the direction of Lake Learmonth to cut thistles, because under the 'Thistle Act' every farmer is under heavy penalty to commence thistle-cutting before the end of this month.

December
Haymaking

Nine mates in the hut. They are noisy and restless. The circumstances do not encourage writing and reading. The Master has gone to Ballarat to fetch a dozen more Chinamen to help with the harvest. He already has twenty-five hands here. Here, a mixed crop of corn and hay is termed hay. The reaper has started cutting the barley and hay which the Chinamen bind. Three horses in one of the three reapers. I, and another, follow the scyther, binding wheat. Thermometer registers 135°F (*sic*) in the shade. I drink large quantities of whey and oatmeal water to quench my thirst. Ice blocks are brought from the factory. It turns chilly in the evenings with the temperature falling to 35°F. Cartloads of gooseberries and cherries are ripe and are wasted.

To help with the hay-carting they have field and yard elevators. These lift a whole loadful of hay on the wagon as one operation on the field, and similarly in the yard it lifts the load to the rick which may be forty feet high. Horses are numerous and cheap; they are worked very hard. Most of the land, and the best land about here, is owned by one man called the 'Big Clerk' (*sic*). He places much of it in the hands of his agents to make the best of it. Wilson is one of them.

The hay harvest is over, unwanted labourers are paid off immediately and have no work for seven months of the year. There are insufficient public works which could employ some of them. Some of the oat straw is so strong that at meal-breaks the binders make musical flutes of them, as well as other instruments, and form a regularized straw band which plays quite good tunes.

On Christmas eve, many of the workmen bother the Master for money. I collected three sovereigns, and walked ten miles to the Welsh eisteddfod at Ballarat on Christmas day. There I recited twenty-two verses of greeting while I stood on the staircase and was warmly applauded by the few that could understand the verses. I was also awarded the first prize of £1 for the best englyn which an Englishman would find it difficult to recite:

Hwch a moch, un-goch, gachog-
  pherchen
Ei pherchyll yn fferchog.
Och, och yw rhoi llyw na llog
Yn llaw yr analluog.

The twenty-two verses which formed his address are also in Welsh and are recorded in his diary, and are of commendable quality.

Four horses were dispatched to bring the steam engine, the threshing and winnowing machines, the shaker and the straw elevator. The last three units were left behind because the driver, who was drunk, got stuck somewhere. He was paid off immediately. I was detailed to build the straw rick; the straw elevator was worked by hand and a boy of 14 could handle it. All the machines worked well.

1870

January *Following the threshing engine*

Was up at 4 a.m. on the farm of John Wilson, Spring Garden, Mount Blow Hard, near Ballarat. The threshing machine's whistle blows at 5 a.m. and all hands attend for work. Rain stopped operations for two days, when the mangolds were singled, and more corn cut. When threshing recommenced nearly 1,000 bushels of corn were sacked, but the work is as yet only half-completed. The machines and their teams are preparing to leave. I went to the office to draw my wages, and was given a cheque for £5 and 10s in cash. Mr Wilson wanted me to stay, but I decided to join the threshers, for my inclination was to follow the engine in order to see different parts of the Colony, and acquaint myself with the different modes of farming. I went to prepare my swag and went to the hut where I prepared to sleep in spite of the cursing and swearing among the card-players.

Took up my heavy swag and walked three miles to Mr Thomas Kinnersly's farm, Burrombut (*now Burrombeet*) where the engine was in position to start. It became very hot and many of the men had their noses burnt. A strong blade of oat staw entered my eye as I was building the big stack. I could not eat my dinner and went to lie in the stable. It improved with time, and I resumed work on the stack. The corn consists of wheat and barley. The grain looks healthy and the yield is twenty-seven bushels an acre. The farm is orderly and the meals are good, while Mr Kinnersly presides at table, and the meal is unhurried. It is so pleasant to be governed by somebody. We moved to another smallish farm, and again to a bigger one near the town of 'Lake Learmonth'. Here I met Joseph Griffiths from Carmarthenshire, a widower with three children who has been here for eighteen years. The farmer here is David Kinnersly, Thomas's brother. I get a splendid view from the top of the stack, but the grass-land looks miserable; no feed except the withered strong Colonial grass. The machines have returned once more to John Wilson's farm, Spring Garden. It is very hot, 120°F in the shade. There are forty-five people at work here, eighteen of them attending the thresher. I send £5 to Mr John Lewis at Forest Creek. The rain comes and fills the tanks about the house. The temperature has dropped to 40° F.

We next moved to Mr William Scott's farm near Creswick, and this too appears to be a tidy unit. The food is good, and Mr Scott seems to be one of the most superior types of farmer I have met out here, but I must not speak too soon, having seen people kissing on entry and cursing on departure. Had a paper and two letters from home.

February *Clue to his bed of straw*

The straw stack measures 16 by 40 yards. They do not care much about the wheat straw here, and all is used for either bedding or litter. The rye straw is kept for thatching, and the hay-oaten straw is carefully kept for animal fodder. A servant girl deals with the produce of thirty cows. It is hard work and she deserves the good wages of 15s a week. We threshed nearly 600 bushels of good wheat during the afternoon. Did my customary ablutions on the Sunday.

The engine moves to Andrew Scott's farm after working eight days at his brother, William Scott's farm. He keeps many young apprentices to learn this important trade of farming. He keeps 30 milch cows and 120 other cattle, many young horses, as well as store and fat pigs. Young girls of 14 are learning how to milk. The engine moves back once more to John Wilson at Spring Garden Farm where there is only one stack of barley to thresh. It yielded forty bushels to the acre. The straw had rotted after remaining in stooks for six weeks.

We have moved to the Rose, Thistle and Shamrock Hotel. We (eighteen of us) sleep in a small stable which has six stalls, and there we threshed 300 bushels of wheat.

Arrived at Spring Brook Farm, Miners' Rest, near Ballarat. This farm of 600 acres is kept by H. F. Leech. It is encircled by creeks and the soil is fertile, but only part of the land is cultivated properly. It holds over 1,000 sheep which enrich the pastures here as elsewhere. Mutton is plentiful at meal times, and three sheep are killed daily to feed the big staff.

I have never before seen such a brilliant moon, and similarly stars. They enable one to read the smallest print. Anyone looking too long at this moon would be temporarily blinded, and develop the malady known as 'moon blindness'.

Around here they burn the stubbles, and consider that this provides good manure. I think so too provided rain follows, otherwise the strong wind will blow it off the surface of the soil, and render the process useless.

I am up early on a beautiful morning. Numerous cockerels are crowing. I pity the water fowl. The geese and ducks look miserable for the want of water and moisture, for the adjoining creeks have dried up.

They are running short of bags to hold the grain, and Mr Leech has purchased a bale of 300 at 13s a dozen. They are imported from Britain and each bag holds four bushels. In Cardiganshire, they would cost 18s a dozen!!

We are now at Mount Blow Hard Farm, managed by Robert Ward. It is close to the Ballarat coach road, Ballarat is nine miles away. Some six or seven coaches pass to and fro daily from Castlemaine-Clunes.

Passengers are charged 3d a mile by the ordinary coaches, but can ride cheaper by the opposition coaches. The thresher was next taken to a Mr Morton's farm, Libona, which I named the 'Tyrant's Couch'. All in disarray here, and no civil word from the Master. We were glad to get away.

While travelling from farm to farm following the threshing machine, he sleeps on straw under the machine or in a barn. From his diary recording these excursions, bits of straw fall out, revealing the nature of his bedchamber. The interleaved stalks of straw have rested therein for over a century.

March *Advice to his son, Tom*

He continues to travel from farm to farm as one of the team of eighteen, to thresh the newly harvested corn. It must have had the appearance of a real 'travelling circus' with horses dragging the machinery consisting of the engine, winnowing machine, and elevator, and with the men trailing behind in the procession. The diarist was entrusted with the task of building the straw-stacks.

Consecutively, they visited the following farms: James Allen, Mount Cavern Farm, Ascot, where he pours praise on the best team of four horses he had yet seen in the Colony. Since the wells had dried up, water for the engine had to be transported from a distance. This was the curse of a fine country. At W. Finlayson's he found things in good order, and the food was excellent. John Shaw kept well nourished pigs and twelve milch cows. William Young, farming near Ascot, told him that his only daughter was killed by lightening on the farm five years before. Back again with James Allen, when it was very hot with temperature 102°F in the shade. John Doyle, farming at Cogle's Creek had nine children, he was neglecting the land, and meals seemed unimportant to him. They re-visited David Kinnersly's farm at Lake Learmonth.

On Good Friday, the threshing engine lies idle, and he composes a poem in Welsh, in which he gave advice to his son, Tom.

Cyngor i'w fab Tom

Advice to his son Tom

O! gwrando, f'anwyl blentyn,	*O Child! regard my warning,*
Tad arnat sydd yn erfyn	*Attend your father's pleading,*
Am gym'ryd pwyll, rhag myn'd ar gam	*Take pains lest you should walk astray,*
Gwna fel bo'th fam yn gofyn	*Heed well your mother's bidding.*
Pan delot ti mewn oedran	*Know well when you grow older,*
I ffurfio barn dy hunan,	*Your own opinion render.*
A 'imaes o law dy dad a'th fam,	*For when you leave your parents' care*
Cai ateb am y cyfan.	*You have yourself to answer.*
'Rwy'n teimlo dyled arnaf	*I feel it is my duty*
I dy gynghori'n gyntaf,	*To first advise you rightly,*
'Waith ysgol profiad geir o hyd	*But in the end experience tells,*
Yn hyn o fyd yn benaf.	*And in this world counts mostly.*

Dysg ddarllen a 'scrifenu,
Dysg rifo a sillebu,
Dysg roi dy feddwl yn ddi-fai
Ar bapur a'i fynegu.

Rhag treulio oriau segur,
Dysg gadw 'dydd gofiadur';
Caiff rhywrai addysg yn ddi-os
Wrth edrych dros dy lafur.

A dysg ddefnyddio'r nodwydd,
A gwellaif a'r gwniadydd
Dysg ledro'r bel a'i bwrw i'r wal
Ar ddwy law fel eu gilydd.

Dysg borthi'r fuwch a'i godro,
Dysg nodi'r oen a'i gneifio,
Dysg hau a medi mewn iawn hwyl,
Dysg gasglu'r yd yn gryno.

Learn to read as well as write,
Learn to count and spell aright,
Write down your thoughts in proper
    form,
Explain them too in clear light.

No idler be, hold sloth at bay;
Record events each passing day.
Some one will profit from your work,
And praise your deeds alway.

Do learn to ply the needle,
The shears and the thimble.
Throw back the ball with either hand
With equal skill and mettle.

Learn to feed the cow and milk it.
Learn to rear the lamb, and shear it.
Do sow and reap in proper time,
Bring home the corn, and store it.

∽

Cynila ffrwyth dy lafur,
Daw'th enill eto'n gysur;
A phaid cam elwa pethau'r byd,
Er poen i'th gyd-greadur.

Paid coelio pob peth glywot,
Paid chwenych pob peth welot;
Paid meddwi'th serch, waith dyna bla,
Am wrthrych na chyrhaeddot.

The fruits of well-earned labour,
Preserve for thy gain later.
Don't ever gain from worldly things
Through pain to fellow-creatures.

Believe not all you hear,
Nor all you look at either.
Don't aim at goals beyond you reach,
Nor grasp things far and near.

∽

Y penaf peth it' wneuthur,
Cydnabod Awdwr Natur;
B'le byna' byddot ar dy daith,
Mae Ef a'i waith yn eglur.

Holl ddyled dyn sy'n amlwg
Mewn geiriau byr a diddrwg;
Car dy gymydog fel dy hun,
A'th Dduw fel un mewn golwg.

Cais aros yn dy annedd,
A'i gadw mewn tangnefedd;
Addola Dad sydd it' môr dda,
Mewn ysbryd a gwirionedd.

Above all else remember,
To praise the World's Creator;
For whatsoever path you take
You're bound to Mother Nature.

It is man's bounden duty,
Throughout his life, and daily,
To love his neighbour as himself,
And serve his God Almighty.

Give unto Peace its merit,
And make its calm a habit,
And worship God where'er you go.
In truth as well as spirit.

∽

The absence of entries for the six months, April to September is explained on the 4th December, where he records that his diary among many others of his treasures were stolen. He castigates the thief in verse:

I've lost the labour of my brains,
Invaluable treasures, future gains;
If I had lost a cheque for cash,
Compared with these, it would be trash.
You honest man I crave on thee
Return'st my writings back to me.
The biggest knave, the worst of tramps
Wouldn't keep my books for sake of stamps.*

(Included among the lost property were six shillings and three pennyworth of postage stamps.)

October *In praise of work*

I called at Spring Vale Farm, Learmonth, and saw the Master, namely David Kinnersly. When I inquired if he could give me work he directed me to the cookhouse for breakfast. This was good news for a hungry man. He asked me to finish building a wall and instructed me to cart stones which would be suitable for the coping. I was glad that I had been accepted, because I was tired of perambulating about in the Bush, lugging my heavy swag. The stones were not to my liking for the purpose of wall-building, for they were hard and global and were similar to the projectiles that the Prussian and French armies have been hurling at one another, although some of the stones I used weigh 3 cwt. How much more pleasant though it is to work at a well-conducted farm, instead of carrying a heavy swag around the country, and bearing the titles of beggar, loafer and worse:

Of all the stations man may have,
From mighty monarch to the slave,
The daily workman gets the best
In health, in joy, in meals and rest.
He has no cause within his span
To hate or envy any man.
This world revolves in form and fame,
But let him pray to stay the same.

November *Defeat of Napolean*

The English mail has arrived and I see it reported that the Pope in Rome has been unseated from his see. The papers also confirm the complete victory of the Prussians over the French, and that Napoleon III is a prisoner along with 150,000 French soldiers and 20,000 wounded or invalids. Also captured have been 3,000 cannon, and 40 million francs. Paris is in a state of siege, and the Prussians are preparing to bombard it, but they are first holding a prayer meeting!

A severe thunderstorm has broken out, and severe flooding has followed. My wall holds well. On Sunday I did my customary ablutions and settled down to read a complete sermon in an old 'Australian Journal' which has the heading 'A lay sermon by "Humbug" '. Especially true are two quotations, the one biblical and the other by the poet Pope:

'By their fruits ye shall know them'. (Matthew vii.20)

'For modes of faith let graceless zealots fight,
His can't be wrong whose life is in the right.'

(Pope, *Essay on Man*; Epistle III)

I had not read Pope's essay before coming to the Colony, but I have written lines which have borne the same meaning.

Harvesting barley. Up 5 a.m. which gives me time to dress and wash, and feed and groom the horses before the breakfast bell goes at 6 a.m. The English rye-grass in the paddock is knee-high. One half of it had been top-dressed with farmyard manure and the other half with bone manure. I am unable to tell which of the two is the better crop.

A large number of swagmen in search of work, call at the farms, but they fail to be employed. A letter from home and posted there on the 5th October arrived here on the 25th of November.

December *Robbed* I was having a talk with the Master's brother-in-law, Oliver Barclay, and we had an argument about honesty. He maintained that every man should be considered a rogue and a thief until he had proved himself to be otherwise. I disagreed with him. *Ironically, three days later he was robbed. He lost his wallet, his diaries (already referred to), account book, dictionary, book of poems, private papers, postage stamps, certificate of voting rights, recommendation paper, and other valuables.*

While the other workers were engaged on the hay I was sent to plough. The ground was very hard. At times I was glad to stand in the shadow of the horses to protect me from the rays of the scorching sun. Last year promising crops of wheat were cut down as hay:

Which resembles a warlike strife
To cut the wheat when blooming life.
Good thriving crops are cut for hay
So bread may well be short some day!

Just discovered that my penknife which I have carried in my waistcoat pocket for nine years, is missing. I seem to be unlucky these days in regard to losing things. Abundant crops of gooseberries and cherries which are sold for 2d a pound. We have started to reap sixty-six acres of barley.

It is Christmas day. How different to the one last year; then it was so hot I could not bear any covering at night. Today (Sunday), I feel it too cold to sit down to write under a clod roof.

After finishing reaping the barley, we separated to do different jobs, some to weed mangolds, some to scarify the fallow, some to fill drains, some to dig wells, some to cut brushwood, some to dig around the roots of recently planted trees. I took a horse and cart to get coarse grass from the lake-side out of which thatching ropes are made.

1871

January
Appreciating Shakespeare

This is my thirty-second diary and the third in this Colony. I am still in the employment of David Kinnersly at Spring Vale Farm, Learmonth. The first day of this year falls on a Sunday, a day for washing my underclothing and later to write letters and to read. I have written a seventeen-page letter to my eldest daughter Margaret, and twelve pages to a friend in London.

He writes two verses on 'Gold' and three verses on 'Life' in Welsh, conveying many commendable truisms.

Today I have read several pages of Shakespeare's writings and I regret that I did not get the opportunity of acquainting myself with his works earlier in life. Although his plays were written some 270 years ago the views expressed therein apply equally to today's events.

Nearly a score of swagmen pass by in search of work, but to no avail. I finished thatching the barley stack and prepare to thatch the big hay stack. Severe thunderstorms. Three people were killed by lightning near here three days ago, a hay stack was set on fire, and cattle killed.

We went to reap and bind the wheat. The crop is poor and full of thistles and weeds, and is unlikely to yield four bushels an acre of poor sample. It cost about £3 10s an acre to produce.

Many swagmen are around looking for work; they are refused food and drink. The farmers are retaliating, because in former times the swagmen would not work for any money. The idiom, 'The strongest hound takes advantage of the bone-picking' applies.

Rebellion breaks out in Ireland, and emigration to the Colonies increases. Four hundred sheep arrived at the farm. They are in good condition and they were bought for less than 1s a head. Altogether there are over 2,000 sheep on the farm.

February
'Too many cooks'

Twelve men were engaged on threshing barley. The work stopped abruptly when the big driving belt broke. A messenger was sent to the local stores for a few pounds of copper rivets, and hours went by before the belt was mended. (*Four days later a new belt arrived from Melbourne costing £21; it was strong and liberally rivetted.*)

The shaker of the machine ceased to work because of the loss of a small key, and each member of the team had suggestions how it could be put right. Swans and ducks in large flocks on the adjoining lake appeared to be mocking us as we engaged in our engineering disputes. All was confusion; one said this and the other said something else.

'The key is lost'. 'No such and such'.
'Stop, I will mend the shaker'.
So every man knows quite as much,
And more than any other.

Each day he enters in the diary the time he got out of his bed, mostly expressed precisely as 'I was up at 4 a.m.' or more generally in terms like, 'I was up before dawn', 'I was up before the sun appeared', 'I was up in the light of the moon', 'I was up before anyone else was astir', but on Sundays the usual expression would be, 'I was not up before 6 a.m.' Throughout his twenty-five years' sojourn in the Colony he rose very early.

I followed the thresher to another farm, 'Labona', where we were to thresh two large stacks of wheat and barley for a Mr Morton who was a magistrate and an ex-M.P. The governor of the engine broke, and the bad-tempered magistrate was cursing and swearing, demanding that the engine should be driven without the broken part. Later, he sacked one of the men because he could not speak proper English, and the horses were jibbing because they could not understand his words of command. So, the would-be 'grammarian' paid off one of his men for bad English!

This magistrate was to demonstrate 'Justice from the Bench'. When he discovered that he had over-paid four men, he deducted 3d from the wage of the remaining eight members of the team!

The Franco-Prussian war continues and France is getting the worst of it. In the course of building a wall I crushed my thumb and two forefingers of the right hand.

I maimed my favourite fingers,
The reporters of my brain.
I would rather lose five others
And suffer twice the pain.

March *Takes up his swag again*

Two loads of wheat went to Ballarat and sold for 4s 6d a bushel, together with a load of good potatoes at 30s a ton. It is rumoured that we are to be paid off because Mr Kinnersly is going to give up cultivating and going in for grazing. His grain land is covered with hog's weed. He now has 3,000 sheep in three flocks of 1,000 each. When I was paid off, I asked the Master for a testimonial and he certified me as a 'skilful man on a farm'.

I went by train to Ballarat, a distance of twelve miles, and paid 2s 6d for the ticket, yet the fare from Ballarat to Castlemaine, a distance of 54 miles, is the same. I went by cab to Sebastapol, a journey which only cost 3d.

At Ballarat I visited Mr Roberts, the photographer, and asked him to take my portrait in three circumstances, namely at work, spending the wages, and swagging the Bush with my billy-can. He agreed to do it for £1 5s. (See frontispiece) *To each state he composed a poem, devoting twenty-four lines to the first, twenty-two to the second, and twenty-four lines to the third. A sample only of these is given here:*

At work:
The proudest man was never made
To laugh and scorn the pick and spade.
Our duty is to do our best
Before the time we'll have to rest,
And make this world as we go round,
A better shape than it was found.

Spending wages:
Now here I am in great renown,
With twelve pound cheque* to knock it down.   *Recent wage.*
I talk of politics and land
With one eyed 'Argus'** in my hand.   ***Australian daily newspaper.*
I have no more guardians when I'm flash,
The wet-store keepers smell my cash.
The landlord now will shout and greet,
When all is gone he'll show the street.

Swagging in the Bush:
Here I am like a roving thrush
Parading through the lonely Bush.
I have the Natives' spear in hand,
Though Forests' beasts I can't command.
The olden maxim tells the man,
That he would lord the Forests' Clan.
To cook and eat, to sleep and pray,
Where forest music dawns the day,
Is gift of love in spacious hall,
Is reading room from God to all.

I obtained employment with a Mr McAndrew of Cattle Station Hill (or Five Mile) Farm, situated between Creswick and the Clunes. He is a Scot and his wife is Welsh.

News has just reached us that Paris has surrendered. The proud city was starved out. I remember the Duke of Wellington saying that a fortified Paris could be starved out by any strong and skilful enemy. Generals Molke and Bismarck have proved him true.

This is St Patrick's Day (17th March). It is kept holy and wet by the Irishmen, for nearly all of them get drunk.

I rise at 3 a.m. to plough a paddock which is a mile long. I plough 1¼ acres each day, when the horses travel fourteen miles pulling the plough. The ground is very hard after the frost, and the plough-shares need frequent sharpening.

April *Economics applied to ploughing*

A census has been held, but it cannot be an accurate count, for thousands of swagmen sleep in the Bush.

Mr McAndrew has acquired a double-furrow plough, so my services are dispensed with. Machine power leads to redundancy among labourers. In this instance, the work carried out by the two-furrow plough, needs one man and three horses, while the equivalent task performed by the single-furrow plough needs two men and four horses, so I am declared redundant, get the sack, and take to the road once more.

Few honest persons, with rightful law
Do keep this world together.
The major part cares not a straw
If John should tumble over.

I presented my wages-cheque at the bank, but they refused to cash it. There should be a 'Swagmen's Home' in every town which would provide overnight accommodation for swagmen, as an alternative to paying 1s a night in a hotel, or sleeping out in the Bush. The last arrangement is my present lot. I find my present swag three times too heavy for travel, and too light to meet the bitter cold mornings. My medical chest now only contains cayenne pepper and eye-water. My laudanum bottle, which I brought with me from Liverpool has broken. I have found it to be excellent medicine when I used it on four occasions. I have also run-out of quinine. I am walking towards Bullarook forest, calling at several farms on the way, but none needed labourers. Potato-digging is in full swing, but they don't want my help. Potatoes are sold for £1 5s a ton, and it costs 6s to 7s to dig them. I meet with upwards of fifteen swagmen every hour on the road. For every labourer at work, there are five out of work, and yet the fertile land calls out for proper husbandry.

May *A wayside feast*

I was frying a meal of mutton chops and potatoes, and went some thirty yards' distance to collect some watercress. On my return I found that nine pigs had consumed all. The pigs were owned by the local butcher, and fortunately he had witnessed the hogs feasting at the swagman's table, so he invited me into his shop and presented me with a liberal consignment of meat.

I came upon a brook with a constant run of spring water. It could drive a big waterwheel and develop eight-horse power, but they prefer here to rely on the plentiful supply of firewood to drive their steam engines.

The failure of the grain harvest has left the farmer impecunious and unable to pay for labour. Thousands of wild duck fly across my path and there are plenty of rabbits, but I have no gun which could bring a little delicacy to my table. Still tramping and calling uselessly at farms for work, some five miles from Dean. Presently I sit on a log enjoying a meal of beef steak and potatoes. Neither the Queen of England, nor the Pope in Rome, have partaken of a better repast, but I wish I could get work. I asked a farmer if I could sleep in his barn; he declined, so I spread my swag in my 'spacious bedroom'.

Arrived at Smeaton where I was two years ago. The two qualifications required of the young are dancing and piano-playing, not milking and butter- or cheese-making. Smeaton district, once considered the garden of Victoria, is now a ruinous area from continued exhaustion of the land. The farms are over-run by weeds. There are numerous deserted homesteads. Landlords are letting their land for 5s an acre to tenants who have no capital to improve it. Two-thirds of the farmers are unable to pay their rates which only amount to 1s in the pound. I walk back again in the direction of Bullarook's potato gardens and cheap meat. I start ploughing at David Miller's farm near Smeaton. Miller himself is a good ploughman and is preparing to compete at a ploughing match.

June *Ducks galore*

As I plough I see a fifty acre field black with wild duck. Hundreds of thousands of them! Enough to provide a tasty meal for every London family, and over a million would be required for that.

I received the sad news in a letter from my brother Benjamin that my mother had died at the age of 77. *Two days later, after returning from ploughing, he acknowledges the letter and writes an englyn to fit the occasion.*

Severe toothache keeps me awake at night. I would like to visit the dentist, but he is twenty miles away.

Went with a party to shoot wild duck. One young boy had a dozen in no time. They could not help bringing them down. It was unnecessary to take aim, and random shooting always brought them down.

I finished the ploughing and went for my wages amounting to £3 11s 4d. Mr Miller said he could only give me 15s, and said I could have his watch which had no hands or glass in lieu of the remainder.

Took up my swag and went to buy some necessities for the road. I bought a nine-penny loaf for 10d. I could eat it at one meal. Twenty-eight pounds of potatoes cost me 6d and I could have bought a ton for £1 10s. Best method of cooking them I found was to wash them and remove the eyes, wrap them in wet paper, and place them in the fire. They emerged clean, dry and well-cooked.

Two-thirds of the farmers have to buy foreign wheat and other grain. They are petitioning the Government. I visited the butcher. He was short of meat so he was charging twice the price for the little that he had. I must leave this poor neighbourhood with its rich uncultivated land.

July *A swagman's sonnet*

Called at scores of farms, large and small, but none could offer employment. In most instances they could not afford to pay wages. In

23

one place I felt that I had more bread in my swag than they had in their larder. Everywhere the answer would have been the same, 'We are a full house'. Had they told the truth I believe the answer would have been something like this, 'My dear man, we are sorry to tell you that we have plenty of work which needs doing, and employment for many workers during the whole winter, but we have no capital, and we cannot afford the wages of a single labourer. In fact, we cannot pay our dues to the store-keepers until the next harvest'.

I have lost my frying pan, but I found a discarded spade without its handle and this serves me well. I aim at having three meals each day.

He writes a sonnet of 130 lines, entitled 'A swagman's rhyme', in which he describes man's attitude to life. Two stanzas only are given here:

This world is always full of strife
Our age is only a race for life.
Some are pleased to run uphill,
And some run down against their will.

But few can here be found
Who always run on level ground.
I cannot run, but slowly drag
My ninety pounds of heavy swag.

He quotes as follows from the census of the 3rd of April 1871 — 'The population of the state of Victoria is 729,654, which shows a growth of 189,332 since the previous census of 1861. There were 17,813 Chinese and 859 Aborigines. It is curious that this last group, the true natives of the country, are not considered worthy of or entitled to be counted as of the population.'

After rising early I walked in the Smeaton district. O, what a beautiful country! It will be turned to good account some day for the comfort of man and beast. In the meantime there is no money circulating here, and meat and bread are twice the price in other places. I turned into a butcher's shop for six pennyworth of meat, which was all the money I had. Although he had plenty of mutton and beef on display, he refused to sell me a small morsel of it.

He must have gained a better response from another butcher, for the next morning he reports breakfasting on beef and potatoes which brought on colic later in the day, and which he dispersed with a strong dose of cayenne pepper that warmed his feet.

I called with a farmer who asked me to hand-sow a four-acre paddock of barley as he was unwell. This I did, and following me with the harrow was a young musician. I envied him for he earned 4s 6d each night through playing a guitar at a local hotel. I regretted that I had not acquired this accomplishment in my young days.

Visited a lime kiln where the white stone was as hard as marble. It was expensive to burn, and it sold at £2 9s a ton. I took a sample of the burnt lime to test its virtues later on.

I agreed to fell two standing red gum-trees, one of them having a girth of nine yards. It branched 70 feet from the ground and was 120 feet tall! I was promised more permanent work at a wage of 12s a week by Mr Paul McPherson, a decent Scotsman, at New Market Farm and Hotel, near Carisbrook.

August-September
Oxen draw the plough

I took hay to town in a waggon drawn by six strong oxen. I erected log-fencing at this fine farm of 300 acres, then ploughed a paddock as flat as a pool of water. I ploughed with both oxen and horses, but much prefer the horses.

I received letters from my daughters Margaret and Nell, posted seven weeks ago. They had received the portraits I had sent. One letter which I had addressed to Wales was returned to me from Melbourne post office because of insufficient stamps. It only bore a 2d stamp although I gave 6d to the person that posted it.

The weather is wintry and squally. Very few barometers available in the country. There is general talk of the wind veering round with the sun, which is hardly consistent with Newton's theory.

I continue with ploughing, planting potatoes, and preparing the garden for carrots. Ploughing mostly with oxen; each one answers to his name and takes his place at the plough when called. Heavy loads are drawn along the roads by both horses and oxen, which are cruelly abused.

People who call here on Sunday get their drinks unlawfully at the back door.

October *The Queen is ill*

Building a calves' shed; finished it in two days. Built a pig sty one afternoon after 4 p.m. Walked to Maryborough to buy some necessities. I purchased shoes, shirt, a length of flannel, soap and tobacco. The ground round here is auriferous, and both alluvial and reef gold is sought but is scarce.

I read in the 'Californian Mail' that the Queen was recovering from her indisposition, and this is good news for the Colony and the whole world with the exception of India.

A mob (sic) of sheep stop at the farm every Wednesday night on their way to the market at Ballarat.

November
'Boomerang' money

It has rained heavily all night. Those who recently were growling for rain, are already shouting 'enough'. I see two sides of life here because it is a public house as well as a farm, and it is common custom in the Colony for hoteliers to own an adjoining farm on which swagmen are engaged for a small wage. They are expected to spend this on drinks at the hotel, and of course they do this, so the hotelier gives with one hand and takes back with the other. I spent the morning picking peas for market, and hay-harvesting in the afternoon. Hundreds of swagmen pass by looking for work.

December
*Confession
of a fatalist*

There is a good crop of potatoes which had been planted in the sludge which had been left when the flood receded into the creek which runs near to the house. It is very hot, and the temperature is 105°F in the shade.

The Master ordered me to unload from the waggon hay which I had just loaded. I was told to come down from the load. I did, and left to collect my swag in spite of appeals from the Master and his family to resume work.

I was engaged to mow hay by another hotelier with a farm. He employed five other workmen. After a week I was given the option of picking stones or going to the races. I elected to leave, and the parting was amiable.

I was hired at another farm near Learmonth, managed by Mr Bennet, a Cornishman. I was engaged to mow wheat with the scythe for a weekly wage of £1. Thanks to instruction from my father I was able to handle this implement with ease. Signs of dry weather. Swagmen are now in demand to help with the harvest.

Later, I was one of two binders following the reaper. I wore a new pair of canvas trousers for which I had paid 4s 6d. It was in rags before dusk because I followed the practice of kneeling on the sheaf to compress it as I tied it.

I settled on a new contract with Mr Bennet for harvest-time, and I aim to get a wage of 30s a week. The Tartarian oats are not so plump as those I used to see at Morfa Mawr in Cardiganshire. I believe that this climate is too warm and dry for this pedigree of oats.

On the last day of the year he indulges in the following philosophy:
Who would imagine about three years ago, that I would be bidding farewell to the year 1871 in this part of the world? Not I. I can assure the reader that it is all a mystery. It is our duty to paddle our coracles as well as we can and keep away from the reefs and the breakers if possible, but what of fate? Has man his own will and ideas to follow? The farmer may think today that he will cut down a quantity of corn tomorrow. There is no harm in that, but many circumstances besides illness and death might impede him entering the field. Yes, even a rainy day would do so. What use is it for men to speculate and rely on his speculation? We are creatures obliged to abide by circumstances as they happen. The great God never gave to mortal man authority to will and to work out his own plans, but I think and firmly believe that He, the harbinger of all thoughts, has ordained for man to be rewarded according to his knowledge and experience of things. Should he go wrong he will feel unhappy, if he will go right he will rejoice, and that is the best way to find out the right course to steer. Adieu 1871!

1872

January, February, March *The rain takes its toll*

This diary is badly mutilated, especially that parcel of it which deals with the early months. Thus the writing on the upper half of the leaves has faded and the paper is friable; obviously it has suffered from either immersion in water or it has been exposed to the rain. This mishap causes no surprise having regard to the nomadic life he leads, and the strange places where his swag containing his diaries, rests. He is still working at Mr Bennet's farm at Learmonth.

Later, I join the threshing team and visit separate farms. I am responsible for keeping the engine supplied with water which I have to get from a great distance, and heave it up from a deep well with a bucket. At one farm is Mr Hoiles, a minister of religion. He is no hypocrite and seems a decent man. When a horse jibs he does damn it, but not loudly!

Loading two carts with wheat to take to 'Mount Bolton Mill' for grinding; ten bags, each containing 250 lbs, in each cart, and only one driver for the two vehicles. On John Parish's farm, I arranged a trough from which five cattle could drink water at the same time without soiling the water with their feet. It continues to be very hot, and I am distressed by the continuous bellowing of cattle for want of fodder and water.

To read and write in comfort on Sundays, I arrange a veil over my face to keep the flies away from my eyes which are sore. The heat is unbearable, and the thermometer registers 107°F in the shade. I am engaged on thatching, a job I like, but not in this heat. Hundreds of thousands of wild duck on one marshy field.

Helped Mr Parish to unload thirty bags of ground corn from the mill. It was cold and raining heavily. I felt miserable as I was unable to dry my clothes in the absence of fires. In this district firewood is scarce and dear, although it is not so very far from the Bush.

I was bitten by a snake and I was troubled all night with dreams. I cannot comprehend dreams, but I believe the circulation is not well when one does dream.

April *Unjust censures*

Still at Mr Parish's farm carting farmyard manure, ploughing paddocks and the garden. I was up before dawn and before anyone else had stirred, when presently the Master shouted angrily, 'Come on Joe, it is broad daylight and time to shake'. I answered, 'Yes, I am shaking and riddling this chaff away from the horses' feed'. 'Alright' was his only answer. Resumed ploughing; the soil is very dry and the going is hard. One of my horses, 'Sam' is tired and lies down as soon as we stop, so I have to drive on, and not risk stopping. Water is scarce. Two horses on a neighbour's farm fell when they were taken to water, and I was called over to help. They were suffering from what has been termed 'the horrors' (in Welsh, 'clefyd pumbys', the five-finger disorder). We lifted them on their feet by means of pulleys, but they again flopped down. I suggested they were shown a bundle of hay, and they got up immediately. Here, the horses are worked far too hard, and even when well fed they are unable to hold out.

My two horses are named 'Captain' and 'Sam'. Sam has a bandy leg and walks in the furrow when I plough.

Ploughing with the double-furrow plough, followed by shallow harrowing does not loosen the deeper soil so that the seed does not get deep-rooted. The farmers here cannot bear criticism, founded on practical experience, and their usual comment is, 'What is that to you, mind your own business'. The Master works his horses far too hard, and while harrowing they are driven at five miles an hour. The ploughing too is difficult because of stones and roots.

Some of the farmers thresh wheat by hand with the flail. I would like to try this because I can use my arms better than my legs, and so dislike much walking.

The farmer, John Parish, called me to him and accused me of breaking one of the waggon's shafts, which in fact he had broken, and charged me 18s. I could not suffer yet another false accusation from this man, so having written an acknowledgement of his cheque as part-payment of wages, I took up my belongings and left.

May *A Royal Birthday*

I left for Ballarat where I had a good dinner at the Times boarding house for 6d. The next day I gained employment at John MacWhelan's farm, Warrenheip, and was asked to sow wheat. The Master was sowing with both hands, but he gave up when he discovered that 'Taffy' could cover more ground and scatter the seed more evenly with one hand than he could with two hands. I applied a bushel of seed to the acre.

They are keeping the day (24th) holy to celebrate the Queen's Birthday, that quiet lady who always works for peace among all nations.

For the first time ever I went out to sow an hour before daylight, when the moon guided my footsteps on a frosty morning. My fingers were numbed by the cold. I am complimented by the Master because he is in a hurry to get the seed sown, so that the horses can be rested and the men can go swagging.

June *Gambling on the Sabbath*

I went in search of my billy-can and other valuables left in a coach a fortnight ago, but there was no trace of them.

My main work consists of ploughing, sowing and harrowing, and for these activities I rise each morning at 4 a.m. The Master has paid 7s 6d a bushel for his wheat seed, and earlier on had sold his own for 4s 9d. The seed has been pickled in lime and blue stone.

The chaff-cutter does its work indifferently for it lacks speed which should approximate that of the drum of a threshing machine. The horses which drive it are tired because they have to trot in order to attain the necessary speed. On my recommendation the machine has been laid aside for modification.

The Master is fond of playing cards for money. Returning late one evening from Ballarat he took me into his confidence. He said that his farms, productive as they were, afforded him neither a meal nor a bed, nor a shilling to pay his labourers. I did not believe him because he has his four-wheeled chaise to drive Mrs MacWhelan to town once a week, and a thoroughbred steed to take him into the company of his friends. Returning from a walk one Sunday I found that twelve card-players had assembled at the house. Eight gallons of beer and a consignment of brandy had been delivered there. Before Monday morning the Master had lost £7 10s to a neighbour. My hut was not far removed from the gaming tables, and their disputes and quarrels kept me awake most of the night, so I elected not to work outdoors that day and forfeited my day's wage of 2s 9d. I wished to leave the farm, but the Master persuaded me to stay and to hand-sow the wheat. He appointed me as a 'working about man', so I was engaged in doing odd jobs like cutting up and salting two pigs and a bullock.

July *Justice justly dispensed*

I drew my wage of £4 16s for six weeks' work and left the farm on my own accord. I paid my debt at the local store, and added to my swag to the tune of fifty-shillings' worth. I took to the road in the direction of Learmonth. I arranged an 'award' in favour of my two brothers in Wales, and got a magistrate to witness the affidavit.

I obtained a summons against my previous employer, John Parish, to recover 18s, being arrears of wages. I was awarded the claim by the court. Subsequently, I had to appear in court to face a counter claim by John Parish in respect of the broken implement. The complainant brought with him his cook, whipper-in, and his wife to testify in support of his claim. The case was dismissed!

I took a boat and rowed on Lake Learmonth. Staying at the Stag Hotel, resting, eating, and reading. A good life as long as the money lasts, and this gave out in four days.

August *Patronizing barbarism*

I took up my swag and walked to David Kinnersly's farm (Spring Vale Farm), near Learmonth. There I was ordered to sow a paddock of twenty acres with barley. The cereal crops are poor this year. Oats sell at 4s a bushel. Chaff-cutting here is satisfactory, for the machine, with its two blades, travels at a reasonable speed.

The English mail has arrived, and I read in the 'Weekly Mail' that the Capital Punishment Bill to repeal hanging has been rejected. O murderous England!, how long do'st thou intend to patronize barbarism?

The month has been wet, except for one week of warm and genial weather. There was frost and snow for a brief period.

September
Shearing draws the swagmen

Dogs are worrying the sheep on the farm, and they have killed a dozen. Many swagmen pass along the road, bound for the sheep-country where the annual shearing has started. Twenty-six prize-rams were brought to the farm today, and which had been bought at Skipton show by Mr Kinnersly who proposes to develop sheep breeding on a large scale. The rams' feet were examined for infestation before they joined the flock. At the moment the sheep are expensive to buy and cost 18s each.

October *A snake strikes again*

The Master gave me a cheque for £4 6s and does not require me for any more work. So I once more go to stay at the Stag Hotel. I fear that I have to face two months of idleness, and it is a great disappointment that my chest condition does not allow me to join the shearers.

At Learmonth there are three churches and one chapel. Roman Catholics are most numerous, next the Wesleyans, while members of the Church of England and Scotch Presbyterians are the least numerous.

I cannot stay long here because it is too expensive. The repair of my watch which came from home has cost me £4 3s 6d. I am sure it would only cost 7s 6d in London, and it would be a better job. I am walking to the Bush at Mount Bolton where I join with another to cut firewood. We worked hard for eleven hours and split four tons of timber at 2s a ton. Our meals alone amounted to 4s. I was doing the cross-cutting and my mate the splitting. I made nine cuts through a log which was twenty-one feet in circumference. I enjoy Bush-life in Australia! It is misrepresented by many writers.

I have been bitten by a poisonous snake. My hand is swollen and painful. It keeps me awake at night. My father had a cure for poisoning through snake-bites, and scores of people visited him. My mother received father's permission to tell me the remedy, but she died without imparting to me the ingredients of the secret balm. My hand has begun to fester.

I watched a man gelding colts. I have never witnessed such butchery in my life.

We continue cutting up the logs, but my mate does not possess an equable temper. When he meets with a tough and knotty log he goes into tantrums, throws his mole away, kicks the iron wedges, and takes off his hat and stamps on it.

November *The songster of the Bush*

I do enjoy myself in the Bush. The melodious song of the magpies can make a man forget all his troubles. These magnificent songsters are caught and sold as cage-birds, which to my mind is a most pernicious and despicable practice, and should be stopped.

The monthly English mail has arrived, but there is no letter for me, and no acknowledgement of the 'award' from either of my two brothers. It is remarkable how many people who have resided here for thirty years do not know the difference between oats and barley.

My mate and I have been cutting up firewood for a hotelier, and although we work hard for twelve hours of each day, we cannot make ends meet. My mate is going to seek farmwork and so must I.

December *The Adam in him*

I bind oaten hay after the reaping machine at Post Office House, Learmonth, but there is no work to-morrow, so I leave to seek it elsewhere. This is excellent agricultural land, but the farming of it is poor. I was promised two days' work mowing and binding a swathe round a 200 acre field of Cape barley in preparation for the reaper machine, but it rained the second day. I was paid and I went to the township to buy provisions.

At another place I offered to mow, bind and stook a field of barley measuring six acres for 30s, but the farmer would not agree. I found work at John Hawkins's farm near Coghill's Creek. I was sent to hoe in a large orchard which holds 3,000 fruit trees. The vineyard measures four acres. The gooseberries are as big as young hens' eggs. I confess that I cannot behave myself in the orchard one whit better than my ancient parents at Eden.

I was sent to bind wheat. I was the best binder on the field, but let not the reader accuse me too soon of egotism, for I was the only binder there. On Christmas Day I received a cheque for £1 for twelve days' work, but was not invited to any Christmas meal.

Harvesting corn is very laborious, so I have written to an engineering firm in England and suggested a way of building a machine which would combine to reap and bind the crop in one operation.

The Master is an industrious man and cooks the breakfast for the household including his wife and three daughters. They are four healthy and robust women, and we are warned not to talk loud at breakfast, in case their sleep is disturbed! (*The diary for 1872 concludes with a description, covering five pages, of how to treat a snake-bite.*)

1873

January *The wrong and the right of it*

If this fine land were to be properly cultivated, I do not see that she could find a market for the sale and comsumption of her products anywhere nearer than Europe. During this present harvest, farm labourers are far too numerous. Nearly one half of them are out of work and the other half is obliged to work hard for a wage of 4d an hour, and are harassed by their employers into the bargain. Moreover, young Colonials are employed to the exclusion of the labourers, so that some two per cent of the fine crops is wasted through the employment of unskilled hands instead of paying proper labourers to perform the work in a husband-like manner:

The staff of life deserves to be
In more efficient hands;
Let ev'ry one, in his degree,
Perform what it demands.
The land is rich from North to South,
From West and East the same;
We would not meet a hungry mouth
Should all add to its fame.

The state of Victoria may take many, yes scores of years, before it is converted to its proper use. A general craving for gold completely checks any advancement in this direction. Only the squatters have the urge to plan for posterity. As long as mutton and wool are harbingers of the general welfare, it is short-sighted to rear one sheep to the acre when twelve could be husbanded with little additional care and labour, while we read that a million people have lately died from hunger in Arabia, and the hard-working man pays so dearly for his loaf of bread.

Our present and former legislators are to be blamed for handing over so much good land to the same people. When land is taken from one tenant and given to another, it is expected that the latter improves it, but the lands of Victoria have diminished in value from the time they were so barbarously taken from the natives, and when the golden rules of humanity were so deliberately flouted.

Working at John Hopkins's farm, Coghill's Creek, at a wage of 4d an hour, but I am loaned to work on John Hawkins's farm, where I get no wage. Engaged in binding wheat. The land is poorly managed. Land must be exceeding rich to produce 15 to 24 crops in succession and without farmyard manure. It will be more difficult to bring it under proper cultivation than when it was first cleared of scrub. The parcels of land are too large and their management is undermanned. Relations between farmers and labourers is bad.

I have just heard of the death of Napoleon III. *He composes an englyn on the occasion.* I have been hoeing between the tines in the vineyard. *He composes two verses in praise of wine.*

They have finished with the harvest, so I shouldered my swag and I am tramping the road again in search of another job. I rejoin a threshing team, and work sixteen hours a day, even threshing by moonlight:

To rob the short moonlight, to lengthen the day,
Is trespass on Nature, I would say.

The wages are at the rate of 2d an hour. Yet, even at this small wage, scores of swagmen are unemployed and hunting for work. *He cries in anguish, either to his Queen or the Colony's State, 'O Victoria! Victoria!'*

February Neglect of the land

This country's soil and its climate cannot be surpassed by any country, but the law and the lawless cannot be so classed. So wanting are high principles, humanity and morals, that people from all classes of society hold that no honest man should set foot in Australia. I would not complain of the labourer's wages, if he were respected and be constantly employed. Now, a labourer is not employed for longer than 12 to 17 weeks of the year. Consequently, the land is neglected and exhausted. Presently, one man is allowed to hold a million acres of land with good surface-soil without obligation to employ a single labourer, while the same land is neither rated nor taxed. On the other hand, the small farmer has to pay a tax of 1s in the pound to support public roads, although there are no roads serving the squatters.

I found work with a William Ross at Newlyn, Bullarook, where I made sixty-five ropes, each of them ten yards long, to thatch some very tall stacks. He notoriously ill-treats his workmen, and drives them like slaves. At dawn he called us all up so uproariously as to give us the impression that the house was on fire. He often called on me to harness the horses at 3 a.m. On Sundays he denied us the Sunday-dinner.

His pet son, aged 7, is a chip off the old block; he drives without mercy the two horses which work the chaff-cutter. He also has the makings of the tyrant-father, for while I was sitting quietly he fell on me, stabbed me twice in the body, and ran into the house to tell his bemused parents what he had done to 'old Joe'. His father did not admonish him.

On Sunday morning I took a walk along the paddocks, but I had to retreat soon because a thick shower of locusts or flying grasshoppers darkened the sky like a snow cloud. They were moving northwards as orderly as any army. As they passed, some dropped to devour the paddock's grass, the leaves on the vine, and the potato haulms.

Both my mate and I decided to leave this scoundrel of a Master. His cheque to me was 5s short of the contract, and he deducted 4s from my colleague's wage because he had broken a tool which was already weakened from general wear and tear.

March *Impounding of poems and cattle*

On St David's Day (1st of March) our diarist was wont to attend the Eisteddfod at Ballarat, but he was unable to do so this year. His brother John Jenkins (Cerngoch), however, was victorious in a similar competitive meeting in Wales in respect of an englyn on 'Y Morwr Colledig' ('The Lost Sailor'). In that it is held to have outstanding merit, it is given here with its literal translation:

Iach hwyliodd i ddychwelid, — ond ofer	*(Safely he sailed to return, — but futile*
Fu dyfais celfyddyd;	*Was the device of craftsmanship;*
Y mor wnaeth ei gymeryd;	*The Sea took him;*
Ei enw gawn, dyna' i gyd.	*His name we have, that is all.)*

I went to the dam for a swim, hoping it would cure my rheumatism. Had a three hours' chat with Dr Roache. I promised to write out for him my remedy for a snake-bite.

I slept by night in a hut, and walked in search of work by day. I agreed to thresh a quantity of peas with a flail for 4s. I gathered my swag and arrived at another farm at 5 a.m. to find the Master cleansing himself before breakfasting. He told me that I had arrived too late to do a day's work, and that I might go about my business. So I left in the direction of Kingston. I came upon three men talking together. One of them required a man to sew bags to store the corn thrown out by the threshing machine. The other two men refused the job. I was asked if I could sew bags, 'Yes, Sir'. Had I needles? 'Yes, Sir'. 'Come with me and get your breakfast.' The work was finished before lunch, having repaired nearly 200 sacks. No more work, but good tucker and wage from the kindest farmer I have so far met in the country. They are two brothers, T. and J. Meredith from Montgomeryshire in North Wales. They are both bachelors, and of course (sic) live comfortably. I stay with the philanthropic Merediths, but presently take to the 'wallaby track' by day in search of work. At a big farm (Oak Farm) owned by David Davies, I was told by Mrs Davies that most Welshmen in the Colony were drunkards; she wished they would be an example to other members of different nationalities, but regrettably the contrary was the case.

Engaged by H. Glendenning to stack wheat and barley straw which had passed through the thresher, at a wage of 4d an hour.

I read that President Grant of America had said that he would exterminate the Indians for the sake of civilization. O Lord deliver us if we must civilize the world through killing those whom God has stationed on the land!

I walked to Glendonald's post office where two years before I had left portraits and poems in the care of the postmistress. She refused to surrender them unless I paid £10. What an imposition! I left them there.

I called with Mr Martin, editor of the 'Creswick Advertiser' and offered for publication my recipe for the treatment and cure of a snakebite. I considered this to be a great favour to him and the public, but he would not accept it; so the secret may remain uncovered for years. The remedy is simple and harmless, and there is nothing in it that would hurt a person of the most delicate constitution, for it is applied externally, except for an accompanying dose of cayenne pepper.

Thatching at Oak Farm again for David Davies. He, his wife and three sons are well versed in the scriptures. The sons in turn read a chapter of the Bible at night. No time to read in the morning when the troubles of the world have to be faced.

The big barn has stone walls and the roof is of Carnarvon slates. The building could last for 1,000 years.

I travelled towards the plain of Smeaton where three years ago I witnessed well-kept farms. Alas! they are now over-run by Scotch thistles, sorrel, and other obnoxious weeds.

I have a sore eye and I ache from rheumatism. While sleeping in a stable, a horse trod on me, so an injury is added to my other complaints. I am a lame and crippled swagman. Davies has just impounded eight of his neighbour's cattle.

Carried on my course in order to visit Clunes, which not many months ago was named the Golden Town, for its streets were said to be paved with gold. I did not see any sign of the precious metal. On the other hand an inhabitant of the town did pick up a shilling of my small store of silver, and that in respect of a very common and scanty meal.

I turned right in the direction of Mount Beckworth, passing well-fenced farms, but with exhausted land; this needs to rest fallow or be treated with farmyard manure, and such truth has to be realised quickly to save it.

April *The stars are his lamps*

Paid another visit to John Hawkins's farm at Coghill's Creek. Invited to taste the plentiful fruit in his fine orchard and vineyard. Grapes are sold for 2d a pound. The flies are numerous and eager, even the common flies bite here.

Arrived at a fresh farm, Glendarnal, near Clunes, and offered a week's work by the farmer, Mr Thomas McMurray. His horses are in a very bad condition. Three of them are sick. Each morning I groom their skeletons. The Master growls all day long over trifles. He refuses to admit that the horses are lean and underfed. I am spreading dung all day, but it is distributed so thinly that it will have little effect on the exhausted soil:

The ploughing and the season
Are blamed by all the farmers.
They won't give ear to reason
That all the blame is theirs.

I work hard all day and well into the night. The stars come out and shed some light so that I can see what I am doing. I am only allowed five minutes for meals. Swarms of locusts have descended here, and they destroy the grass in the paddocks as well as the potato crop. On Sunday, I went to wash my underclothes in a nearby creek. McMurray followed me, and ordered me away, so I had to travel into the Bush before I could pursue my ablutions.

May and June *A swindler and tyrant*

The farmer, McMurray is 'penny-wise and pound-foolish'. He has 200 tons of straw in the yards, yet he will not permit bedding for the horses which would help in the making of suitable manure for the impoverished soil. He believes in ploughing deeply which is a mistake. He denies the horses good feeding, keeps them in poor condition, so that they are too weak to do much work. He sows unevenly, harrows superficially, provides bad quarters for his workmen and a hut devoid of a fireplace or means to dry their wet clothing; he would not spare me a candle so I have to make my bed in the dark, and he is a continuous miserable grumbler. In spite of his greed and meanness I predict ruin for him. His recipe for a tired horse is, 'Give him rest tomorrow, don't feed him tonight, he will have plenty of grass tomorrow; give him half-feed in the morning; let him into the stable after supper on the resting day, and don't give him anything to eat, for his belly is full enough, and he will be fresh and active tomorrow'. He accused me of not driving the horses quick enough in the harrow and took the reins from my hands. I left to pick up my swag, but he ran after me and begged me to go and plough. I diffidently agreed. My grandfather told me that in the 17th century, the farmers in Wales, as soon as they had completed seeding their crops, took their horses to the hills for two months to get rest and grazing, while the men engaged in fishing, wrestling and fighting. On this farm the horses are in harness all the year round, get no rest, and are grossly underfed. Similarly the labourers work hard and for long hours (sometimes seventeen hours in the day) for a wage of 5s a week. My present Master is a scoundrel, swindler and tyrant!

The carrots here are eighteen inches in circumference! Some of them should be fed to the horses. (*He repeats over and over again the shameful state of the over-worked and starved horses.*)

McMurray asked me to stay over the winter at a wage of 2s 6d a week. I left for Ballarat where I found the Labour Office full of men seeking work. The wheat price is up, and the 4 lb loaf costs 8d. I walked back to Glendarnal to get my working clothes, and was invited in for breakfast. No men employed on the farm now till hay-making time. Two-thirds of the 400 acre farm is under cereal crops.

July *The Bushman's accoutrements*

Walking from farm to farm, I passed a paddock of 240 acres where they were holding a ploughing match. The farmers set the dogs on the swagmen unless the latter carry a revolver. I do not possess one.

Lodgings in the towns are too expensive, and the Government will not sell less than forty acres of land and this deep in the Bush, and probably without a water supply. I walked into the Bush and to the hut which I had built for myself earlier in the year. The tools which I had then left in it, had disappeared; they were worth £3 10s. I returned to the stores and purchased 2 axes, 21 lbs of iron wedges, 2 cross-cutters, 2 pairs of mole rings, 2 files, and other handy tools. I also took with me 2 suits of clothes, underclothing and bed clothes, as well as a supply of soap, candles, tobacco, yarn, thread and needles. It was necessary to turn to the Bush because I had walked twenty-five miles without a sign of any sort of a job. Work on the railway was in the hands of subcontractors. Leaving the district of Mount Bolton I ran into a heavy shower of rain:

The timely shelter of a hedge
Shows some reform in Nature!
You farmers ought to take the pledge
And patronize such culture.

When I returned to the hut, the fine cat which I had left behind me gave me a great welcome. I drew water, split some logs, retired to my bed, and slept well. I awoke to the magnificent song of the magpies, and the hilarious chuckles of the laughing jackasses. On Sunday morning I washed thirty-five articles of clothing, and then read some chapters from both the Old and New Testament. Later, I darned some stockings and mended my underclothing. Next morning I made the American axe fly into action. The weather was boisterous, but it was strange that while the farmers would be grumbling, the feathered tribe of the wood was pouring out melodious music.

I felled a tree five yards in circumference, but its core had rotted and served as a home for several opposums which are innocent creatures, shaped and smelling like a fox. Their furs are in great demand in Europe. Thirty-two of their skins make a rug which is sold for £2. It also makes a light and warm coat for the swagman. My watch keeps good time, but its jewels have been pilfered by the last man who repaired it.

The timber is hard and tough to split. It sells for 2s a ton. In 10½ hours I was only able to split 2 tons, and 21 tons in fourteen days. My hut, which is situated on Mount Bolton, is draught- and water-proof. My employer told me to fell the best trees I could find, but a man visited me today and gave orders not to fell a single tree, but to split the ones which were already on the ground. I must look into the matter. I have rheumatism in my arms again, so I must take more mustard with my meat.

August
The swagman's shopping list

Mount Burton belongs to G. G. Morton Esq. who is chairman of the magistrates. Thousands of ewes and lambs graze there, and at the moment, grass is plentiful. There are lots of lizards about, some of them as big as young alligators.

I made sixteen moles to help with my log-splitting. Not many people can make a straight and firm mole. It is a knack. My Master whom I split the timber for, is the landlord of the Stag Hotel, who sells beer at 6d a glass while others retail it at 3d a pint.

My weekly shopping list costs me 12s 4d and is made up as follows — bread (2 loaves) 1s 4d; meat (12 lbs) 3s; sugar (2 lbs) 10d; tea (2 oz) 4d; potatoes (14 lbs) 6d; salt 1d; pepper 1d; tobacco 1s; matches 1d; medicine 4d; candles 6d; thread 2d; oatmeal and flour 6d; newspaper 6d; mustard 2d; onions 4d; soap 7d; tools and clothes (wear and tear) 2s.

A dark native, that is an Aborigine, paid me a visit. He was looking for bees. He mentioned that when a native discovers a hive, he invites the neighbours to partake of the honey, but when a white Christian discovers it, he keeps the produce for himself.

Many people are worried that the locusts will destroy their crops next year, for they allege that they have found thousands of eggs in the soil. I cannot express an opinion, and in the meantime the tough timber is my worry:

Dellto nid hollti allan.	(Breaking crossways not down the main,
Dâl yn groes, nid dilyn grân.	Tears apart nor follows the grain.)

September *Four acres and a cow*

A heavy thunderstorm has just passed. The hail was as big as marbles. Snow followed. In the last copy of the 'Leader', I read the following:

Let him take, who has the power,
And let him keep, who can.

Such appears to be the policy of the Government. The land is starved and there are no good farmers to feed and cultivate it. I have suggested to the Minister of Land, that for every 100 acres of land apportioned to a farmer, 4 acres should be allocated to a labourer which he could fence, build on it a house, keep a cow, and bring up a family. Should he vacate it, it should be conditional that he must not sell it to any farmer, nor to the one from whose parcel of land it was separated. (*In suggesting this scheme he had forestalled Lloyd George's plan, 'Three acres and a cow', by forty-five years.*)

It is reported that a labourer's wage is from 7s to 9s a day, but this is only at harvest time, and for only a few days in the year. I have never received a wage in excess of 5s for a day of fifteen hours, that is at a rate of 4d an hour. The swagman's labour is required for only three months in the year, the harvesting lasts four weeks on an average, threshing for only a limited period of a week or so, and the seeding season for some seven weeks.

A few men in the Colony own over a million acres of rich land which was taken over from the Aborigines. They have effected no improvement of such land except to build on it an elegant homestead and erect boundary fences. They employ cooks, grooms, overseers, store keepers, buggy drivers or coachmen, a man or two to feed the sporting dogs, and they hire a team for the wool-clipping season. This last section of employment is limited to the few, for three years ago I sought occupation at thirty-two shearing stations, and although I was proficient in this art on my own farm at home, my services were rejected because I could not cut close enough to the bone. The way it is carried out here is nothing short of butchery. Some squatters shear twelve tons of wool. The farmers in this district cart straw to the market, while their hungry paddocks cry out for farmyard manure.

The stock-riders have been assembling 1,700 ewes during the past two days for the purpose of gelding or castrating the lambs. Three lambs only five days old, broke away from the flock and were lost in the Bush. They passed my hut the morning after and then followed the track which the flock had traced. The three arrived together in the stockyard a mile away. Such is instinct!

I received a letter from my daughter Elinor. She gives an account of farming at Trecefel, but does not say whether it pays or not. She reports that a choir of 500 voices sang successfully at the Crystal Palace, and was introduced to the audience by the Prince of Wales.

October *Knotty timber poses a knotty problem*

I kept all my cobbling tools in a box; it was stolen, along with £4 worth of an assortment of nails. The trees at Mount Bolton are very difficult to split, as the barrels are hard, short and knotty. They are easier at Bullarook forest where the trunks are 70 to 90 feet high without a single knot, and that is why they have so many 'splitters' there, so I must stick it out here in spite of my lower output.

November and December *The missing implement*

I visited the Smeaton National and Spring Show having walked the fourteen miles from Mount Bolton. Why don't they produce a special dung cart which will distribute farmyard manure? (*British agriculture had to wait over sixty years before this most useful implement was made available.*)

My employer and his driver have been carting away my measured piles of timber during the past fortnight, seventeen tons of it on some days. I now have only two unmeasured piles left.

Among the implements exhibited at the Smeaton agricultural show were both single and double furrow ploughs, the former were of a good design, but the latter were cumbersome. A potato seeder and potato digger were two good machines. The harrows were too heavy, scarifiers were not the best. There were good scrubbers, and two winnowers imported from England. The chaff-cutters were good and of different kinds. There were two attempts at manufacturing a binder-attachment, but although unlikely to work, it showed promise.

Hay-making has commenced, so I must leave the Bush and seek work on the farms. I dislike leaving this lonely place:

I love a lonely life.
All peace without temptation.
I hate disputes and strife
In towns with their corruption.

I am employed at Mrs McKay's farm near Learmonth, to do binding after the reaper, and stooking. My right arm is weak after so much log-splitting, and I can hardly handle the scythe. Mrs McKay is the sister of the landlord of the Stag Hotel.

I move for three days' work at hay-scything at William Vallance's farm where I am paid 6s a day. I have never earned so much.

Having joined the 'Hand of Friendship Lodge' at Learmonth, I became a member of 'Good Templar's Society', so that even on Christmas Day, I drank neither beer nor spirits.

1874

He records the events of 1874 in a hard-cover official diary measuring only 6½ by 4 ins, where each day is printed, and four days apportioned to each page. On the 11th of January he regrets having started it because he can only enter a third of the happenings of the day. He admits that when he first kept a diary he found it a little irksome, but for many years now it has afforded him great enjoyment, and he cannot sleep unless he has recounted his day's activities.

January *Work is second nature*

I never dreamt in the year 1839 when in Wales, that thirty-five years later I would be recording my diary in this distant and rich country. I went to see the doctor in Ballarat about the rheumatism in my right arm. He attributes it to working too hard when I was young, and when I got up each Saturday morning at 3 a.m. to thresh loose barley in order to provide straw for thirty-eight heads of cattle on the Sunday. Of course I continue to work hard, but this is no longer a hardship because it has now become second nature.

On this New Year's day I was up at 4 a.m. and walked twelve miles to see the English Eleven play Ballarat at cricket. All the shops were closed. It seemed a holy day as well as a holiday, because the topic of conversation revolved around Grace and graces, not about those pious qualities of course, but about W. G. Grace, the illustrious English cricket captain and his brother, the other Grace and cricketer.

Later, I took a boat and sailed over Lake Wendouree to visit the Botanical Gardens. The return trip only cost 6d. It was worth a pound at least to see the gardens. I took the coach back to Learmonth at 4 o'clock. The locusts are at it again, devouring the crops wholesale.

Binding oats at Mrs McKay's farm. The binders hold out for a wage of 6s or 7s a day so they remain unemployed. I believe in a quick 9d rather than a slow 1s. I was paid £3 15s in respect of wages for fifteen days, that is 5s a day. Carting wheat from paddock of forty acres; many of the sheaves were thrown aside because they were mostly made up of thistles. We threshed the wheat and I thatched the stack of straw.

Called to my previous employer, David Kinnersly of Spring Vale Farm, Learmonth, to cart rye-grass and white clover from a field of thirty-three acres.

February
Complacency in fair weather

This is the testing month for a farm's crop yield, and on this farm it has been satisfactory. The wheat crop yields 32 bushels to the acre, and the English barley 36 bushels. The former sells at 6s a bushel and the latter at 6s 9d. It is true that some badly managed farms only yield 3½ bushels of corn to the acre, but I hold that when land here is properly cultivated, it has no equal in the whole world.

Heavy rain has fallen and spoilt the hay which should have been carted a long time ago, for there has been no rain for six weeks! The crop would have made two stacks worth £400 each, and is now only worth £50 for bedding the animals.

Peth diflas yw segura	*On rainless days when sun shines bright,*
Ar adeg y cynhaea,	*And hay or corn needs harvesting,*
A ffeth colledig iawn erio'ed	*'Tis sinful quite, and not alright,*
Rhoi gormod o'd i'r hindda.	*To lie and laze doing nothing.*

The sheaves of wheat are huge, 6 feet tall and 5 feet in circumference. It is wonderful straw, but the head is a little light. Thatching a stack of barley carted from a paddock of sixty-five acres; its roof measures 75 by 36 feet. Threshing rye-grass with a flail which when winnowed produced eighteen bushels of seed. The thresher comes to the farm, drawn by two teams of bullocks, and is employed there for a week. It is no joke to cook meals daily for thirty-two lusty people. The stubble is burnt; this is bad farming, for the wind blows the ash away. A flock of 1,000 sheep was turned into a clover field, and in two hours' time they had to be turned out again, for over-indulgence would kill them.

March *Harvesting through silage*

The Master has decided to give up cultivating for cereal crops and is to devote all his attention to sheep-farming. He grows acres of clover, harvests it and then feeds it to his flock of 2,000 sheep, providing them with five loads daily. This month is a trying one for graziers, and this is one good method to ensure food for his sheep during a prolonged period of drought.

There is a sheep sale on the farm tomorrow, and fifty-six gallons of beer, and four dozen quart-bottles of whisky and brandy, have been carried into the house. I spent two days erecting straw stacks as shelters for the sheep.

April
'No till' seeding

For a week I have been engaged in sowing perennial rye-grass and white clover on unploughed land. What a splendid country this is! Anything grows here. A grass paddock of thirty acres was sown with perennial rye-grass about four years ago, and has since supported 260 sheep which are in good condition. (*A century later in Wales the sowing of grass seeds on unploughed land is being tested, but it is likely that mechanized direct seeding is needed as a final exercise in the scheme subsequent to initial weed-killing. Even then this labour-saving device is worthy of trial.)*

Having completed the re-seeding of the pasture land, it is likely I shall have to leave this fine farm and seek work elsewhere, for only experienced shepherds will be employed. Already there are 5,000 sheep here of the Blowhard and Windermere breed.

A cheque, dated for yesterday, has been handed me so I must take my swag and go in search of another job. I cannot hope to meet with a better Master than David Kinnersly of Spring Vale Farm.

May
Time (-piece) flies

I stayed the night at the Stag Hotel at Learmonth. I read a little in the library, and later took a walk in the cemetery, inspecting the tombstones. There was only a single record of a demise of one older than myself, so that mine is not likely to be long postponed.

At the Labour Exchange I was directed to a William Clarke at Mount Cameron. My swag was very heavy because I had bought two blankets which cost me £1 2s. That night I slept well under a stack of straw. Arriving at the farm I was ordered to plough in a paddock of 140 acres, which was stony and rocky; I was thrown to the ground twice, for my two horses drawing the plough were travelling at 4½ miles an hour. I sleep on the floor in the barn which holds 200 bags of corn.

I don't know the name of this farm, but I call it the 'Eight Miles' farm, because it is eight miles from Talbot, eight miles from Clunes, and eight miles from Majorca.

I sow over 30 bushels of wheat each day. The Master sows with both hands, but I cover more ground with one.

Two men came here to kill the pigs; they murdered (*sic*) three. My wage here is less than 2d an hour.

One of my ploughmates bought a silver watch for eight guineas. He left it in a leather bag at the headland in case it broke while ploughing between the boulders of stone. A crow took it out of the bag and flew away with the watch, but dropped it some distance on, and the timepiece was found broken.

It rains heavily, and the corn blades appear in the newly sown paddocks.

June *A lawyer's fee*

This is the most miserable place I have ever worked at. Both man and beast are worked hard and poorly fed. I am up each morning between 4 and 5 a.m. and finish work at 9, 10 or 11 in the evening. The eight horses are similarly cruelly treated through hard work and underfeeding. I have no fire for drying my wet clothes. I sleep in a narrow passage leading from the barn to the stable. My blankets are trodden upon by all who pass. William Clarke has no children but a nagging wife. She and her sister milk the cows on one side while the calves suckle on the other side. They maintain that the cow yields her milk better through this method.

The horses have developed the 'horrors', no wonder for they drag the plough uphill for fourteen hours each day at four miles an hour, and are beaten mercilessly by the Master as he curses and swears at them all day.

I cannot suffer the conditions any longer so that I have taken to the road again. I am paid 6s 8d in cash (which is recognized as a lawyer's fee at home), and a cheque for £5. I have tried to change this cheque at several places, but without success.

I have been robbed of a new pair of boots, books and postage stamps. These were in a parcel which was tied by string to my swag. The thief cut the string with a knife, and ran away with the parcel.

I was attacked by colic and was advised by Dr Howells (a native of Carmarthenshire) to take a good measure of the best brandy in the town (Marjorca), but as I wished not to break the 'pledge' I took cayenne pepper instead.

July *Hospitalization*

He was taken ill with quinsy and diphtheria and was admitted to Maryborough Hospital at Majorca. It would appear that he was desperately ill. He remained in hospital for forty days. In spite of his illness, he continued to record fully the events of each day, and even pronounced on the state of the weather together with the direction of wind, since he was able to see the weathercock on a distant church, from his hospital bed. Common to so many other patients he had many complaints concerning hospital life: discipline was too rigid; his bed was too far from the fire-place; open windows meant to provide fresh adequate ventilation, he regarded as a source of unbearable draughts; disturbed nights from the coughing and groans of ill patients; and the proximity of the beds. He felt better when sitting up in a chair, but the rules prevented him assuming this more beneficial posture.

Two yards away from his bed lay a very sick and lean Aborigine, labouring under great shortness of breath. Presently, he dies. No more heed or notice is taken of his passing than if he were a fly or a moth, although during his illness the doctor and ward watchers had given him every attention. On the occasion of this death, the diarist composed a poem of twenty-four lines, twelve of which are given here:

The skilful surgeon did his best
To lessen pain and ease his rest.
The faithful wardsmen played their part
To feed, to warm, and cheer his heart.

All class of people, race and tie
Were born to life, and live to die.
This world of strife is nothing more
Than tragic shipwreck near the shore.

> So save yourself, and try to land
> To give some one a helping hand.
> Let everyman perform his best
> Before the time he'll have to rest.

August *Standing on auriferous ground*

After leaving hospital I stayed the night at a boarding house at a cost of 1s. The bed was not as comfortable as the one I occupied at the hospital. Left in the direction of Majorca, calling at several farms, but no offer of work. Called at Buck Hall station with its 30,000 acres of rich land, employing only half a dozen workers and four shepherds. My services were not needed. Travelled by coach (fare, 2s 6d) and rail (fare, 3s 2d) to Castlemaine. Getting stronger every day, but also getting further into debt. Joined my old friend David Evans who is still prospecting for gold. I left four diaries, some books, and clothing in his custody while I journeyed on in the direction of Mount Inkerman and camped for an hour on the very spot where a nugget of gold weighing 210 lbs was found six years ago. Thence I climbed over the top of Mount Malega and Mount Mackyntyre (*sic*) where three lumps of gold were found, and were sold for £13,000. One specimen was flat like a pancake and confined between two layers of quartz which lay a few inches below the surface.

David Evans and his son were lucky again today for they found two nuggets one of which weighed nearly a pound. Gold sells here at £4 2s an ounce. He has a system. Each day he spends eight hours digging for gold and three hours erecting buildings on his farm. He keeps silent about the amount of gold he finds, but he certainly thrives. I dug two holes, but found nothing.

I do not feel well, so continue to stay with David Evans at his home in Old Berlin or John's town, and help to dig the garden and to erect fences.

September *Further decline*

I left David Evans's home in a spring cart and made for the farm of Thomas Johns in the Bush at Couts' Creek, and accompanied him to cut up some timber, but I feel very weak and can scarcely use my arms or my legs. Paid several visits to the doctor, but his treatment seems of no avail. He does not name the complaint, but terms it a 'chronic and hopeless case'. Board and lodgings at this nice farm cost me 15s a week. My weakness is confined to my hands and legs, and there is no pain, while my appetite is good. I return to stay with my friend David Evans. I cannot button or unbutton my coat. It is paralysis of a kind.

October and November *Hospital but no hospice*

Another doctor has examined me and has ordered me to Inglewood Hospital. Mr and Mrs Thomas Johns came to see me, brought me some nice things, and said they would be glad if I returned to work for them later on.

How I pine to leave this miserable place. Kindness and even civility are in evidence only when the doctor is around. The reckless and sluggish wardsmen undo the benefit wrought by the work of the good doctor. The proud and nasty cook goes around scoffing at everybody. Last night a nearby window was left wide open, countermanding my request. I prefer sleeping in the Bush than be caught in this cross-current.

When we were allowed out in the grounds during the day and resting on seats conveniently arranged in the shade or facing a northern aspect, we chatted on various topics. One time, the Australian natives (the Aborigines) were discussed. The majority of the patients held it was a right and even a Christian obligation to be rid of them all. In the name of everything, whence came such authority?!!!

After a month's stay in hospital, I escaped from its clutches and vicious draughts, and made my way to David Evans at Old Berlin. I was much improved from the palsy of my limbs, and wanted to test my strength, so I helped him to enlarge his orchard.

News arrived that a nugget weighing eight pounds had been picked up in the vicinity by a Mr James Carr, a quiet and respected bachelor. I had a long chat with him, and found that he had good taste in poetry, although we disagreed concerning one subject — he preferred Milton's 'Paradise Lost', and I placed greater value on his 'Paradise Regained'.

December *A night with Venus*

I walked nine miles through thick Bush in the direction of Newbridge. There I found 150 harvesters craving for employment at a low wage. I managed to obtain work with a farmer, William Brownbill of Rosewood Farm. I was engaged at 6s a day or 5d an hour, stacking the cut wheat. I am regaining strength, but not feeling very fit yet. My hands are tender following the palsy. I am like Wellington at Waterloo, praying either for the night or for Blucher's assistance.

After a busy day, reaping and binding corn, when there was much thunder and lightning, but no rain, I returned in the evening to prepare instruments to observe the movements of Venus. (*He does not particularize the nature of these instruments.*) It was plainly seen. It appeared as a common spot on the disc as on an ordinary white table plate. What this planet contains remains a puzzle.

Searching for another job near Edington. A stack of lucerne required thatching at the Farmers Hotel. I offered to do it for 30s, but the hotelier would only give £1, so I left in the direction of Deep Creek and Carisbrook. I arrived at Ballarat, and after dinner which cost me 6d at the Times Hotel, I walked towards Warrenheip where I met John Whelan who employed me at a low wage to reap a wonderful crop of peas. (I had worked on this farm before in June 1872.)

Enjoyed a good dinner on Christmas day. Two roasted geese among five of us; plenty of good beef and plum pudding as well. They have plenty of geese on the farm. I counted ninety in one flock.

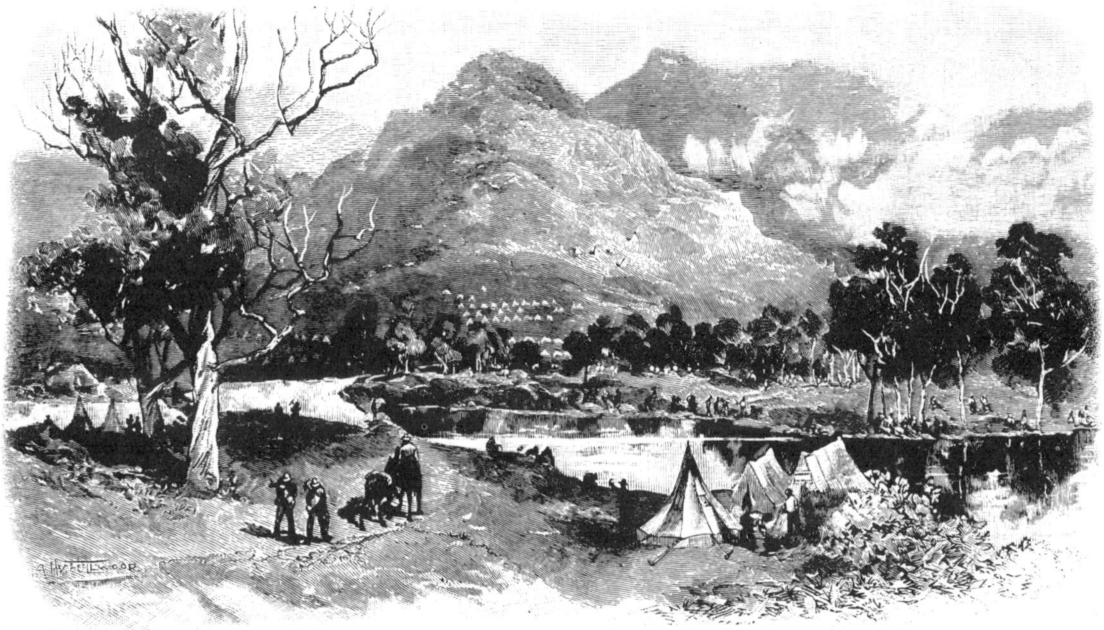

1875

This is my thirty-sixth diary, and my sixth in the Colony. In that I am unable to procure an official diary, I have cut up paper to size and bound it. (*The end-product is a commendable exhibit. The cover is made of stiff cardboard lined with hide.*)

January *'Turkeys and geese' magistrates*

The Master, John Whelan, declared New Year's Day as a holiday so I left by train for Ballarat, four miles away. My return ticket cost me 6d. Having purchased a few necessities, I went to watch the New South Wales cricket team play Ballarat's, but soon the rain stopped play. When I commence a new diary and look back on the old year, I realize that I am on the wing, not *Time* as commonly expressed. No one can prove to me that Time was not in existence before Creation.

I was ordered, along with four other workmen to weed the garden. We collected tons of all kinds of weeds in the course of a long tiresome day. The plum trees are overloaded and there are plenty of gooseberries, but no apples. The wheat crop is beginning to turn yellow. Parcels of land in the locality hold barley which is ready for the sickle or scythe, for it is too short for the reaper. We look forward to the morrow (Sunday). The working man would welcome a resting day every other day.

Carting hay and timber. The engine arrives to thresh peas from paddocks which yield forty-nine bushels to the acre. The work is indifferently done because the peas are damp and are not for that reason marketable, so that the Master is out of humour. We had a dispute over the water-cart and he called me a liar. As I had been in the right, I left. He kept back my wage for Christmas and New Year's Days which was wrong in that I was hired by the week. It was useless for a swagman to dispute this in the courts before the 'turkeys and geese' magistrates. Whelan has hundreds of geese and turkeys. I slept at the Limes Hotel, paying 1s for a bed and 6d for a meal.

Took the train to Geelong, fifty miles away. This is a pretty town with a sea port that can accommodate big ships. Four long jetties extend to sea to meet large vessels at ebb tides.

I made contact with the two poets, Tom Hughes and Jenkins, and they introduced me to a gentleman by the name of C. Ibbotson who has a fine mansion and farm in the country about eighteen miles east of Geelong. I was given a letter of introduction to his bailiff and I left immediately by coach (fare, 2s 6d) and arrived there at 5 p.m.

The farm (Spray's Farm, Bellarine East) runs down to a beach in Hobson's Bay. I can see the Heads in the distance where the World's big ships enter for Melbourne. Here, a tongue of land juts out into Hobson's Bay and divides the water into two channels, the northern one taking the ships to Geelong, and the southern one to Melbourne and Williams Town. O what a beautiful bay!

I was directed by the bailiff to thatch a hay stack. They work here from 6 a.m. to 6 p.m., some four hours less than at other places. Graceful living here. Too good to last for an unfortunate man like me. The cattle and sheep are imported. One big paddock under cultivation. The main crops here are carrots, potatoes and onions. Hundreds of acres of onions around here. Last year they sold at £75 a ton, but £3 this year.

The children are most mannerable, and their daily salutation is, 'Good morning to you old man'. I killed a snake four feet long on the veranda. It is very hot, and the thermometer in the shade registers 113°F.

February
Giant onions

Sad news comes from Melbourne where many die from the effects of the heat. Many fierce Bush fires are burning. Nothing like it since 'Black Thursday'.

Harvesting peas again. The welcomed rain comes to fill the tanks and dams. Weeding lucerne. Sowing rape seed. Bad news from home; my great friend John Miller of Morfa Mawr, Llanon, shot himself in a fit of depression.

Threshing peas with a flail. They yield well. Carting bricks (14s a thousand) to erect an extension to the mansion.

The children pick and harvest the onions. Many of them measure 15 to 18 ins in circumference. The present crop is the twelfth in succession without manure. The onion seeds are drilled in May; thereafter it is only a question of weeding. A neighbour sold his onion crop on the ground for £3 a ton. In a few days the price rose to £9. The buyer was a Jew.

The real value of a thing
Is just as much as it will bring.
No article ever can command
More than the market will demand.

Ram-lambs of pure breed nurtured on the farm fetch £60 each when eight months old. The sheep in the Colony drink a great deal of water; they drink like a thirsty horse. I believe they drink from custom rather than from need.

I helped to bathe and doctor an old favourite horse. Many pensioners apart from him are cared for on the farm. Would that old men were similarly treated among the so-called Christians.

I have a birthday (27th of February). It is my 57th.

March *Fear at Quarter Day*

When Mr Ibbotson came home he looked very pleased. He had won a law-suit which brought him £2,000.

I went for a swim. Drank two pints of sea-water. It took effect soon. A thunderstorm broke out. Potato-digging appears to be a big daily chore here.

A heibio'r wythnos fel un dydd,	The week goes by as if a day.
A mis fel wythnos gron;	The month seems too as but a week;
Mi ganaf nawr os felly bydd,	So mote it be, my earnest prayer,
Mai mis wna'r flwyddyn hon.	That the year may pass the same.

He again praises the gracious living along with the good food, 'thanks for the appetite built up for the meal, and the means of digesting it.' He gives the Welsh translation of the customary grace said in Victoria before and after a meal.

St Patrick's day (15th March) is a great day in the Colony and is kept as a public holiday.

Many of the paddocks are infested with weeds. For their eradication it is important to deal with them before they seed.

Brought home a load of lime for use in the building of an extension to the mansion here. It costs £20 a ton so that it is too expensive to use on the land.

Mr Ibbotson who is a station-holder in many parts of the Colony, says that he will lose at least 10,000 sheep unless the rain comes early next week. I fear the approach of Quarter Day lest my services here will be dispensed with. I don't want to leave this fine place.

April *Blessed are the meek*

The rain has come which pleases man and beast. I am engaged again for a further quarter at a monthly wage of £3. The overseer and his wife are engaged for £75 a year. Travelled four miles into the Bush for a load of firewood which is expensive in these parts. The flies worry the horses at this time of the year.

Received two letters, one from my daughter Margaret and one from my friend David Evans of Old Berlin who informs me that he received £5 from my wife. Acknowledging his letter I added the following lines:

We walk uncertain through this life,
And always prone to pain and strife.
I was quite pleasant when I wrote
And sent to you this friendly note.
A chip of wood, with speed did fly,
And caught my left and tender eye.
I cannot blame another hand,
The axe was swung at my command.
It made it sore, took half my sight,
I could not sleep a wink last night.
Keep this letter safe and well,
Might be the last, we cannot tell.

I groom three horses in the mornings and feed 150 head of cattle. Master has promised to get another man to help, but he is forgetful like myself.

Frosty mornings do me no harm,
The stable duty keeps me warm.

Ibbotson visited me while I was sowing rape. The millionaire probably did it himself when he was young. I find Sunday to be a short day; I busy myself mending my ragged things and reading. I have finished reading the Old Testament for the fourth time, and the New Testament for the third time. I prefer the latter which gives Christ's teaching. *One Sunday he composed a poem of 150 lines, taking as his theme the verse, 'Blessed are the Meek for they shall inherit the Earth.'*

May *A niggardly burial*

I have learnt that the £5 sent by my wife to my friend David Evans was meant to cover the funeral expenses because she had presumed me dead. She ought to be told that a man cannot be buried decently in this Colony under £14. (A grave in the cemetery costs £2; hire of carriage or hearse, £5; undertaker's fee £7).

Toothache has plagued me off and on for weeks; it disturbs my sleep. The overseer's wife has had her first child, and it is rumoured that the overseer will have to leave soon. I think this is rather an unkind act. I was asked to compose a verse on the occasion of the birth, so I wrote twenty lines on Sunday evening. The rumour is true, for Mr and Mrs James Fenie are to leave Spray Farm and are replaced by Mr and Mrs Webley. There are only four workmen here when there should be twenty-four.

I was accused by the new overseer's wife of carrying into the house a snake along with the firewood; it was a lizard and not a snake.

The onion crop occupies a field of forty acres. It yields forty tons of onions to the acre, and onions fetch £30 a ton. So, it brings in £4,800.

June and July *Foot and mouth disease*

A cow dies, others are ailing. They froth at the mouth. (*Is not this Foot and Mouth Disease?*) Two more cows die. It is obviously something contagious. A Government Inspector attends here. Yet, two more cows die. Another two cows die, making seven within the month of June, the wettest ever recorded in any part of the world. Sparrows and rabbits are the farmers' worst pests. The new overseer sported a revolver:

Overseer:
He asked me three times or more
If I had seen the like before.
'Tis either Colt's or Adam's work,
And one I brought with me from Cork.

Diarist:
Revolvers are unwelcome tools
When held by man and angry fools.

August *Timely word on contagion*

Cattle continue to die here from what they call the 'Pleuro'. (*Probably an abbreviation of pleuropneumonia, namely pleurisy and pneumonia, but it is now clear that it must have been an outbreak of Foot and Mouth Disease.*) The disease is obviously contagious. If this is so, I cannot understand why they drag dead animals for a distance of a quarter of a mile across pastures on which the other cattle graze. (*This was a commendable observation, and showed astuteness greater than can be accredited to the Government Inspector.*)

I had some sharp words with the overseer. He had taken my stable fork and had broken its handle in two. The Master had bought it for my sole use on condition that I was to take care of it, otherwise to pay for it. It had cost 7s. (*It would seem derisory for a millionaire whose onion crop brought him an income of £4,800 to haggle over a broken tool worth 7s, unless it be to enforce the truism of the old adage, 'look after the pennies and the pounds will look after themselves'.*)

I sent John Lewis of Forest Creek, Castlemaine a post office order for £4. He previously owed me £2, so he now owes me £6.

The horse 'Tom' goes to the blacksmith to be shod. He is a bad blacksmith, he hacks at the hoofs to make them fit the shoes, so the hoofs are so brittle that they fail to hold the nails. (*Instead of 'Sunday', on this occasion he names the day of the week as 'Swagman's Washing Day'.*)

September *More begets less*

I have made myself a pair of clogs and they are a good and comfortable fit. Troubled with toothache again. This is the most pleasant time of the year, the flies are not about yet.

I am astounded at the overseer's ignorance of farming matters. For example, he has sown that quantity of peas in a two acre paddock as would cover one of sixteen acres. As a result they will not grow as well, and it will cost £2 an acre to single them.

The waggon goes very frequently into the Bush to acquire firewood, and the journey takes half a day.

Every morning before breakfast, I groom, clean under, and feed three horses.

October *More thrift by the millionaire*

I received a cheque for £9 17s 6d in respect of wages for the previous quarter, and I was engaged for a further quarter when my weekly wages during the harvest month will be 25s. I agreed, because it is better than swagging the country, and spending my hard-earned money, searching for work.

The Master's two daughters, with their servants, have arrived at the mansion. Carting shells from the beach during the afternoon. The shell-laden sand is not heavy, and is a good fertilizer for the land. It is scattered in the sheep shed. The yearling ewes are sold for £20 each. A bell is sounded at breakfast time, a flag is hoisted for dinner, and supper is at 6 p.m.

O what a glorious country this is, and the present climate is ideal! One ewe from a flock of seventy-two has died. The Master paid eighty guineas for each. He mourns the loss of the single ewe, more than the twenty-seven cattle which have recently died from the contagious disease, 'pleuro'.

I have just paid £1 6s being my year's subscription for the weekly paper, 'Leader'. I work four hours longer than the other four who work here. No hay is gathered here for two reasons, they do not know how to harvest it, and the Master does not want to face a heavier wage-bill. As a result the cattle will starve for want of fodder in January. The abundance of grass is allowed to rot because it cannot be wholly grazed by the stock.

November and December *Wool, the Colony's undug gold*

No one places value here on farmyard manure, and great quantities of bone dust is bought and applied to the land annually.

As usual I volunteer to chop some firewood for the morrow. I am under no obligation to do this, but I find it to be policy to please the cook.

I am disappointed that no papers have arrived recently from home in spite of the fact that I regularly send Australian papers to them by each mail.

The sheep, of the Lincoln breed, all captured first prizes at the Geelong show. Three of them are priced at £600 each. Their wool is 13 inches long, and the average weight of a fleece is 22 lbs. Nearly a ton of wool was obtained from ninety-two sheep. Some 9,000 bales are exported to England annually at £22 10s a bale.

How I wish I could acquire twenty acres of land to farm it on my own!

1876

He begins his diary, reminding us that this is his thirty-seventh with never a blank day. He exhorts that diaries should be in book-form and not as loose scraps of paper which at a later date could be rearranged to stake a claim that they had presaged certain events. He maintains that even the notable poisoner, Palmer did not adopt such a disguise. He then proceeds to write his own epitaph:

Here laid beneath, a man in name,
But short of form, feat, and fame.

January *Seeds are the parents of weeds*

Up early to mow, to clear a road round the paddock to allow the reaper to commence cutting. The machine, an early invention, does not work well. The wheat is rusty and will neither yield well nor prove a good sample.

Weeding peas after dinner and gave up an hour before sunset, leaving the Master in the field working by himself. He is cross today because of the excess of weeds. It is now too late to overcome them. Weeds need to be dealt with early and before they seed. At such a time one man could keep the paddock clean, but now 100 men could not clear the weeds without destroying the crop.

The Master mounts his mare at 4 a.m. to ride to New Town. He does the twenty mile journey in an hour. Not bad for a man of 70 years.

Two blacksmiths worked in opposition in the town. The last to arrive had his tools stolen, his dwelling house burnt down, and his bellows ripped. Suspicion falls on the other smith, but the two local policemen choose not to act.

Another of the cattle is attacked by 'pleuro'. This contagious disease is a long time leaving the farm.

I read the Sunday papers after washing thirteen articles. They record news from all parts of the known world; they tell mostly of murders, thefts, cruelty, and quarrels among Christians.

Severe drought in South Australia, but the ground keeps moist in Victoria. A heavy thunder storm has just passed. Four sheep sheltered from the storm under my veranda.

I was sent to a new job, namely to bush-harrow the paddock, the idea being to thresh the seeds from the grasses, and save them entering the sheep's wool.

Went to the beach and had a pleasant swim. The water was clear and still. I dropped a pin into the water which was three feet deep. I could see it more clearly than when it was placed at the same distance on land. Presumably it was the incidence of light that accounted for this in addition to the clarity of the water.

Had a letter from my friend, David Evans reporting further luck at gold-digging. Abundant fruit in the orchard. Peas productive. Apricots are ripe, some of the onions are forty-four inches in circumference! The dams and tanks are full to over-flowing which is a rare happening this time of year. The Master has brought with him another millionaire who is from New Zealand. Plenty of music here. My co-workers play the harmonica and concertina under the veranda. I prefer to read a book.

The mower fails to cut the lucerne crop. They don't understand the machine, and they won't listen to advice as to how to put it right, so it is laid one side. The farm hands went for a swim in the morning and had to walk 200 yards before reaching knee-deep water. I waited till the afternoon when it was full tide, and was able to plunge immediately into four feet of water which had been warmed through passage over the stones and shells heated by the sun's rays. The dog 'Rover' came with me, swimming in front, and giving me signals when I should turn back.

February *Fodder-storing appreciated at last*

At last, my Master has opened his eyes and realized that he has to prepare something for the cattle when the grass is no longer available to them as fodder, so that he has harvested more hay this year.

I was sent to thatch one of the hay stacks. I could find neither ladder, nor thatch. The overseer, a London cockney, argued that they were unnecessary. This new country contains too many gamblers bent on horse-racing, football, coursing and cricket.

Following a four mile walk to Clifton Springs I composed forty lines, exhalting the health-giving properties of its waters and which appeared in the 'Geelong Times' on 23rd of February. *He autographed the poem with the letters F.R.S. which he said stood for 'Farmer and Roving Swagman'.*

I work hard and for long hours, for I feel it is my duty, and I am happy doing it. I am thankful to my parents for encouraging and even compelling me to work in all branches of farming. This fortune I retain and no one can deprive me of it. A heap of gold could slip out of my hand in a few hours. Health and work are man's greatest assets, and provide for contentment and happiness.

Onions are selling for £3 15s a ton, and an acre of land grows from 10 to 15 tons. A blind man and his guide called at the farm. The guides are paid 15s a week, so it is a paying occupation.

Three rams died from snake-bite; at £20 a piece, the loss was considerable. From 700 to 800 cattle beginning to suffer from the want of grass, all for the want of foresight, and a hopelessly inadequate agricultural labour force to provide green crops like clover and lucerne. The continued drought means that the cattle will be at the hay before I complete thatching the stack. Thatching reminds me of an incident on my father's farm forty-seven years ago. When the old and lame thatcher employed there had gone into the farmhouse, I sneaked up the ladder and continued the thatching. When the old thatcher returned, he commended me on the piece I had done. Thereafter, he would address me like this, 'Come Joe, do this lay for me as I feel tired', and away he would go to rest for an hour or two.

Sharks are in the bay and they have just killed a young man. Dysentery has again overtaken me as it did when in Wales, so I have taken twenty drops of laudanum and shall go early to bed.

March *A tall story*

Still no rain in most parts of Australia, New South Wales excepted, and the cattle and sheep are suffering.

I am engaged in threshing peas and beans, and grading potatoes. Consulting my previous year's diary, I was doing precisely the same jobs then. The ears of maize begin to fill; some of the stalks are over eight feet high. The flies are so troublesome that I have arranged a net to cover my head and protect my eyes.

The Master has returned from New Zealand, and reports that the corn crops there yield 100 bushels of grain to the acre. A tall story!

As another Quarter Day approaches, I reflect that I have now worked on this farm for fourteen months. What is now in store for me? I await the verdict.

April *Unearthing the precious metal*

I was given a cheque for £20 5s. The sum of 5s a week had been deducted from my wages during six weeks of harvesting, a time when it should have been increased.

Mr Ibbotson has announced that he is giving up farming. He gives no reason, but I can supply it. A ship cannot float and sail without a navigator on board, especially when it is among reefs.

I tramp to Castlemaine, and at the Albion Hotel in Wesley Hill I find myself among my own people.

Although the land round here is rich, the land is Nature and Nature is honest. You may only take from it what you give to it. Thus, the farmer must reward the soil for the yield he draws from it.

I ride in a farmer's cart through the Bush for a distance of fourteen miles to the home of John Lewis at Llwynteg, near Walmer. The farm measures 250 acres and they are actively engaged in fencing it. The soil contains quartz so it is not very fertile, and at the moment shows no grass. The neglect to sow foreign grasses like lucerne and clover, leaves the cattle short of fodder during the dry season.

I paid the Labour Exchange 5s for putting me in touch with a farmer, but nothing came of it, so the money is wasted again.

Started my swagging along Wallowby's track, and found the adjacent farms in a miserable state, with never a sign of any attempt to treat the soil as it should be treated.

I arrived at Tarnagulla and stayed at the Golden Age Hotel. The proprietors were a Mr and Mrs Edward Lewis. Mrs Lewis hailed from the vale of Aeron and she knew my father-in-law, Jenkin Evans of Tynant and his eldest daughter Betty with whom she was in school. She recounted to me my personal history, most of which was grossly distorted, before I had revealed to her my identity. She heard my version and invited me to stay as their guest for a week or longer, but I left the next morning for I had planned to visit my friend David Evans at Old Berlin. I walked eleven miles carrying my swag of eighty pounds, and felt very tired after an uncomfortable journey of sixty miles which I accomplished in three days.

I went to visit the site of the new 'gold rush' which is only four miles from here, and consists of a rugged hillock surrounded by trees and scrub land. Some 1,500 canvas tents and all sorts of temporary buildings had been erected there. It already has the appearance of a small town with stores, banks, hotels, butcher shops and bakeries, a printing office, saw mills, carpenter shops, blacksmiths and police headquarters. The ground surface is hard, showing a sort of pipe-clay and cement consistency. Some were engaged in blasting the rock, others were using steel chisels and hammers. Picks are useless. Each claimed-plot measures 20 square yards, on which they sink pits varying from 15 to 30 feet in depth. Depending on the seam which carries the gold the diggers may have to prop up the roof. The area is all taken up by prospectors and hundreds of would-be diggers leave without the chance of trying their luck, for the exercise is luck rather than skill. 'Claims' which do not yield gold are expensive because of the scarcity of water to wash the excavated earth, while the carters get 6s a load for transporting it. What puzzles the diggers is why the seam bearing gold runs zig-zag along the ridge of the hill, so that one man strikes it, while two or three adjacent claims provide nothing. Some get as much as fourteen ounces per load of washed-earth. This gold sells for £4 2s an ounce, or £58 per ton of bottom gravel.

I suffer from quinsy again, but the pain is eased by a stiff dose of cayenne pepper. I walked twenty miles, calling at half a dozen farms, but found no employment. The continued drought has made the ground too hard for ploughing. Settlers in the Bush hold farms of 320 acres, 20 to 40 of which are partly cleared and cropped continuously, but since they receive no manure they soon become exhausted. The occupiers find themselves unable to clear the remainder of the land so they sell. Those who have only taken up 20 to 40 acres, flourish, for they are able to cultivate these small allotments properly.

I travel another twenty-five miles, calling at several farms, but fail to find work. My funds are running out. Exhausted land everywhere. Give to the land, and the land will give to you, is a truth which the would-be farmers seem not to know, nor does the Government. I estimate that 1,000 labourers, employed at £2 a week could reclaim the land which I covered on my journey today.

There was talk recently at the Legislative Council that the 'Thistles Act' should be repealed on the grounds that the weed provided food for cattle. What ignorance! This very day I passed fields full of green thistles which were untouched by cattle although they were starving from want of fodder.

May *Hercules in the pigstye*

I turned in at William Clarke's farm at Mount Cameron where I had worked previously some two years ago. I was engaged on piece-work because at my age I am not able to follow a team of strong and well-fed horses tilling the paddocks. There is no hut for the labourers on this farm, but I intend taking more care of myself than I did when here before. Clarke collects his wealth, not through good judgment on farming methods, but through his frugality and niggardship. He has thousands of pounds in the Bank, but he is so mean that he does not provide candles either for dressing in the morning or undressing at night. Neither does he provide soap.

This being Sunday I visited the creek. There I found a big stone which served as a chair; another one I adopted as my writing desk, which suits admirably because it does not shake. There is nothing here to disturb me. The water murmurs as it runs over the pebbles in the creek, the magpie sings melodiously overhead, and there is every prospect of a goose for dinner. I am deliriously happy.

Up at 4.30 a.m. I take out four horses to draw the double-furrow plough. They can hardly pull it through the hard ground, but the rain has come. In the Colony the rainy season usually starts in April, but sometimes it arrives as late as the beginning of June. It now rains heavily, a blessing for both man and beast. The tanks begin to fill, and water flows into the dams.

I was kicked in the thigh by a colt, and it is very painful. Mrs Clarke ordered me to clean out the two pigstyes. They were last cleaned nine years ago. The litter was over six feet deep. I had to take off the roof before I could enter. It is written of Hercules that he did much heavy work, but it could hardly be heavier than the task of cleaning out those pigstyes. When I completed the work, Mrs Clarke's only remark was, 'Wash your boots before you come in to supper'.

I was up at 3.45 a.m. sowing a mixture of oats and barley in a paddock of twenty acres far removed from the house. The siting of the farmhouse in Victoria is usually wrong, in that it is erected at the periphery of the farmland, while the planning of town allotments is done with greater care.

My contract with William Clarke terminates today. I am paid-off in a friendly manner, and asked to call again.

I walked to Clunes, and went by train to Ballarat, where I stayed at the Times Hotel. Reporting at the Labour office, I was directed to a farm in the middle of the Bush near Bullarook, occupied by a widow, Mrs Bourke. The farm consists of 270 acres, but it is not all cleared yet, although she has had it for twenty years. I found many workers in the hut, and I was obliged to make my bed on the floor. I started to plough between the tree stumps. It is cold and there is thick ice on the water-pools.

Trees here are 70 to 80 feet high. Many have fallen, not from the axe, but as a result of the storms. Often a fallen tree leans on a standing tree. The grubber tackles the half-fallen trees. It is good land and when properly cleared produces ten tons of potatoes to the acre. The horses are fed half a bushel of boiled potatoes daily and no corn. Both horses and cattle are in good condition. There is a good crop of clover in one field. The man employed on digging potatoes gets a wage of 5s a ton; he can dig one and a half tons a day, so he is better paid than a ploughman. Potatoes are sold for £2 7s 6d a ton, and pigs at 8s a score.

The bailiff or whipper-in is a nigger-driver, and only takes three and a half minutes at a meal. He wanted to dismiss me, and asked Mrs Bourke to do this. She refused, saying that she had received a testimonial in my favour from the Labour Exchange far better than she had read in the case of any previous farm-hand.

Here they place the wheat seed in a solution of blue stone overnight and sow it next day.

June *Evangelism in the swagman's hut*

Ploughing for ten hours each day. I feel tired because the horses travel very fast. Five pounds an acre is too little pay for clearing this farm of timber and stone, but if this were done, the crop-yield would be trebled. Why don't they do it? *He writes an englyn criticizing farming methods in the Colony, and the neglect and starvation of the good land.*

Received news from my daughter Margaret that my father-in-law, Jenkin Evans, had died at the age of 94 years, as well as three other acquaintances. One was my brother-in-law, Jenkin Griffiths of Pontfaen, a distinguished sea-captain, who fell from his horse and was killed on the 20th of March last, on the road between Llanrhystyd and Llanon, when returning from Aberystwyth market.

Sea Captains are so skilful,
When steering ships abroad.
But never as successful
Astride a metal'd road.

Heavy snow has fallen, and it freezes hard with ice nearly half an inch thick on the water. It is Sunday, but no one from here goes to either Church or Chapel, and we remain inside the hut in which a big fire burns all day. My Bible was in use, but I could not persuade any of my colleague-workers to read our Saviour's 'Sermon on the Mount'. They say they cannot comprehend it, but they maintain they are able to understand the real meaning of the words found in the book of 'Revelation'. Dr Clarke (*presumably a local Divine of the period*) cannot explain them.

I am obliged these days to work for my tucker in order to make up the loss during the wet days. The whipper-in has accused me of being slow, saying that I was robbing my mistress who was paying me wages in respect of work which I was not giving her in return. I replied:

There is a boss near Bungaree,
A self-conceited fool,
Who always shouts 'I', 'mine', and 'me',
Can't use the simplest tool.

I plough between tree stumps, and boulders in a field called 'Paradise Paddock'. In a slice of it, 5½ yards wide and 7 chains in length, I negotiated the following hazards, 11 tree stumps, 7 standing trees, and 150 big boulders of stone. Some paradise paddock!

It is the hardest frost I have experienced in the Colony, yet I start ploughing at dawn when I can hardly bear to grasp the handles of the plough which can hardly break through the soil's crust. Finished sowing wheat and oats, but forty-five acres have yet to be sown with barley, peas and potatoes.

July *The embryonic warrior*

Out of work again, and the beginning of winter too. The prospects of getting work are bleak. Before I left the farm there came into the hut another elderly swagman. He seemed respectable. He was accompanied by a dog and he carried a double-barrel gun. He had a silver watch and wore a gold chain. He displayed on his breast a Waterloo medal, but in his pocket he only had a threepenny bit. He seemed too young to be a Waterloo veteran, and could not bear cross-examination on the subject by a critical historian. Even had he enlisted at 15, he would now be 76, and he looked less than 60, so he must have been fighting as an embryo! Mrs Bourke believed his story; she was an open-hearted woman who had married a ploughman and had since 'paid him off'.

Called at the Labour Office at Bungaree and was advised to stay in the town for two days to await possible visits from prospective farmer-employers. Employed the following day by William Westcott of Sal Sal Farm and Gardens, Moorabool Creek, near Bungaree. He has thirty acres of orchard and garden. A load of some kind of produce is taken to market at Ballarat, twelve miles away, daily. Now, two tons of potatoes, which sell at £3 12s 6d a ton, are taken in each day.

I was asked to plough a twelve acre field which is clear of stones and roots, and free from stumps and standing trees. What a change from 'Paradise Paddock'. A ploughman in this Colony is expected to plough an acre of land each day. I plough 9 to 10 inches deep in the orchard where 100 fresh gooseberry trees are planted, for tons of gooseberry jam are prepared here.

They are very religious people, and a service is held in the house after supper each Sunday evening. The gardener plays the organ and some thirty people attend. The country cries for rain. Sheep are dying from want of grass by the thousands. One squatter has lost 100,000 sheep. The land is over-stocked, and no winter-food is prepared for them. Why! Even the bees are not so negligent. Man is the greatest drone; he tramps upon, and gores his fellow creatures and has no thought for the beasts of the field; at the same time he talks of humanity, civilization, and Christianity. *He asks repeatedly, 'Why don't they cut and store the grass when it is heavy on the land?'*

All the men here are decent people, and all the workers, apart from myself, have a stake in the farm.

At the service on Sunday evening I was given a hymn book. The shepherd boy, who arrived during the week, is a Roman Catholic and does not attend, because his priest forbids him from attending other denominational meetings, in this case, Wesleyan.

August *Godliness ousts cleanliness*

I plough all day in a paddock in which four potato-diggers are working ahead of me. I am fast closing in on them. They pick no more than ten bags a day which earns them a wage of 5s, for they get 6d for each bag. They live mostly on potatoes and salt which costs 2d a pound. It is cold and freezing. The sheep are lambing and grass is scarce. Some winter provisions must be prepared for cattle and sheep in this fine country, for the land remains dormant for 3 to 4 months during winter.

A neighbouring farmer called here to geld a foal. He provided himself with two sticks four inches long. These he split down the middle and tied the two halves together at one end. He then made two cuts in the scrotum and brought both testes down, which he then clamped with the split sticks, through tying the other ends. The testes were then allowed to hang until they dropped off, a process which took a long time. A curious and most cruel procedure!

Ewes are dropping their lambs, dead or alive, by twos and threes. Although grass is beginning to appear, it has come too late to enable the poorly nourished embryo in utero to survive after birth. The ewes too are in a poor condition and less than one-third of them will be able to rear even one lambkin.

I have nearly completed the ploughing so I expect that I shall have to leave and take up my swag soon, and depart in the heart of winter. Spring, however, is at hand. Birds of the forest are nest-building, the geese are sitting, and the hens are laying more eggs which brings the price down to 10d a dozen.

They are very religious people here, and they will not allow me to wash my underclothing on the Sabbath day, and of course I have no time to do this on a week-day. I rise at 4 a.m. and work sixteen hours a day for a wage of 3s with which I am well pleased.

Very often the Minister fails to attend on Sunday evening to take the service, and on these occasions Mrs Dent, the cook, reads the sermon,

Mr Dent, the gardener, plays the organ, and the singing is very good. Being shabbily dressed, I feel uncomfortable among the well attired people who habitually attend the service.

I asked the cook for half a bar of soap. I was offered it on condition I would not wash my clothes on Sunday. Since I could not fulfil such a promise, I proceeded to the village stores and bought soap. It's funny, they expect me to groom the horses on a Sunday morning, but they regard it an unforgivable sin to groom myself.

September
Jam by the ton

The new shepherd turned the sheep on the road where there is good grass. In some places the roads are three chains wide, and they pass through very rich land. Few men or beasts travel along them. They were originally planned by the squatters to get their sheep to market.

I went into the Bush to get a supply of tree bark to start my fire in the evenings. The customary divine service takes place here. The Minister is in attendance. The tenets of the Wesleyans are more Calvanistic than I had thought possible. The Minister's undernourished horse is well fed when here. The cook is collecting money to buy a new horse. I contributed 2s 6d.

Two girls are cleaning and applying kerosine and oil to the blighted fruit trees. I do not understand the nature of blight because it affects some trees and not others. There is severe frost. When I rose at 5 a.m., I found a thick layer of ice on the water. It was the severest frost that I have witnessed in the Colony, and yet at 8 a.m. I was so warm that I had to cast my coat when at work.

A gale blows creating a sinister roaring noise in the Bush punctuated by an occasional crash from a falling tree. No floods this winter for there has been little rain. The cattle are suffering, and the young corn crops look poorly.

After supper there was a concert. Every member of the household played some musical instrument with the exception of myself, but this seemed reasonable to me since someone should act as a listener.

Three or four sheep are killed here each week 'for the pot'. Jam was taken to Ballarat market. Tons of jam are prepared here, and they are in no hurry to get rid of it; it will keep for years.

I spend hours hoeing between the fruit trees in the immense orchard, usually from 5 a.m. to 9 p.m. They have a good cook and the food is capital. Plenty of tea and sugar. Three or four sorts of jam on the table, fresh mutton, excellent bread puddings, buns and pancakes.

My wage is 17s 6d a week. I enjoy good health. Sometimes, I think I should be at home training my two boys in the way of living, but my conscience is easy, because it was not my fault that I absented myself from my, and their, home.

October
Speculating in land

Vivid rainbows in an angry sky, with heavy hailstone showers. No preacher attended for the evening service so the cook's husband read the sermon from the Wesleyan magazine.

Midday is warm, calm and bright; it may be a 'fox of a day', it is too much like summer. Forty-five dozen bunches of rhubarb sent to Ballarat market; they sell at 3s 4d a dozen.

The young girls are out cutting thistles, and brought back the first snake this Spring, a brown venomous variety, three feet long. Carted timber from the Bush and killed another snake four feet long. I wrote another letter to the editor of 'The Leader' on the virtue of farmyard manure, and the need to feed it to the Colony's soil.

Back in Cardiganshire they talk of working hard, I earn 3s 11d a day and do more work in the day than two men working for me at home.

Rhubarb is despatched daily to the market. Today 1½ tons were sold! I was very pleased to receive a letter today from my daughter Nell. Mr John Jones of Dolau Cathi was shot dead, and his daughter wounded, by his butler who also killed himself. *He pays high tribute to this man of unequal usefulness in the community, a liberal landlord, critic, antiquarian, philanthropist, and able lawyer. He dedicates several stanzas in Welsh to his memory.*

To buy land from the Government at £1 an acre has not been a bad speculation, for the timber alone from the acre is sold for £3; a good deal of firewood is needed by the gold-mining projects. The timber may be twelve miles from the market, but the buyer has to provide transport, uproot the timber, and cut it up.

Snakes are abroad and numerous. They are of many kinds, black, carpet, tiger and whip varieties.

Among the snakes and withered timber,
Some dead branches often drop.
My life's exposed to constant danger,
It is suicide to stop.

November
Daily devotion

Treating cabbage, turnips, rhubarb, and young raspberry canes, with liquid manure.

The weather has suddenly changed and has become boisterous with heavy showers of rain and hailstones. The fruit trees suffer. The gardener says that every bud on a raspberry cane is worth 6d. Scores of thousands of them are on the ground today, so the financial loss is great.

Mr Westcott came home today in a new waggon drawn by three horses. After breakfast each morning it is his custom to read a chapter from the Bible and he follows with a prayer when all members kneel.

The Master handed me a cheque for £1 8s so that I might pay my subscription in respect of my weekly paper, 'The Leader' which is a great comfort to me, supplying me with pleasure, information and knowledge.

Thirty bags of potatoes go to the market today; they sell at £2 15s a ton. The waggon brings back twelve tons of sugar for jam-making. We have commenced to shear the flock of sheep.

I learn from papers sent from home that my daughter Margaret was married on the 8th of September. *He salutes her on the occasion in poetry.*

The apple crop is a complete failure this year. This is the wettest day I have experienced since I came to the Colony. The great agricultural show has opened at Smeaton, where £1,000 is awarded in prizes. I was disappointed to learn that no *'dung-cart and spreader'* is on show this year again.

Mrs Westcott, her daughter and son, are in the country in order to comply with the residence clause of the Land Act. We have started on the hay harvest and eleven workers are now employed on farm work.

December
Orchard produce takes precedence

The fruit-pickers are forgathering here. Some fifty, mostly women, will be employed for the next two months. Continuing to take rhubarb to Ballarat daily; two people engaged pulling them, and three tying them in bundles. Seven workers pick gooseberries, and they collected 1,000 quarts today. The cherries are also ripe, and many tons hang from the trees. A waggon, heavy laden with rhubarb, gooseberries, cherries and currants, starts for the Melbourne market at 3 p.m. and will not arrive there before the morning.

The Master has too many irons in the fire. They are so busy with the fruit and jam, that the hay and mangolds on the farm are neglected. The mangolds have not yet been singled and they are already as big as a goose's egg. The weather is hot and ideal for hay making. The hay crop is heavy and it comes into the yard in good condition, but it is thrown into the barn in lumps, and there is no attempt to distribute it evenly, so I do not think it will keep well.

A letter from my daughter Mary tells me that my youngest child, John David, fell when riding a donkey and broke his arm. *He composes three verses in Welsh on the occasion.*

People attending Sunday evening services come early during this month, so that they can walk through the garden and orchard.

I have been informed that my wages will be advanced to £1 5s a week during the next six weeks of harvest time. I had thought of leaving at Christmas, but I have now decided to stay in preference to swagging for a day or two here and there for 6s a day.

1877

January *Drought takes its toll*

The eisteddfod at Ballarat on next St David's Day is to be more of a concert where singing takes the place of composition. I do not consider that singing alone is of any advantage to keep up the language of the Ancient Britons. I cannot imagine what the patrons of the 'Eisteddfod Fawr Caerfyrddin' would say to parading this concert as an eisteddfod. At the Carmarthen eisteddfod there were present Iolo Morganwg, Ifan Tegid, Daniel Ddu, as well as all the renowned bards of Wales and England.

Up at 5 a.m. and groomed the five horses before breakfast. Mended the broken strap of the chaff-cutter. The fruit-pickers are busy getting a load ready for the waggon proceeding to Melbourne. Sleet fell at noon. Hand-hoeing and singling mangolds. My mate at a job in the morning has gone on strike in support of a demand for a half-day holiday during each week. It is likely that his services will be dispensed with.

Many young boys apply here for work as fruit-pickers, but they are turned away, for girls are favourites for the job.

Directed to fetch a load of sugar from Ballarat for jam-making. They use a tremendous quantity of sugar for this purpose. Peas are ready for harvesting and the corn is ripening.

It is Sunday and I washed seventeen articles of clothing. I conducted this operation in secret, for they in the house object to this being carried out on a Sunday, although they expect the working man to be clean and tidy at table and during evening service in the chapel.

Fruit-picking and jam-making are in full swing. One man is employed solely in making packing cases to take the jam to the market. Rain is wanted badly. Beasts are suffering from want of grass. Bush fires rage, and the atmosphere is foul with smoke. Five miles from here many farms have been burnt out. Went to town for a load of sugar; I had already brought a load yesterday. The sugar is boiled with the fruit, and two girls are employed to stir it continuously.

Calm and hot. Cattle suffering from want of water and fodder. All the water holes are dried up. The fine grass that should have been prepared for hay is now withered, and this renders it very liable to fire from a careless discard of a lighted match.

Although it is Sunday I was up at 4 a.m. I wish to make it a long day because I have five papers from home to read as well as this week's 'Leader'. The Arctic explorers, and their ships, 'Alert' and 'Discovery' have returned, after their failure to reach the North Pole. They were hampered by the ice and were subjected to frost-bite and scurvy.

I have never experienced it so hot as it was at midday. When I spat on the scythe blade it seared. Indeed, a piece of beef steak placed on the blade could be satisfactorily roasted. Storage of water and hay grossly neglected in the Colony.

Fruit-picking and jam-making continues; thirty-five people attend at meals. Thatching a pea stack. The reaper is mowing oats and I am one of eight binders. I find I can bind a sheaf as quick as the younger men. Killed a fat brown snake, six feet long. There is a great need of rain. Enormous stretches of waste land covered with sapless withering grass. Thousands of sheep lie dead. This calamity could be avoided through foresight, employing more labour to harvest more hay, and raising artificial grasses like lucerne and clover. I wrote a letter to this end to 'The Leader', but one of the boys on the farm got hold of it and tore it into shreds. The behaviour of the rising generation is a disgrace to society. My wage of £1 5s a week is likely to be reduced next week. There are now forty hands here, many of them are girls under 9 years old. Fruits are dead-ripe except for damsons, plums, pears and apples.

February
Fashioning a shirt

Finished the corn harvest, and I cannot see any prospect of more work. Very little thatching needed in a dry season, and too early as yet to plough.

Three men employed continuously here labelling jam-jars. Each labels sixty in five minutes. A Bush fire broke out five miles from here, but fortunately it has been brought under control. The long and withered grass ought to be in stacks in order to feed the animals now starving for want of fodder, but the graziers say that labour is too expensive. The price of one head of cattle saved would ensure enough hay to feed twenty for months.

The rain has set in accompanied by thunderstorms. Twenty pickers have left the farm today. I have started ploughing and covered eleven acres in eight days, and have moved to another paddock of fifteen acres of oat-stubble. Perhaps it would have been better if I had stayed at home to train my two young sons in the arts of ploughing and handling horses instead of teaching the young casual workers on this farm.

Although a Sunday, I got up at 5.30 a.m. because I had seven yards of flannel from which I made a shirt for myself. I was well pleased with the finished article but I was blamed by the sabbatarians for breaking the Sabbath day.

The thresher arrives at the farm. One thousand bushels of oats, the product of a field of thirteen acres, passes out of the machine. Cutting rushes and reed, to thatch a stack of the straw, in a swamp which teemed with black snakes. I saw five and killed two. Had a warm contest with one of them.

Today (27th of February) is my birthday, and I have entered my sixtieth year. This is a peaceful place, but I work hard and for long hours. I wish I could obtain piece-work for at my age it is tiring to follow young and spirited horses.

March *Neither a lender nor a borrower be*

I visited an adjoining farm. They roasted a turkey for my coming. Swamps need draining. Farms of 100 to 200 acres are badly managed, and since they have only a single labourer, the land remains in its original state, so these units continue to be useless both for the farmer and the Colony.

I am very pleased with my thatching of the stack of loose straw:

Rhêd y dwr ar hyd y dâs	*(The water runs off the stack*
To diddos, toiad addas.	*A water-proof roofing, a good thatch)*

I was paid up to last Saturday and received £27 14s. Mrs Westcott, her son, and daughter, have left in a spring waggon for their other station in the Colony, a journey of three days.

I am ploughing in a fifteen-acre field which is being cleared of fallen trees. There are two drainers and three grubbers on the farm digging ditches and clearing scrub-land. They do not get much of a wage. They cross-cut and split three tons of timber in a day. A ton of timber is got from forty feet of tree trunks. The trees here are easy to split. A terrible thunderstorm accompanied by a downpour of much needed rain has just happened. They are still jam-making here because the plums have ripened, and another load of sugar has been brought from Ballarat.

I was given three days' leave and journeyed to Castlemaine, where I met my friend Walter Jones who drove me fifteen miles to the farm of Mr and Mrs John Lewis. There I examined my box of clothes and books. I took away with me the lyrical poems of Iolo, some clothes and a new pair of boots.

I lent Mrs Lewis £20, and since there was an outstanding debt of £10, John Lewis gave me an I.O.U. for £30. (*This debt was never redeemed.*) I returned by train and felt more tired than if I had been at work.

Mr Westcott bought fifty fat sheep, so we are assured of plenty of mutton. He will not slaughter any of his pedigree stock.

The Master has asked me to be up at 4 a.m. to drive him to meet the first train from Ballarat, for he is leaving for his other Colonial station where he will stay for seven months.

General election here soon with contests between Whigs and Tories, between Free Traders and Protectionists. Some want a Land Tax, while others wish to keep it free so that they can monopolize it for their own use.

Completed a bedstead for myself for I dislike having my bed on the ground because of the many snakes that are around. I made two feeding boxes for the horses, because the mangers were also on the ground.

The millionaire, Andrew Chirnside, who possesses 220,000 acres of the best land in the Colony, shot a farmer, and awarded him £100 as compensation, together with other privileges. Another man, a gardener, adopted a similar practice and shot a boy loitering near his vineyard.

April *Worshipping God and Mammon*

It is a great mystery to me that although the selectors have lived in this neighbourhood for 15 to 25 years, the productive land which they have held has remained uncleared. It could be cleared for £4 to £6 an acre, while the first crop, namely potatoes, would fetch £20 an acre.

Engaged in dragging stumps and burning them after the grubbers, some of them so big that a team of fifty willing oxen could not move them. Having ploughed one and a quarter acres, I carry on busily in order to earn honestly a wage of 2s 11d a day together with good victuals.

I have sowed and harrowed three acres with grass seeds. The crops look promising in this glorious country, but the farmers are shockingly neglectful of the productive soil. The horse flies are a nuisance, but the magpies sing melodiously.

On Sunday the eleven cows are milked before breakfast, but after breakfast on week-days. Two preachers attended evening service. As soon as it finished the young hands turned to card-playing when £5 notes changed hands. What religious people!

Ploughed fifteen acres in fourteen days with a single plough and a pair of horses, and in addition clearing away many tree-stumps. Many swagmen on the road, but none offered work by the short-sighted farmers, for should they employ them, it would bring profit to themselves, the workers, and the country. Potato-digging commences. The crop pays three times the cost of reclaiming the Bush. They harvest eighteen crops of potatoes without applying any manure. The potato crop is good, which is a blessing, for it is a splendid substitute for the expensive bread (a 4 lb loaf costs 7d). Mutton and beef are cheap.

Whilst ploughing in the orchard I came across a leafless apple tree. One of its branches bore blossoms, another carried a ripe apple, and on yet another branch there were small newly formed apples.

The welcomed rain was accompanied by hailstones of a peculiar kind and resembling crystalized metal, for they don't melt in the pocket, in hot water, nor in the fire!

It has rained heavily; it was greatly needed, but already people are complaining, and they don't appreciate what a blessing the rain is. Of course it is unpleasant to have to work in the rain, and today I am wet to the skin. The worms, the birds and the bees are in their prepared holes. The Queen-bee does not send out her swarm to collect honey for Her Majesty on a rainy day.

I have just read that Russia is going to wage war on Turkey in defence of Christianity, and France is preparing to fight the Prussians for revenge and retaliation. I do not think I shall live to see the swords turned into pruning hooks and plough shares. Very likely England will stay out of it and keep her gold.

May
The bad shilling

Raining most days, and the grass grows well. Grass seeds sown a few weeks back, are now a carpet of green covering the ground. The growth-rate of grass, cereals and trees, is much greater in this Colony than in Wales.

The English and champion pugilist, Jim Mace, arrived in Ballarat. This renowned missionary from the Christian country may succeed to improve our morals through compulsion, for the bishops and priests have failed through preaching and persuasion.

On Sunday I remained indoors most of the day reading Iolo Morganwg's psalms which I find a great comfort. I value them greatly, and as in the case of the Old and the New Testaments, I now understand their messages far more clearly than I did when at home. I cannot understand why the separate denominations neglect their preachings and follow such as Martin Luther, Wesley, Calvin and others.

I have just undertaken the disagreeable job of taking my co-worker and friend, John Williams, to meet the coach. He is leaving the farm after a stay here of six years. His departure has resulted from a few cross words with the bailiff. Man is born to affliction.

All wages have been raised except those of farm workers. Carpenters are to get 8s for a day of eight hours.

The Liberals have been returned to govern in the general election just held. Each parliamentary member gets a salary of £300 a year. This will be very acceptable to them, for the majority are not only poor, but are illiterate as well! The Liberals are mostly protectionists, and the working man is not likely to benefit from them. Why should I have to pay thirty per cent duty on my clothes and boots, while ladies' silk and toilets are exempt from duty?

While dragging logs into a heap to be burnt, the horse jibbed and several hooks and chain-links were broken before my mate and I had to abandon the job. It reminded me of a character back in Wales named 'Twm o'r Nant'. His favourite phrase was 'use your brains'. He could move timber with one ordinary horse when others considered it foolish to try without the help of a score of willing and strong oxen. His power rested with his 'brains and methods', but a jibbing horse always puzzled him, and his plan then was to deal with it as with a bad shilling, namely get rid of it.

My workmate Dick is leaving tomorrow to assist his father to dig potatoes at 6d a bag. Thirteen bags are considered to weigh a ton. I wrote a twelve-page letter to my daughter, Margaret.

I miss the company of my friend, John Williams, and I cannot befriend the new worker who has taken his place:

For three things, your time don't spend,
For a whole and faultless clan,
For a brave and faithful friend,
And an independent man.

Since I broke my watch whilst ploughing, I find it difficult to allot my duties in relation to the time of day, and I mistake the moon-lit mornings for the dawn. I have found that the moon sets at 10 minutes to 5, so I arrange to complete my stable work which involves feeding and grooming the horses, and cleaning from under them, before the moon disappears below the horizon.

Spent 16s in the town on sundry things which included a Bible, hymn book, calico, shirt, needles and tobacco.

On Sunday evening at the farm we had a short and purposeful sermon on the text 'Let us not weary in well-doing'.

June
A sculptor at work

Many swagmen walking the road. They are driven away from farms by dogs. They offer to cut firewood for a meal.

Rams in the Colony are strong beasts. This week a butcher was butted by one and killed on the spot.

At a public auction, fifty-four acres of ordinary land were sold for £1,100. Land is as dear in Australia as in Wales.

Tons of jam continue to be despatched to Ballarat from the farm. Up at 4 a.m. to start ploughing for oats again. I have many letters to answer, but this Sunday I have found the day too short to complete this task.

I overslept, and was not up before 5.45 a.m. so that I went in for breakfast before grooming the horses, but I was able to feed them before having my own meal. This is only the second time this unpunctuality has taken place since I joined this farm. Even so, I was out ploughing before dawn. Two young horses draw the plough, and we travel at four miles an hour. In the evening I sharpen the plough shares and mend traces and harness. I received three newspapers from home, so it was midnight before I retired.

Last night a co-workman scoffed at me for bothering to write this diary which records my daily movements. I answered, 'Through doing this I am building and carving my own monument, whether it will be good or bad.'

July
The farmers' code

I attended the customary religious service after tea on Sunday. I am never invited to the supper that follows the sermon. Earlier I took a walk into the Bush where I picked up a needle case holding twenty-seven needles which I had lost two months before. It had been carried there by native cats; some of the leather had been eaten away. In that I had placed the needles in goose-quills, they had remained shining bright.

Carting mangolds. They are small, one of Charles Ibbotson's would outweigh two dozen of these. The horse 'Captain' jibbed when drawing the load. The bailiff said it was because he was too fat, so I was blamed again for that. The horses drawing the harrow are driven very hard; they are foaming and frothing from sweat. There are three characteristics peculiar to farmers in this Colony — exhausting the land, abusing horses and exploiting the labourer.

I posted a letter to Wales which will arrive there on the 3rd of September. I spent all the day harrowing; the job does not suit old horses and old men. Finished ploughing, harrowing, and sowing oats in a paddock of 13½ acres in fourteen days. Helped a ewe to lamb, but it was born dead.

The attending minister this Sunday preached to the same text as did the one a week ago, namely 'Jesus wept over Jerusalem'.

They always warn us from this text
To shun the World and love the next.
But in this World we yet abide,
And for the same we do provide.

Wheat is 7s 8d a bushel, and flour is £16 10s a ton. Less rain fell in this month than in any July for twenty years. Weather favoured the sowing of the cereal crops. The fruit trees are budding and some are in blossom. My health is tolerably good except for toothache.

August
The dry winter

Attended a ploughing match where the best ploughmen of the State of Victoria competed. Many contestants turned out work that was pleasing to the eye, but closer examination showed that the turned sods were not cut clean from the ground underneath on the right side.

Frosty and unusually dry days. It is the driest Winter since 1838 in the Colony; that winter was followed by very dry Spring and Summer.

Continuing dry without any sign of rain. The cereal blades are withering for want of rain, and the cattle and sheep are dying for the want of food.

September *Clerk of the weather is bypassed*

I have finished ploughing the mangold's ground, and have ploughed and harrowed for barley, sowing five bushels of it. The land is in an exhausted condition, and is fouled with sorrel. It is no use talking to the farmers about preparing farmyard manure to fertilize the land.

They are holding prayer-meetings in New South Wales to plead with the Almighty to send rain:

The mortal man, half rotten clod,
Attempts in vain to mock his God.

Instead of engaging in such futile exercise it should be for them to prepare dams and even tanks to conserve rain water from the roofs, for the use of man and beast, providing for the period of drought. Moreover, the farmers should cultivate the land and grow artificial grass as lucerne, cocksfoot grass and clover, which all flourish during the longest period of drought ever recorded in the Colony.

Nine milch cows here produce seventy pounds of butter for market each week in addition to the quantity which eight people consume at table. The butter sells at 1s 2d a pound.

A ten-acre paddock, the sixth on this fine farm, has been cleared of scrub, and not a single stump remains in any of them, but the best half of the farm land is still uncleared.

Cultivation of the land is for young men following young horses. I would like to engage in piece-work. Sixteen hours daily of hard work is too hard for one of my age, and I feel tired.

October
The diarist invents a farm implement

The products of the farm are still being carried daily to Ballarat, which include jam, rhubarb and potatoes. The cottager can buy a strong pig and a ton of potatoes with which to feed it for £1, both commodities delivered at his door.

I always appear to have a work-mate who is fond of music. My present colleague on the farm has three musical instruments, concertina, the pipe, and a Jew's harp. I like the last best of all, although sharpening a hand saw would please me as well. Doubtless, the next generation will be able not only to record the noise we make, but also preserve it for posterity.

I enjoyed my customary Sunday walk round the farm, and I never witnessed a grander sight than the fruit trees in blossom when I entered the orchard. The grass is growing tall and luscious, the corn blades are thriving, and the animals are in good condition. O what a beautiful country for man and beast!

I always clean and grease my boots each Saturday night. I invented and built a drill to sow mangold seeds. It works well and is easy to handle. With it I completed twelve drills, each of ten chains in length, in the course of an hour.

Last night I listened to the sound of the wind and of the thunder. These have not yet been recorded, but they will be by a future generation. In the meantime, through the written word we have been able to keep count of sounds and events. How valuable this has been, so that the fine sweet psalms of the prophet David have given us so much pleasure through reading, and have not reached us through the sound of his harp.

November
Religion and humanity to ride tandem

My mate and I walked ten miles to inspect the countryside, but we saw no farm as prosperous as this one.

I was disappointed that today (9th of November) was not kept as a general holiday, to pay tribute to the Prince of Wales on his birthday. I hope that no-one informs him that there is so much disloyalty to him in this part of the Colony.

The family have returned from six months' sojourn in their other home in the country. Mr Westcott inspected the orchard and was highly pleased with what he saw, namely the trees laden with fruit.

water in the water-holes. The fruits were frozen to the trees. The frost wrought wholesale destruction. Yesterday, many would have been glad to purchase the produce of the orchard for £500. Today, they would not give £10 for the lot. The Master bears the loss quietly, and without a growl against Nature:

Yesterday, gladness; today sadness.
Disappointment, but no bitterness.

The hard work and the long hours are too much for one of my age, so I gave notice that I was leaving. I was paid my wage of £27 4s 9d, and I agreed to stay on a few months longer if my health and strength permitted, but I elected to leave for two weeks' travel. I cashed the cheque and deposited £20 in the Savings Bank.

I stayed at the Bridge Hotel at Ballarat which was in the keep of Mrs A. Thomas, paying 1s for my bed and 1s for each meal.

I made to attend the Smeaton annual show in an overloaded cab. The horse jibbed, so I had to walk, although I had paid my fare of half a crown.

Wandering round the streets of Ballarat, which were thronged with people from morning to midnight, I met Mr and Mrs Westcott, and they wanted me to return with them. I readily agreed in order to be rid of the town with its pride and vanity.

After filling twenty bags of oats for market, I felt tired so I did not attend the evening religious service. As the Master was away, his wife did the reading and the praying. On Sunday I was up at 5 a.m. and as it was a late breakfast I stole out before the scripture reading and prayers. I was severely admonished for this.

The family drove out to evening service. I was asked to accompany them, but I refused and said that the horse needed to be rested because he had already been overloaded with work during the week. They evidently drove him furiously, because when they returned the horse was frothing all over. Religion and humanity ought to go hand in hand.

In an entry on the 22nd of November (vide), which is written across part of the day's record, he speaks of a letter from the editor of the 'Daily Telegraph' requesting him to send an occasional letter on practical farming for publication.

An all-timber building is being erected att the farm. Carpenters earn 8s for a day of eight hours. Most of them are rough or 'Bush carpenters'. The one working here says that he was a 'ship carpenter'. On my voyage to the Colony I noticed that every aged sailor practised that trade at sea.

It has been an exceptionally dry November, and the public continue to hold prayer-meetings and pray for rain. They are candid enough to admit that the drought is a retaliation for *our* sins, but when questioned, the complainants attribute the faults and the sins to *others*.

December
*Admission
of weariness*

My home-paper, 'The Welshman', dated the 12th October, records the death of the Reverend Latimer Maurice Jones, Vicar of St Peter's, Carmarthen. He was my landlord, and one of the Trustees over my children until my return to Wales. My father-in-law was the other, and now both are dead.

Lots of plum—and cherry—trees have been cut down, and replaced by raspberry canes which are more profitable. The gooseberry-pickers have arrived late in the evening. They are a rowdy lot and there have been two stand-up fights already. A prayer meeting followed. What a mixture it has been.

Swearing, fighting and thieving continues among the pickers, and I get no peace to write my diary.

I have remained in a fair state of health through the year, and have been able to do my work with pleasure, even if it has been rather hard at times, for I have never worked so many hours each day in any year before, and which at my advanced age has told on me. My joints are not as pliable now, so that it will be difficult to tackle new jobs.

1878

January *Man's inhumanity to man*

At the commencement of this my thirty-ninth diary it occurs to me that should all my manuscripts be kept and examined, it will be found that no days or even hours have gone unrecorded in those thirty-eight years. This has given me more pleasure than labour, and I am in sympathy with the phrase, 'Habit is second nature'.

See yonder poor, o'er-laboured weight,
So abject mean and vile,
Who begs a brother of the earth
To give him leave to toil.
(From Robert Burns' poem, 'Man was made to Mourn'.)

Should that witty poet be obliged to swag this country at the present time, he would find that these four lines of his would be most appropriate. The working men in this Colony are suffering from want of the necessities of life, both in regard to aliment and shelter, where millions of acres of the richest land in existence, remain in their natural state, and which have been claimed by a few 'dogs in the manger', who do not keep a single sheep on each two acres of such productive, but neglected land.

These deny a fellow-creature even water from their creeks and reservoirs to quench their thirst. It is plain that the world is steeped deeper and deeper in tyranny. How different from the days of Abram and Lot, for Abram said unto Lot, 'Let there be no strife, I pray thee, between me and thee, and between my herdmen and thy herdmen, for we be brethren. Is not the whole land before thee? Separate thyself, I pray thee, from me. If thou wilt take the left hand, then I will go to the right, or if thou depart to the right hand, then I will go to the left'.

Shortly past midnight, I was awakened by a loud report from guns nearby. This hailing of the New Year was new to me, and it seems a foolish idea. The Scotch and the Irish regard it as a sporting day. They assemble at the Sal-Sal falls where over 3,000 attend horse-racing. There is too much gambling in the country, but the people will have it. Most of the race-goers were farmers, and half of them had neither water nor grass at their farms for the cattle, all through lack of preparation against drought conditions.

Bush fires are likely to be numerous before the end of the month because of the dry grass. To drop a lighted match, carelessly or deliberately in revenge, can burn fifty square miles of grass and corn, as well as homesteads and animals. The guilty person is not always the one punished. When a rogue is well dressed he is very often mistaken for a gentleman.

A load of timber boards arrived from Melbourne for the making of jam-boxes. Many thousands have already been made. They measure 2 x 1½ x 1 feet. The man that makes them gets 5s per 100 and he makes 130 a day. At home I doubt whether carpenters would manage sixty in a day. Labour on this farm is got on the cheap.

I have finished singling a three-acre paddock of mangolds. A sermon at the house as usual this Sunday evening. I cannot understand why people in the face of common sense, believe in the teaching of John Calvin.

It was a miserable journey by waggon to Ballarat. At times visibility was down to two yards from dust rising from the rough road. Dust lies six feet deep in parts; it drifts like snow in the hollows. Since the 1st of January the toll gates no longer function.

I opened roads in the cornfield with a scythe in preparation for the reaper. It was so hot that I could not handle with my bare hands the stone to sharpen the scythe.

Bush fires rage and the air is foul with smoke. Some think it is caused by heat from the sun on broken glass-bottles, others consider it is caused through negligence, but most happen when hungry swagmen call at farms in search of work, and are sent away by ferocious dogs and foul words. A lighted match in the dry grass is their way of retaliating.

Harvest men are numerous and are obliged to sleep and starve on the dusty roads. They will not be employed before Monday in order to save their Sunday meals. The drought continues. No water for man or beast. Prospect of a scorching summer, and a dry Fall to follow. It is time for Joe to leave the husks and return to Wales!

I managed to mow 2¾ acres of barley in 11 hours and 5 minutes, and that by one in his sixtieth year. I must never repeat this frolic.

Ten days ago I could not hold the stone to hone the scythe because it was so hot; today I could not hold the rake and fork because of the cold, so changeable is the weather. The mangold crop is a complete loss, the vegetable is devoured to ground-level by the locusts, and they have now started on the potato haulms.

Took the waggon to Ballarat for a load of sugar for jam-making. I arrived there at 11 o'clock and found that my watch which had not been cleaned for twenty months coincided with the time by the town clock.

The temperature is $103°$ F. The Master drove back in his heavily loaded carriage from a journey of twenty-six miles. The horse was covered in white foam from sweating. There is no sense in it.

February
Hard drinking

Sheep are sold for 4d each; they are dying from the severe drought. The Sunday sermon was read by Mr Westcott because the minister did not turn up. These ministers often break their promises, and their excuses gain credence, and yet they criticize such faults in others.

The Master usually sells scores of tons of fruit in addition to fifty tons of jam, but this year he has to buy quantities of fruit in order to serve his usual customers with jam.

The heavy rain has arrived and the snakes come out in large numbers; they don't surface during the very dry weather.

Farmers and their wives swarm the roads nowadays. The women usually drive the buggies. They stop at hotels to drink ale and spirits. The husbands are generally hen-pecked, but they are never denied an abundance of drink.

Master on his return journey from Ballarat, drove the fourteen miles of an uphill road in less than two hours. This is not good enough for heavy farm horses.

At the Sunday evening service, the Minister said that faith will do without good works, but good works are as nothing without faith. I prefer the idiom, 'He can't be wrong, whose life is in the right'.

March
Men of manners

On St David's Day (1st of March) I made to attend the annual eisteddfod at Ballarat. I was in time at the coach station, but found the coach already over-filled with my countrymen, so I had to walk on. It was very warm, and I made my way to Warrenheip station, but missed the train by half a minute, so I had to walk the five miles to Ballarat. On the road I composed four verses of eight lines each, by way of salutation to the eisteddfod (*these in Welsh, are recorded in the diary*), but I missed the morning session. In the afternoon I delivered my address and verses to the well-attended gathering, and was given a standing ovation, when flowers were thrown on to the stage. I entered a competition for the best englyn to Stanley, then exploring the Nile in Africa, and was successful from among six competitors. Again, I was unable to get a place in the coach on the return journey so I had to stay the night in Ballarat, occupying Room 19 at the Bridge Hotel.

I started ploughing again. Surveyors on the farm deciding the course of a proposed new railway track. Two routes in view, both passing through this farm which will spoil it. Many snakes about by day and night; one entered the kitchen. My cottage is well built with a fire-place in one of the three neatly-papered rooms. There is one draw-back, namely that I have only a few spare hours in the week to wash, mend, read and write.

On Sunday two Swiss gentlemen came to visit Johann the gardener. They are fine men of good manners. In fact the Swiss, Germans and Americans are the most civilized men in the Colony, and are an example to the English, Irish and Welsh.

Two tons of jam to Ballarat again today; scores more tons in store here. I held that the farm-work was being neglected for merchandise, so I was ordered to go and plough tomorrow. Very dusty at Ballarat with visibility down to three yards. Drapery hanging outside the shops were a sorry sight.

April *New Testament to save boot-leather*

Finished ploughing a fourteen-acre field in eleven days, and later harrowed it three times. I never realized the importance of proper harrowing before coming to the Colony. My brother Griffith gave me early lessons on this theme, but I did not agree with him then.

The horses are much troubled by the flies so that they proceed at the trot all day. Consequently, both they and I are very tired at the end of the day. As I trudged back through the Bush I was reminded of those lines of Gray's elegy which my uncle, David Davies, Castell Hywell, translated thus:

Dacw'r ychen gwâr lluddedig	The curfew tolls the knell of passing day,
Yn dod adre' i fynd yn rhydd	The lowing herd wind slowly o'er the lea,
A'r llesg arddwr yn ymlusgo	The ploughman homeward plods his weary way,
Ar eu hol, o glun i glun.	And leaves the world to darkness and to me.

Sowing lucerne, and allowed for twelve pounds to the acre in a twelve-acre field. So steady was my pace, and so even the sowing, that I had only half a pound left at the finish.

On Good Friday I went to Ballarat to hear the Rev. Thomas Jones of Swansea preach. I composed an englyn exhalting him, but having listened to the views which he divulged in his sermon, I added a verse denigrating him.

I attended the usual Sunday evening service, and found only seven people in the congregation. The preacher should have more sense than walk seven miles over a rough road on such a dark and wet night. Is there not a New Testament in every home?

Visited by very heavy rain and a severe thunderstorm. Hares are a menace for they strip the bark off the young fruit trees. A letter of mine on 'Degrading the Bench' has appeared in the 'Gordon Advertiser'. (*He does not record the contents of the letter.*)

I carry out my customary stable duty on the Sunday, and I am expected to groom and feed the horses, eight in number, throughout the day, but I am prohibited from cutting a piece of firewood for my own comfort, for it is regarded as an unpardonable sin. Attended the usual sermon in the evening, because I am expected to do this at a place where the Minister undervalued and indeed denounced, good actions. When I came out of the service I composed the following lines:

Believe in righteous actions.	Our God, our heavenly Father,
Have faith in doing good.	Demands a pure heart
Be just in all transactions.	As sacrifice to render
Beware of shedding blood.	Before we do depart.

May *The thriving lone farmer*

Carted twenty-eight loads of farmyard manure to the orchard; none to the farmland. The Master's son, Thomas Westcott, J.P. paid us a visit.

A neighbour, Mr Letham, farms 200 acres of good land by himself. His wheat each year measures thirty-five bushels an acre. He treats his fields with farmyard manure and bone meal. He only has a woman to cook for the men who follow the threshing machine for a few days once a year.

Did some shopping at Ballarat; for £1 I bought 6 yards of flannel, 2 yards of calico, 1 yard of moleskin, a new shirt and a jumper. It is frosty and ice, one-eighth of an inch thick, covers the water pools.

As I was coming home from work, the full moon was appearing over the Black Hills. It seemed to be the size of the rear wheel of a farm waggon. The same time last night it appeared the size of a man's face. It was not the figment of the imagination. The astrologists may have an explanation for this phenomenon.

The gardener and his assistant were planting rhubarb, a crop which takes most of the farmyard manure. This is a bad policy. The garden used to pay well when orchards were few and the fruits in demand in Melbourne and other large towns, but now the farm pays best and should have all the natural manure.

June *The rivals*

I have written to the 'Geelong Times' on 'The farm labourers and their rights'. My letter last week on the same subject has already appeared.

A large meeting of the 'unemployed' has taken place in Melbourne, while New South Wales cannot get labourers. Yet, only a river which is conveniently spanned by bridges, divides these two rival States.

Here, many swagmen are walking the road in search of work. They are willing to work half-time to avoid starvation. On this farm, fifty fat sheep have just arrived, and there is always plenty of fresh mutton at meal-time.

In the weekly sermon, the preacher denounced righteousness and good works. He said that Voltaire and his followers were in hell, while John Bunyan was in heaven.

July *The Governor takes notice*

Potato-digging in full swing; they sell at £2 12s 6d a ton. The Master likes the oats sown before mid-July, but it is hopeless to do that this year, because in addition to the ploughing, I have to fill the holes where the trees have been uprooted, with a spade, fork together the tree branches, pick the stones, and cut the roots with an axe.

There has been a meeting of the Assembly at which the Governor spoke. I had the satisfaction of seeing a few sentences of a letter I wrote two years ago in the 'Geelong Times' quoted by the Governor.

I took a long walk over six adjoining farms. O, should this rich and productive land be properly cultivated, it would supply the whole of Europe with all comforts and the necessities of life!

The weekly sermon was delivered in good style. It was mostly about the devil. Poor fellow, they will not leave him alone when things are going well for all. It appears that he himself is an old transgressor, so he is blamed for every dirty action that the creature-man can invent.

I was up in proper time to benefit both myself and my employer as should always be the case, and found half an inch of ice on the water pools. The land is now bare of grass.

Dropped a hint in the house that I would like to attend a lecture at Gordon on phrenology, but as no early supper was prepared for me I gave up the idea.

Two newspapers, the 'Cambrian News' and the 'Cardiff Mail', arrived from home. Two items of news interested me. The one announced the death of my friend Colonel Powell of Nanteos, and the other told of the marriage of another friend, the Earl of Lisburne. (*He composed an englyn on the former event.*)

From a neighbour I borrowed an arrangement for leading pigs into a cart or waggon. The pigs climb up the 'race' without trouble. (*This contraption appears to be the forerunner of the modern trailer for loading animal stock.*) Nine storer pigs are taken to Ballarat and sold by auction. (*Again a forerunner of the modern mart.*) I do not like the system because the commission is heavy, and I prefer the private bargaining between man and man.

The rate-collector has arrived at the farm. He demands 1s in the pound on the land value. The occupier who holds a section of land is only a trustee for the public. The Government loans the land for cultivation for the public's benefit.

I have spent most of the month reclaiming a virgin paddock, clearing it of timber and stone, ploughing, harrowing and sowing it with oats. It was very tough work. There has been a heavy fall of snow, and there are lots of hares about, eating away the bark off the young fruit trees in the orchard.

August
The trouser floats: the jacket sinks

The roads are in a bad condition following the rainy weather, and the waggon carrying a load of flour from town had its axle broken.

All hands are working in the orchard, hoeing it and manuring. The farm is subservient to the orchard for there are more labourers in the orchard than on the farm, and yet the farm pays and the orchard does not. A swagman shares my cottage for the night. He has been on the road for a month in vain search for work. Yet, there are millions of acres of productive land in the Colony remaining uncultivated. O the mismanagement and the shortsightedness!

Johann, the Swiss gardener, told the following story at the supper table. When he was on the voyage to Australia, a certain man on the ship was so shabbily dressed that the Captain ordered him to strip, and provided him with a respectable suit of clothes. When the Captain threw the old clothes overboard, the man went wild for he had 300 sovereigns sewn-up in his coat sleeves. The boats were instantly lowered, only the trouser was recovered.

It is dark when I do my stable work in the morning and again in the evening. I am out of candles, but the mean women in the house will not provide me with either candles or oil, so I walk over a road flooded from the recent thunderstorm to buy from the post office, which is also the local stores, a pound of candles for 1s.

Johann accused me of irreverance because I only knelt on one knee when the preachers that visit the place are in prayer. I made a suitable reply.

Mr Westcott's son had been sued by a worker for arrears of wages in respect of timber splitting over a period of two years. The sum he claimed was £150, but the defendant won the case.

A discussion on Voltaire has taken place after the evening service, and he was denounced by members of the household as hell's chieftan. I maintained he was a disciple of Christ, and devoted his life to publishing the truth against the world.

September *Last walk over the farm*

Visited by toothache again. I abused my teeth badly when I was young through cracking nuts which grew plentifully on the farm. I plough between the orchard trees as the magpie sings beautifully. The trees are overloaded with blossom.

The Gordon-Warrenheip railway is under construction. The hotel keepers will benefit greatly because they are the sub-contractors.

My letter has appeared in the 'Gordon Advertiser' (*he does not mention the subject-matter*). The customary sermon lasted a whole hour. An hour of absolute nonsense!

Received my wages of £20 4s. I deposited £10 in Post Office Savings, and now hold £40's worth. I gave notice that I would be leaving the farm at the end of the month. I hope that I shall never do any more ploughing. I have now been here for two years and two months. *He gives no reason for leaving, but mentions that he must be under the care of his doctor, although he does not give the reason for this. Mr Isaac Westcott has been away at his other station at Boort, some 150 miles away, where he has thousands of acres. The bailiff has found a Mr John Lambeth to replace the diarist here, at Moorabool Creek.*

On the last Sunday of the month I take my last walk over the farm, and I leave tomorrow.

October *Enters the house of torment*

I carry two big bundles and a box to meet the coach that was to convey me to Ballarat where I stayed at the Bridge Hotel, kept by Mrs Thomas. I bought some clothing, ate a good dinner, and reported at Ballarat Hospital. Admitted into a ward of thirty patients. At 11 a.m. next day I was seen by Dr Owen who said he would see me in the surgical room at 11 p.m. There I underwent a most painful operation when something was injected into the base of my bladder. I was in agony. *In spite of his obvious distress, during the night he wrote a sonnet of sixteen lines without any evidence of rancour, and in a spirit of calm resignation as the last two lines testify:*

Whatever trouble the night may bring,
I thank my God for everything.

My spirit is high, and in anticipation of either a natural relief of the pain, or death.

I am unable to walk, and can hardly stand up. Yet I am compelled by the wardsman to make my bed, and later he was obviously dissatisfied with the way I had made it.

Still very painful. This place is more like a torment house than a hospital, but I hope things will get better.

Continue to be painful, but a little better. Dr Owen is most kind to everybody. This is Sunday and visiting day. Nine people came to see me. I cannot guess how they knew so early that I was a patient here.

It appears to me that for the sake of comfort and improved health, the patients are confined to bed for too long a time. To keep men in bed day and night, men that are able and anxious to get up and walk through the fine garden which is attached to this place is indefensible. (*This erudite observation was made by the diarist, a century before its adoption by the medical profession as the right course.*)

I read that in the Legislative Assembly, a Mr Bird stated that a great many respectable people were obliged to travel *second class*, and they were sometimes subjected to inconvenience by swagmen and others who would travel in the *third class* carriages if they were available. (*This is recorded without comment.*)

On Sunday, visiting day, three young men who had worked with me on the farm, paid me a visit. Within an hour three young ladies brought me sweets, cakes, cheese, tobacco and flannel vest. I have no idea who they were.

Operated on again today, but not so painful as the first one. It is a frosty morning, but I hope the fruit trees at the farm have come to no harm. I have now been eighteen days in hospital, and the doctor has given me permission to leave today. My clothes were brought to me, but the wardsman had taken the money I had when admitted. I went to the Bridge Hotel, where I paid 1s for a bed and 1s for each meal. I had my photograph taken and paid for twelve to be sent home.

I left for Castlemaine where I attended the agricultural show. In the implement section I was again disappointed not to find a dung cart and spreader among the exhibits. I accompanied Mrs John Lewis and her son to their farm at Ravenswood, Walmer. There the kangaroos are devouring the crops.

November *Wise use of prison labour*

Unwell again. Very painful and my urine is red from blood. I am in a most inconvenient place to die, for I am fifteen miles from a cemetery,

82

and staying with people who cannot go to much expense on my behalf.

Had a rough ride in dray to Castlemaine Hospital and was admitted immediately.

From this fine hospital I am able to survey the whole town. I refer to Castlemaine as the 'golden town', because it is estimated that £25 million sterling worth of gold has been mined from the immediate neighbourhood. No one would have thought of building a town on this rugged and barren place had it not been for the gold which the surrounding area has produced.

Getting very weak because of the pain and lack of sleep. John Lewis's son visited me today. The family are very attentive. They wish to borrow £8 or £10 from me.

The doctor sees me every day. He gives me no medicine, and appears to rely on his superior, 'Doctor Time'.

I had a visit from my friend, William Davies, the shoemaker, and a native of Carmarthenshire. He is an astute tradesman and employs many hands. He himself has left the last, and buys and sells properties in and around the town. It is alleged that he makes an annual profit of £1,500. Many of my countrymen have come to see me, but their sympathy does not ease the pain. I might be impatient with my progress, but I am anxious to get well, leave the hospital, and lend a helping hand to the farmers to gather the staff of life and bring in the harvest. I was given leave to go to the the Savings Bank to withdraw £10 and loan it to John Lewis. He now owes me £37. My body begins to swell. I would like to see my children once more.

The prison stands near the hospital. Every morning at 7 a.m. I see the prisoners pass on their way to work. They go in gangs of eighteen guarded by three officers armed with rifles. They are employed to improve roads and other public works. That is how the Government and the councils get their schemes completed on the cheap.

I had a painful and restless night. One old man who was groaning with pain gained release about midnight. This and my own tormented state caused me to compose the following lines:

The man whose health was storm'd adrift,
Was eased from groaning pain,
Through death has Nature's heavenly gift
Brought everlasting gain.
When Kings and Queens are deadly sore,
And racked in torment by disease,
They cannot choose, or wish for more,
Than death to grant release.

The weather has favoured hay-harvesting, and it is mostly over in this district. It is clear now that I shall be unable to take part in this one, the first I have missed in fifty-four years.

Very painful again today, but struggled to see part of an American peeping show to which the patients were admitted free. A freak thunderstorm was impressive. The Niagara Falls were splendidly shown, as was Sydney Harbour. The Salt Lake country, where the mormons dwell, in my opinion was the loveliest of all the places shown.

December
Deceived by his countrymen

I now hear that John Lewis is deeply in debt. During my first two weeks in hospital, members of his family visited me daily bringing me little gifts, but after lending them the money a fortnight ago, none of them has paid me a visit.

I had permission to leave hospital, and I travelled to Harcourt by train. Then I walked the eight miles to John Lewis's home at Ravenswood through thick Bush (*remarkable for one in his weak state*), and went straight to bed.

Tried scything corn. I prepare to swag again, but I fear I shall be unable to get work, for my poor health will not stand the strain of hard work. I hear that the present rate of pay is 2s for a day's work of sixteen hours.

The crops around here are destroyed by hares, kangaroos and parrots. Bush fires are frequent because the grass is long, withered and dry. The farmers have not prepared fodder for their cattle. No labourers are needed because the farmers help each other. Rain is wanted badly. It is 103^0 F in the shade and 117^0F in the sun.

At Walmer I collect a registered letter containing four £5 notes. I deposited them at the New South Wales Bank. (*He does not mention the source of this money.*)

I paid a visit to my friend, David Evans, who lives in a hospitable cottage at Rheola. There I made my Will, and left it in my friend's keep, before moving on to Tarnagulla, and afterwards to John Lewis's farm.

1879

January *Exposed to the elements*

The diary for this year is without a cover and the leaves are loose. None is missing, but many pages are badly mutilated from damp. January's record in particular is badly affected. Much of it is unreadable, but the script at the margins indicates that he is remaining outside hospital, and going from place to place in the Castlemaine district. Sometimes he is on a farm helping with the threshing, but mostly he is staying in hotels. It is very hot, and there are many Bush fires. He suffers from toothache again.

The partial effacement of this diary increases the surprise that the volumes should be in such a satisfactory state of preservation after forming part of a swagman's kit while camping in the Australian Bush, working on farms, residing in hotels, and sometimes in hospital, through so many years.

February *Water-divining*

Took my swag to Wesley Hill and I stayed at the Albion Hotel, where I left my swag because it was too heavy to carry. My health has improved, and I walked thirteen miles into the Bush. It is very hot and sultry with the smoke of Bush fires filling the air. No water on the way. Cattle are suffering. Driest summer on record. I arrive at John Lewis's home again, at Ravenswood, Walmer. I have done no work for four months; I am exhausting my money on meals and hotel beds.

No signs of rain, the water pools are empty, the cattle are bellowing, and when they see a human being they follow him around, hoping for something to eat and drink.

Drawing a plan for a new dairy for Mrs Lewis. She wishes to have four feet of it underground, and six feet above ground. I cut out the foundation, and I am to build it for my board and lodgings.

Four miles away there are three chapels belonging to different denominations. They are so close together that they are for ever quarelling. Better the philosophy of the Bedouin in the desert, namely 'Pitch your tents far apart, so that your hearts may be closer together'. Mrs Lewis and her son walked to chapel to listen to a Welsh sermon, and I walked into the Bush to meet my God.

Yesterday, the son Lewis bore a hole a few yards from the house and found water, but this morning, the hole held no water and only a layer of scum remained. Farmers are selling their poor yield of wheat for 3s 9d a bushel.

The cattle are moving about in droves in search of water. They break down the fences and congregate on the common. They belong to different owners, and no-one takes any notice of them. One fell into a well while attempting to reach the water.

I took out my pick and spade in search of a source of water supply. I selected a spot only 100 yards away from the house. After digging to a depth of only two feet, water welled up and filled the hole within fifteen minutes. This farm has several springs, but they are all shallow.

I went out to the Bush to split rails for fencing. It was hard timber and I only split fifteen rails. They sell for £1 per 100 rails, so at this rate it does not promise much of a wage. I was happy working by myself, avoiding idle talk and disputes.

This is my natal day. I was born in 1818 so I am 61. I feel my age. I feel the earth attracting my legs. John Lewis's greyhound caught a hare weighing 8½ lbs.

March

The vicious circle

The drought continues. Cattle are falling for want of fodder and water. The losses are general. The bankers exert pressure on the farmers who have borrowed money, with their crops as surety. The crops have failed. The farmers are selling their crops and their lands, so they cannot employ labour. Consequently, the labourers are unemployed in their hundreds. In that the labourers earn no wages, they cannot buy even the bare necessities of life such as food and clothing from the stores. Thus, the tradesmen suffer. Bush fires are raging. The nation is depressed.

My friend Walter David Jones of Penywern, Cardiganshire, came to see me. He also is out of work. He intends purchasing a gun to shoot hares and sell them. If he is as good a shot as his uncle Jones of Llanio, he should do well. During one season he discharged 1,700 cartridges.

In spite of a sore eye I go to the Bush to split fencing rails, in order to lessen my bill for maintenance which is 15s a week, and sleeping in my own blankets too. The current food prices are as follows, — wheat, 4s a bushel; tea, **1s** 6d a lb; potatoes, £3 15s a ton; meat, 2d a lb; sugar, 4d a lb. Thousands of labourers roving about looking for work. Strong young men are willing to work for three meals a day.

I walked to Castlemaine where I shall stay for three nights. John Lewis gave me the magnificent sum of 1s 6d to cover my expenses for that period! I posted postal orders valued £19 as a loan to Mrs David Evans at Rheola, Old Berlin.

The papers report that the robber, Ned Kelly, and his gang are still at large.

The Labour Exchange at Wesley Hill could not offer any job. I sought work at Mr Moffat's station, but he was not at home. Scores of thousands of acres of good land remain uncultivated, where a single stock-rider is employed to ride round the boundary fence each day.

The fence consists of six wires drawn through strong posts placed three and a half yards apart, with one strong top rail of split wood. It makes a good sheep-proof fence.

April *He tenders for road building*

No sign of rain yet. It is a sorry sight to witness the cattle suffering from want of both food and water. It is the most severe drought within the memory of the Colony's inhabitants.

I tendered for the preparation of a road 1½ miles in length with a drain on one side. My tender was £38 and it was the lowest apart from one from among four. The lowest was one of £18, which is equivalent to 6d a day for a good workman, and he was awarded the contract. The man must be mad!

I prepare to build Mrs Lewis's dairy, using straw to reinforce the mud wall. The bore hole which I had dug is filled with water; what a welcome sight!

It has been announced that an award of £8,000 has been offered for the capture of the Kelly gang, dead or alive.

On this Sunday I read Spurgeon's last Sermon. He approaches the truth in his advanced age. I hold that God is not only merciful and loving, but that he associates pleasure and perfect happiness with what is really good, and misery with anything which is against His Will on earth.

It has turned cold and ice forms on the water. I am constructing a brick archway for the dairy's doorway. (*A paper cutting lies interleaved in the diary advertising an iron fence to stem the advance of a Bush Fire, costing £31 a mile.*)

I continued to build the dairy's mud wall. I have completed two window frames and started making the door frame.

The surveyor came to inspect the extension of the adjoining dam. I inquired if he had a job for me. He replied that the Maldon Council would not employ any man even if that man worked for no wage and fended for himself. O Victoria! (*Presumably meaning the State and not the Queen.*) What is to become of thee?

John Lewis prepares to go to Castlemaine accompanied by Mrs Lewis and a fat pig.

The family have gone to one of the three chapels, the one that accommodates the 'Bible Christians'. The other two are the 'Independents' and the 'Calvinistic Methodists'. The members of each expect to enter heaven, and from there to look down at the other two.

At last torrential rain has come. Two feet of water in the dairy. This is handy to make the mud-wall.

May *Farming costs*

I take my usual walk into the Bush. There I found Nature glorifying its Author with both hands.

I was surprised to be asked to sow oats before the wheat. The farming practices are quite different here to what they are at home. Thus, here they neglect to cultivate the land, they speak against farmyard manure as a means of nourishing the land, and against preparing fodder for the winter and dry summers. They discourage workers on the farm, apart from certain weeks in the year for ploughing, sowing and harrowing, reaping, binding and threshing the corn, and thatching the straw. Farming activities are wholly neglected during ten months of the year, so that workers are unwanted during the whole of that period. The farmers maintain that wages are too high so that only 100 acres on a farm of 320 acres are cultivated. The labour costs for harvesting this acreage relate to the hiring of seven binders for six days at 5s a day, of five men for six days to cart it, of fourteen men for three days to thresh and bag the corn, and of two men to market it during twenty days at 2s 6d a day. In all the labour expenses connected with 100 acres would amount to £54, namely about 11s an acre. Added to this would be 1s an acre for road-rates, making it 12s an acre in all, compared with £5 an acre in the United Kingdom.

How are the farm workers of the Colony to survive nine months of the year without work, and on a wage of 4s a day during two months when work is available? Nowhere can they have board and lodgings under 15s 6d a week.

I have nearly completed the mud-walling of the dairy. I am not tired, but the rheumatism troubles me.

John Lewis takes a load of firewood to Walmer, a distance of thirteen miles, once or twice a week. He gets 6s 6d a load, and 1s 6d of this goes to the splitter. This leaves 5s for a day's work by one man with a horse and cart, notwithstanding the wear and tear over a rough road, so the remuneration is meagre.

I had a fire inside and outside the dairy to dry the mud wall. It dries as hard as a brick. The chimney draws well too, almost too well because it draws the smoke from the middle of the floor. How long will the masons continue to build chimneys that won't draw smoke? It should be a rule that the entrance at the base should not be greater than the exit at the top.

I continue with the mud walling. My hands are sore and cracked from moulding the clay.

Thatching the dairy. I am getting tired of staying here among a lot of ignorant, self-centred, self-righteous, proud, penniless, grudgers. I cannot help the times or such habits, so in the words of Robert Burns, it is best to 'welcome what you cannot shun'.

The walls at the pine ends of the dairy are nearly a yard thick. I was obliged to build high scaffolding with the aid of forked trees, for they have no twine here.

June *The backside of creation*

The folk here are very religious on Sundays, and believe that God is only present in chapel, while the devil is in the Bush. Letters from home are delayed for here I am now at the backside of creation.

Went to the Bush to find suitable timber to roof the dairy and hold the straw-thatch. I have built the chimney of bricks and lit a fire to dry it.

I helped Lewis kill a pig, and later hung the carcass in the newly built dairy.

July *The dairy is completed*

It has rained heavily and all the dams are full. The people begin already to complain of the wet weather.

Only one-tenth of the labour force of the country is employed. Some thirty years ago, the general wage was £1 a day, but now one-half of the people are short of money on Monday morning.

I had hard words with John Lewis this morning for he now denies my loan to him. I finished the dairy today, and I took down the scaffolding. The slaughtered pig became its first occupant. From now on I must pay for my food and lodgings.

August *A sartorial innovation*

I made a new pair of sleeves for my woollen shirt, and then covered the sleeves with calico, so I now have double sleeves.

Two swagmen called at dusk for a 'shake down'. They complained bitterly of the absence of work, and it was yet too early to go to the shearing country. I get undesirable dreams. What can be the cause of such wandering of the mind? They puzzle me beyond anything else in Nature. Franklin and the philosophers attribute dreams to a faulty circulation of the blood. Even so, why is it that in the course of half an hour's sleep, a man can trace the activities of two or three long lives?

Short of rain again. This has gone on for eleven months. The cattle are still suffering, and a walk through the Bush is unpleasant because of the offensive smell from the cattle dead from the prolonged drought. I went out with a friend in search of hares, but they had scattered into the Bush, and like the Nihilists in Russia they avoided capture.

'The Leader' gives an account of rowdy scenes in the Assembly, where members call one another, 'butchers', 'cattle duffers', 'liars', etc. etc. They are too selfish and quarrelsome to do any good for the sick country.

September *The joy of the wattle tree*

I went out with the two sons of John Lewis to hunt hares. We saw twenty. The son Evan proved the best shot for he killed one hare, and wounded one of the dogs!

I went out into the Bush to enjoy the wonderful sight of the wattle in full bloom. The bark of the wattle is superior to that of the oak for the purpose of tanning leather.

Still waiting for the return of the money which I have loaned to the

Lewises. There is no shape in this place although the farm consists of 200 acres of good land, half of which is cleared and fenced. Their cattle are starving for want of fodder and water. They buy bread, tea, sugar, meat and horse-feed. They make no sales apart from firewood, and that transaction is not economical. (*At this juncture the pages of the diary are badly mutilated, and a month later he writes that when he had left his room for three minutes, a cockatoo had got in and upset all his things, and had torn his diary.*)

I have received two papers from home; they were posted in Wales on the 7th of March. A southerly gale has brought down many tree-branches which are strewn all over the Bush. Very few big trees fall because the soil is dry and the roots are fast.

I still await the return of my money, and the quarrel over it continues.

October *Bad debts remain undischarged*

I have been told frankly by the family that they are unable to repay me, and it is clear that they do not intend to. Ultimately, they gave me £10, so that the sum of £42 remains outstanding. Had I kept this money in the Savings Bank it would have saved me much bother and irritation. I had earned this money through heavy toil, working seventeen hours a day, earnings which had never exceeded 3d an hour, earnings which I was laying by to pay for my return journey to Wales.

He composes three verses in Welsh on 'dupeness' or 'dupidity' should either word do as a noun to express the activities of a 'dupe'.

I left for Castlemaine, and ultimately arrived at the home of my friend, David Evans of Rheola, Berlin. On my walk over the hills I met a digger. He was breaking new ground at his leisure. He had made an average of £70 a year while excavating casually.

A Mr and Mrs Thomas Johns called with David Evans. They had returned from a visit to Wales. They possessed land in the neighbourhood whose soil was 'nuggetty', and which had brought them thousands of pounds through letting it to diggers.

November *Cow mothers an orphan colt*

The soil here at Rheola is too dry for the growth of cereals, for the rainfall during the year was only 14 inches compared to an average of 20 inches over the last thirty years.

How different are the conditions in this homely place from that at Ravenswood. No hypocrisy here. Not a cross word among either the family or neighbours. Mrs Evans tubs over sixty pounds of butter each week. The grass is plentiful in the paddocks.

I took a walk among the burrows which the diggers had occupied before I arrived in the Colony, and where a Chinaman found a nugget weighing over 100 pounds in his hole. This was a fine lump of gold which would fetch £4 2s 6d an ounce in Rheola. Although gold is gold, its commodity price differed in the separate stations, so that in

Castlemaine gold was only £3 17s 6d an ounce, while in Ballarat gold sold at £4 an ounce.

Water for ablutions, cooking, and butter-making is obtained from a spring about two miles away. After dinner I took out some digging tools in search of water. In less than an hour, and at a distance of less than 200 yards from the house, I struck water at a depth of three feet, which escaped at the rate of four gallons a minute. The household regarded it as a better find than a nugget of gold. In the morning the spring was still yielding clear water.

The harvest is in full swing in the district, and I scythed one and a half acres of hay.

I made my way towards Bridgewater where I hoped that I would have a job. Arriving at Inglewood, I found it was a general holiday in the town, and I was unable to deposit £18 in the Savings Bank, so I left my book and the money with the Postmaster.

At Mr C. Moore's farm at Bridgewater, I found twelve men working at the hay on 140 acres of a fine farm. Rain interrupted the proceedings, so I earthed up some store potatoes and grubbed some saplings.

A fine mare fell sick after giving birth to a foal. The foal was taken away and was put to suckle a cow. The grand and favourite mare died and was cremated.

I went to scythe barley whose straw was 4½ feet high, and bound oats having straw only 18 inches tall, but it had a good head. I was sent to mow a swathe in the wheat field. Its headland was half a mile long. It took me 1½ hours and it was hard-going.

A steam engine at the farm drives the flour-mill and the chaff-cutter. It also pumps water to irrigate the paddocks. It raises 2,000 gallons an hour from the River Loddon which runs within seventy yards of the farmyard. The river here is 60 yards wide and 32 feet deep.

December *His daughter marries*

The reaper starts on the wheat field of ninety-two acres. I bind in the morning and stack the sheaves in the afternoon. It is hard-going for the reaper is driven at the trot.

I received the 'Aberystwyth Observer'. It reports that my daughter Elinor was married on the 9th of June, 1879, to one of the sons of Crynfrynbychan, and they have gone to farm at Tyndomen.

Four teams are carting to a huge stack of corn. I am in charge of one of them. I feel well, and strong enough to walk ten miles after supper.

1880

January
A bumper harvest

He commences this his forty-first diary, and his tenth in Australia with a query on fatalists:

How can fatalists endorse
Their easy minds or tortures?
If they never feel remorse,
Why judge their fellow-creatures?

I got up this morning at the hospitable residence of my countryman and friend, David Evans of Rheola, who knew me in Wales. Should anything happen to me, my books as well as my Last Testament are in his care, and he is my sole executor.

The day is bright and warm. I left at 10 a.m. to meet the train at Dunerolly, and I booked for Creswick intending to be in time for the late harvest, but on arrival there I learnt that I was ahead of the ripening of the corn, and in common with hundreds of other harvest men I had come too soon. Started for Bullarook six miles away, but I was obliged to stop two miles short of my destination because of the intense heat. I feel as if I was in another country. The grass is green and abundant. The crops look wonderful; they are healthy and heavy, and I have never witnessed their like.

I travelled on to Newlyn and reached Bullarook where scores of swagmen await the commencement of the corn harvest. Food is very expensive — beef 6d and cheese 8d a pound, bread 7d for a 4 lb loaf, although wheat is only 4s a bushel, so that millers and bakers are taking too much profit.

I made for Kingston three miles away. A mate joined me on the road and together we wondered at the heavy crops. Last year Mr Berry and his Ministry were blamed for the failure of the crops, but who will get the credit for this year's bountiful harvest? I was employed by Mr J. Glendenning at his Summerset Farm, at which I worked some six years ago. I was one of eight binders following the reaper in a paddock of oats. I have never seen such a crop, nor ever thought it possible for any soil to produce and nourish such a crop. The straw was six feet tall, and the grain-head was eighteen inches long. I was the second best binder in the paddock, but I realized that my speed was reduced by two habits which the others workers did not follow, namely that I shaped the sheaf before tying it, and then I would gather the stray straws before moving on to bind the next. As we worked in the paddock, the funeral of a neighbour filed past; I counted thirty-one carriages, and there were many people on horseback. I did not fancy supper because I had drunk too much water during the hot day.

Heavy showers of rain during the night, so that there is no work at the corn today while half the workmen were sent away. I expect that I shall have to pay for my victuals.

In three days we finished the harvest till next year. The barley crop is likely to yield fifty bushels an acre.

This being Sunday I remained indoors washing clothes and mending my trouser and shirt which had suffered badly when binding the corn. It is a bad bargain when a day's wage of 5s is offset by a ruined shirt which cost 9s! In the afternoon, I took a walk to visit my friend David Davies at 'Stone Barn'. The farmhouse is so named because it is built of stone, and the roof is covered with Carnarvon slates. When I inquired of Mrs Davies how her husband was, she broke down and cried, because he had died recently. He had left the farm in good order, the crops were good, the fine quick fences were strong and neatly trimmed, and trees in the orchard were over-loaded with fruit.

At Summerset Farm we had two waggons, each drawn by a pair of horses, carting corn. I was responsible for the stack in the rickyard. There are now three Josephs on the farm, the 'young Joseph', the 'big Joseph' and the 'old Joseph' (that is me). It is the second hottest day I have experienced in the Colony, and we had to give up work for four hours because of the heat. The stack is now twenty-seven feet high and it has to take eight more loads.

On this Sunday I climbed on to a hill, 500 feet high, and surveyed the countryside. It was a very pleasing sight with the paddocks packed with stooks of precious grain, gathered through the assiduous labour of the swagman, whom they variously abuse and call loafer, vagabond, and sundowner.

On the eve of a general election, I went to hear an address by the constituency's M.P., Mr Richardson. I asked him a few questions about the state of the working man, and I wrote a letter on the same subject to 'The Leader'.

February *Four Sundays in February*

I again visited the bereaved Mrs Davies and her three sons. The thresher had been there for three days. They threshed 2,400 bushels of corn, and the land had yielded thirty bushels to the acre. In some places the yield has been as high as seventy bushels.

The thresher has arrived at Glendenning's farm. The team attending, are mostly the so-called selectors who hold 320 acres of land, while a few are Chinamen. I applied to join the team, but too many of the owner's relations need employment.

In the course of thatching the straw stack, the ladder slipped and I fell twenty-two feet, but did not break any bones. The cattle are beginning to fall because of the scarcity of water and fodder, but not on this farm, for the dam still holds some water. The potato haulms are withering for the want of rain. I have four bad companions, headache, toothache, earache and sore eyes. Prices of cattle are low, and 22s will buy a good cow.

Some welcome rain has fallen. This is the anniversary of my birthday. I have nothing to glorify in, except the genial rain that falls to cheer both man and beast:

The glorious heaven to earth does pay
Her long and lawful debt,
And yet the weather-growlers say,
'Tis bad and awful wet.

This is general election day. There are several parties contesting, including Conservatives, Free Traders, Independents, Protectionists, Ciphers and Liberals. There are 103 candidates, but only 86 members are to be elected. The Conservatives had a majority of 10 over the Liberals.

This is Leap Year. I can only remember one other occasion when there were four Sundays in February.

March *Holiday without pay*

There is always a big gathering of Welshmen, and especially Welsh women, at the Ballarat eisteddfod on the 1st of March (St David's Day). I could not go this year because I was thatching a big stack of straw and for which I got £1. My earnings will work out at 2s a day, in addition to my rations.

The Master is carting dung, and he was spreading it from the cart. This is as it should be because manure should be spread directly. The seeded grain begins to germinate, and the grass commences to grow; the stubbles have turned green already. I have finished thatching, so I will probably have to leave because the Master himself is ploughing.

At the stores I bought a pound of tallow candles for 6d; tallow itself costs 2d a pound, so it costs a lot to put the wick in!

Digging potatoes for 6s a ton, providing my own victuals. I cannot manage to pick half a ton a day. They sell for only £1 15s a ton at Creswick and they have to be carted there.

Being Good Friday, this is a public holiday, but not for the farm labourer. Clerks and others get fifteen public holidays a year, but the toiling farm worker only has Christmas Day, and that infrequently because of the call of harvesting. Whenever I have been employed by a farmer on weekly terms he has retained my wage for Christmas Day!

April *Neither first nor last*

Digging potatoes day by day. The farmers here pay less for work done than in Wales, not that the wages are lower, but that the work accomplished in a day is greater. Digging a ton among a light crop of potatoes in one day is no joke.

Each morning before breakfast I draw fifty-six gallons of water from a well which is seventy feet deep. It is a dangerous job and I have to take care that my foot does not slip. If the women at the farmhouse had to draw the water, they would not waste so much of it.

There is a glut of potatoes on the market, so Mr Glendenning dismisses the two diggers and I carry on alone. I dig eight bags in eight hours, which for me is good digging. Continuous heavy rain has caused the dams to overflow, and there is wide flooding.

At the local stores I found them raffling two guns. The stakes were 5s for each gun. The result was determined through the casting of dice. The highest score claimed the double-barrel gun, and the lowest won the single-barrel gun. I failed to qualify for either, being 11 short in the former draw, and 4 too many in the second count. Bad luck still trails me.

May *So much to do, so little done*

Boring and morticing fencing posts when too wet to dig potatoes. The Master is busy ploughing.

One thousand sheep turned into the potato field to clean it, but they don't fancy the tall weeds, and prefer the sweeter grasses which are plentiful.

Took a walk on Sunday after breakfast to inspect the working of the Golden Claims a mile and a half from here. One of them pays £250 per cent dividend to its shareholders. I foolishly wished I had a few shares, but regretted the thought directly, and composed the following englyn:

Yr awr hon yw'r awr henaf, — a feddaf	This is my last hour to live,
Heddyw yw'm dydd olaf.	Today is the last of its kind.
Oeraidd yn wir yw'r addo wnaf	Rash is the promise to give
I feddu pan na fyddaf.	What really will not be mine.

A mate shared my bedroom last night, a William Welsh and a native of Ireland. He is an ordinary labourer, and had travelled a full 100 miles in search of work, but to no avail. Poor Victoria cannot afford to pay for a day's work when there is so much to be done, and there is such a loss from the omission to do it.

When drawing water from the well, the rope broke and the bucket fell to the bottom. Poor Joe, what will he do now? Obviously, he must not go after it, so I went to dig potatoes. I picked seven and a half bags. It is reckoned that thirteen bags make a ton. The next day I managed to retrieve the bucket by lowering at the end of a rope a tail of chain with a hook at the end.

A travelling swagman shared my bedroom last night. He looks about 5 feet 9 inches tall. He swears that he was 6 feet tall when two months' old. The story is taller than the babe!

Another very wet day, so there is no work I can do and I shall have to pay for my keep. I retired to my bedroom and made myself a shirt out of Welsh flannel which I purchased at 2s 3d a yard.

June *Ned Kelly and his gang netted*

I was joined by two mates, Cornelius Lewis and Daniel O'Connell of Ireland. They commenced to dig potatoes at 6s a ton, providing their own food. They started briskly, but gave up after five minutes on account of the poor crop, and the smallness of the tubers, circumstances which would not allow them to earn a living wage.

The saddler came here to mend harness. I bought from him a pair of braces. I had purchased my previous pair from Jackie Baker of Lampeter in Wales in 1840 for 9d; they are still in service, and should last another forty years if properly cared for, but I wanted a pair in reserve. These cost me 9s 6d, and I regard this as too high a charge.

Finished one paddock of potatoes, and moved on to another. Freezing today with ice on the water. Toothache with me again.

Eclipse of the moon commenced at 8.50 p.m. (23rd of June), and the moon was clear at 2 a.m. Mr Proctor at the Melbourne University is investigating the behaviour of the planets, and is speculating about their inhabitants too! He does not tell us whether they are up to the same iniquities that infest our planet. Perhaps we should ask Mahommed whether Mr Proctor is right.

Heavy rain which prevented work except for small jobs. This Sunday I remained indoors, reading and mending my clothes. I feel happy when alone. Nothing pleases me more than a quiet life in the Bush. Good things to eat, good water to drink, clothes to wear, and an easy bed. Short of nothing at present but work. I am getting too old to tramp the country, and I would like some little cottage before going to my last resting place.

The newly elected parliament has been dissolved by the Governor. It was defeated over the Reform Bill, and had only functioned for forty-five days. We ought to petition the Governor, praying on him to manage the affairs of the Colony himself and alone. The two houses have done nothing in the past ten years except spend money and quarrel among themselves. The public debt of the Colony when I came in was £4 14s 6d per head and it is now £22 10s. A few unnecessary railways have been built, but far too few water-works have been constructed, for the use of the towns.

The Kelly gang of four young and desperate thugs have been captured. They had shot seven policemen and had robbed two banks. The outlaws came upon the police Bush camp, and they shot a man, Sheritt who had posed as their intimate friend and sympathiser. He was shot in the head by Joe Byrne who sent another ball through the body as he lay on the ground, to relieve him instantly of his pain. The four policemen in the camp dare not venture out to meet their even number, so they hid under a bed. Next day, some fifty policemen cornered the gang in a hotel in Glenrowan where their look-out man was shot. The landlord, another man, and two children were shot inside. Throughout the day, police and outlaws exchanged volley after volley of gunfire. A quarter cannon was sent for from Melbourne, but the hotel was on fire before it arrived. Three of the desperate outlaws were found shot, and two of these, Dan Kelly and Steve Hart, had made a pact to shoot each other inside the burning building, to avoid being roasted alive. They had discarded their steel armour and helmets. One of the gang, Ned Kelly, was captured alive, and doubtless will be hanged later.

The reward of £8,000 has been distributed among the police, and the relatives of the spy, Sheritt, who had been the chief agent of the capture. £60,000 had been spent while hunting these desperate Bushrangers over one and a half years. The four members were Irish Colonials, as most of the police are, so it was a feud between Irishmen. The ghastly affray has shocked the civilized world.

July
A cure for a cold

It is very squally and there has been a heavy snow storm. Two papers, the 'Cambrian News' and the 'Aberystwyth Observer', arrived from Wales.

I managed to pick nine and a half bags of potatoes today. Two new pickers came here. They jibbed at 11 o'clock maintaining that they ought to be paid 8s a ton instead of 6s. They were instantly dismissed.

Unable to get my copy of 'The Leader' today, because it contains pictures of the Kelly gang. Roasting alive has not been a deterrent for Bushrangers, for another gang has been apprehended, but this time without bloodshed.

The Liberals have been returned to power; they had a majority of 15 over the Conservatives. Some of the men with money have as many as twenty votes. I had a bad cold so I took medicine consisting of cayenne pepper, salt, senna, ginger and sugar, dissolved in a pint of warm beer. I was no better next day, so I repeated the same medicine, but on this occasion I took a quart of beer instead of a pint, and immersed my feet in mustard and water. Again, I was no better for the treatment.

At home Gladstone has removed the Malt Tax. Bravo! That and compensation for tenants who improve their land were always my idea.

The Master cannot sell his potatoes. There is a glut on the market, and nearly 1,000 tons are piled up in the station. Here, twelve tons were sorted, placed in a pit, and carefully covered with straw. It was set on fire last night. The police came, but there were too many footmarks. All the potatoes had been burnt up. This is the third malicious act committed here since potato-digging commenced. It has been difficult this year to provide the consumer with an even sample of potatoes because of the second growth which has taken place, and which should be attributed to the tender hand of providence, than to the horny hand of the potato digger.

August *The Boers hit back*

I am vexed by the toothache again. As soon as I earn my first note, it will go to the one that will extract four of them. It will cost another pound sterling to reach the dentist. Everything is five times dearer here than in Wales.

News from home tells that Gladstone is seriously ill, also that the British army has been repulsed by the Boers in South Africa. It had no business to go there in the first place. Lord Beaconsfield (Disraeli) and his Ministry made a sad mistake, one which the Liberal Government cannot amend soon.

Barley was sown today over the dug ground which was in good condition to receive the seed and for harrowing. The harrows could not be seen for the rising dust.

Some years back a 200 lb sack of flour was sold at Creswick for £15. It can now be bought for 16s, but I was told today that it was easier to find £15 then than 15s now.

Whilst drawing water, the handle of the winch slipped, and as it spun at high speed, it hit me on the forehead. I was stunned and fell across the platform, and narrowly escaped falling into the well, which is seventy feet deep. (*He writes an englyn castigating his carelessness.*)

Shearing is in full swing. There are favourable reports on the quality of the fleece. It has been a successful lambing season.

I have completed the fencing, and it is likely that this will be the last job here.

September *Cheated of his dues*

Potatoes are still selling at the depressed price of 15s a ton. Merchants are speculating and holding them from the market so that thousands of tons are piled up at Creswick station.

The Master brought home my watch from Ballarat where it had been cleaned, a service which cost me 7s 6d.

I was only paid half the wages owing me. It has been customary to regard thirteen bags of potatoes as weighing a ton, but the Master maintained that it required twenty bags to make a ton. No means of checking it now.

It was a cold, wet and windy day as I walked around Smeaton, Newlyn, Ballarat and Bungaree. Staying at hotels and paying 1s for a bed and 1s for each meal.

Watched the Diamond Drill from America at work prospecting for gold. It bored through blue rock at a rate of seven feet an hour.

Sleepless. My mind is never easy when I have nothing to do. Both body and mind cannot enjoy rest unless one is employed during the day.

Intend to visit David Evans of Rheola which is sixty miles away. Six years ago I could swag it in three days at an expense of 3s to 4s. Now it will cost me a pound to be conveyed there.

Proceeded by train to Creswick where I left my heavy swag. Walked to Tarnagulla a distance of fourteen miles, where I met many of my countrymen at the Golden Age hotel. I wagered that none of them could relate a verse from the Bible in Welsh. I won. There was a scene. I left and walked to Rheola. No farm work. Things are bad. A cow can be bought for 30s. I talked to some of the diggers. They all said that no one had taken more than an ounce of gold in twelve months.

October *'Lofty', the foxhound*

A neighbour called on David Evans to retrieve a straying bull. At home I had worked out a way of felling an undisciplined animal, into a comfortable and natural position. The forelocks are hobbled together; the two ends of the rope are then brought back on either side and fastened by running knots to the hind forelocks. The two ends of the rope are then pulled and the animal falls naturally.

It has just come to light that a day or two ago, a Scottish Wesleyan Minister found a nugget in this locality. He tried to keep it quiet. He had to dig to a depth of ten feet before he unearthed it. As is usually the case, diggers are now rushing to this place. It reminds me of the old bitch-hound 'Lofty', one of the pack belonging to Esquire Jones of Neuadd fawr. Whenever the pack was checked from a loss of scent, 'Lofty', with nose to the ground, would make a wide circuit, and regain the lost trail, when she would let out a terrific howl, and lead the pack to pursue the fox. In the same way the diggers follow their 'Lofty', but are not as successful as Squire Jones's hounds.

I tried my hand at digging, having measured and registered my 'claim'. Each digger is allowed ten square yards. I dug a hole 5 feet by 3 feet, but found nothing. I took my pick to the blacksmith to be sharpened; he only charged me 1d. I started another hole 5 yards by 1 yard and 'bottomed' at 5½ feet. I then resorted to 'dishing' the auriferous soil, but no trace of 'colour'. I had more 'blanks'. Like David Copperfield I was born after sunset on a Friday evening, during a waning moon, so I am not destined to be happy and rich.

Letter from my daughter Nell to say that she had given birth to a daughter, Elizabeth, on Friday the 13th of August, so like her grandfather and David Copperfield, she is unlikely to be lucky.

The daily attendance at the International Exhibition at Melbourne was only 4,500, which proves that the people are short of money.

I wrote a letter to my daughter Nell, and many more to my acquaintances in the Colony asking for a job during the approaching harvest. Strippers are the fashion now, so that binders, carters and stookers are not wanted. They leave the straw on the ground and burn it. (*So, they had combine harvesters in Australia in 1880!*)

In all I have dug eighteen holes without success. In the last I was joined by David Evans, and another Cardiganshire man, David Jones of Rhiwonen. In one dish after washing the soil I had small specks of gold. I gave the bits to David Jones and he enclosed them in a letter home. One thing is certain that it will not be too heavy! *He then composed an englyn:*

Tri chardi'n chwilio'r aur,	Three Cardis dig for gold,
Ym mysg y pridd a'r cerrig.	Among the grit and stone.
Y cyfan yno geir	Their prize and pay all-told,
Yw lliw neu rhywbeth tebyg.	Is just a speck alone.

November *Knows where the eggs are*

Ned Kelly has been tried and found guilty of murder, and was sentenced to be hanged.

The gold miners are required to work their particular area underground, for the lease determines that it is manned by so many hands, otherwise the 'claim' is forfeited and it passes to another. On the other hand, no similar Labour covenant decrees the working of the surface land, so that one individual can monopolize thousands of acres, and just retain them in their natural state. There should be a decree that the fine land of the Colony should be properly cultivated, to provide plenty of work for the labourer, prosperity for the employer, and benefit for all.

The Melbourne racing Cup was competed for today. It was won by a horse named 'Loafer'. A junior bank-clerk from Dunnolly won £1,000 in a bet.

My colleague Jones and I have started swagging, but Jones is soon employed at good wages, so I swag alone through Inglewood in the direction of Bridgewater-on-the-Loddon.

Today (9th November) is the Prince of Wales' birthday. Not much loyalty here among the lower classes, even to the Queen.

Succeeded in getting a job with Mr Michael Lorkins on his farm at Kinneypaniel. The farm is 2,000 acres, and the land which borders on the River Loddon is flat. The soil is said to be 100 feet deep, but there is one draw-back, there are no wells. My work is cocking hay.

Ned Kelly, the Bushranger was hanged today at 8 a.m. His last words at the scaffold were, 'Such is life'. The hangman was an ex-convict aged 70 years.

More than one-half of this farm has been cleared, and most of this parcel is arable land. There are only the Master, myself and a dray to run it. We are going to cart hay, and I was asked to get the horse 'Ben' from a paddock of 900 acres! We cart continuously for seventeen hours in the day and without rest at noon. I fear that it is too much for me at the age of 60. The hay is too dry. The grass is withering. Rain is needed badly.

The rams are turned in to the flock of 2,000 sheep. I was asked to look for eggs. Does the Master think that I do not know where they are habitually laid? Later, I was asked to wait on Father Hogan, the local priest who drove in his elegant 'carriage and pair'. The Master considered he was doing me a favour; he had miscalculated. I hope to finish a letter to my daughter Mary tonight.

Reaping the wheat, and I am one of seven binders. This year the wage is 5s a day of sixteen hours. Last year it was 7s. The Master has offered me £1 a week, but I wonder what happens when the harvest is over, so I did not accept. Two young inexperienced lads are engaged in stooking the sheaves. It is a mistake not to do this immediately following the binders, for when sheaves are left on the ground for a day or two in hot weather, each sheaf sheds a handful of the grain. The Master suggested to the two youths that they should work quicker; they demanded their wages of the previous day and left: admittedly the boys were in the wrong, but this employer is the most hot-tempered man I have ever met. He is a real slave-driver.

December *Lament of a stack builder*

Still binding wheat in the morning and stooking in the afternoon. It is hard work. No oats or barley around here, only wheat. Five men have been paid off. Two men and myself have been retained for carting. In other places the strippers are at work, so the binders and the threshers will be out of work.

My present job is building stacks of the wheat sheaves in the yard. Twenty acres have been carried, but the stack is not up to its eaves yet. Rabbits are so numerous in the stooks that some of them get carried among the sheaves. The toothache is with me again.

Commenced my third stack whose base measures 4 x 7 yards. Bullock teams are numerous on the roads, taking this year's wheat from the north to Inglewood station. It fetches 4s 4d a bushel.

We have finished carting. It has been a short harvest, a day short of a fortnight. How quickly the farmers of the Colony get their crops cut, bound, carted, threshed and winnowed; on this farm the crop has yielded 300 bags.

This is Sunday, and I walked to the yard to survey the four stacks which I built. I am very pleased with them. They are a good shape. The next day the threshers arrived. The engine and the thresher were drawn separately by two teams of eight bullocks. How sad to reflect that these fine-looking stacks built yesterday, will not be there tomorrow.

The harvesting has been completed here, so I have to leave. The Master saw fit to retain £1 5s of my hard-earned wage. I intend to sue him and others in the courts in respect of this unfair and cruel practice.

I reached Hope Creek, and proceeded to Inglewood. Took the coach to Rheola, the fare being 4s, and the distance twelve miles.

At Rheola I joined my friend David Evans to dig unsuccessfully for gold on six consecutive days. I am very downhearted in that I have neither constant work nor money. Two years ago I could put my hands on £100, but now I am owing in lieu of board and lodgings, and £48 may be counted as bad debts.

The water holes are drying up fast, and soon there will be a state of drought. They ought to make more water holes, and instal more underground water-holding tanks.

More immigrants have arrived, and this will harm the labour market. I leave my books here with David Evans, for it may be my last visit.

1881

January
Berserk for work

Left the home of David Evans and walked in search of work for fourteen miles to New Bridge. Then on to Eddington. The harvest is in full swing, but labourers are not required. The farmers can have the pick of a dozen able-bodied harvest men any hour of the day.

From farm to farm in search of toil,
Begging for it, while we can
Improve and till the public's soil,
Which God ordained for man.

Proceeded towards Majorca, and Mount Cameron, and halted for the night at the Standard Hotel. In the morning I made towards Mount Prospect in the face of a dust storm. Reached Blampied post office and stayed there for the night. I was up before sunrise and was washing myself outside when a young farmer (named Stoyle) tapped me on the shoulder and asked whether I wanted a job. I said 'yes'. He asked me to join him at once. I picked up my swag directly and followed him to his farm half a mile away. I was given breakfast, and later taken to my job which was new to me. It was forking peas before an American machine which harvested the pods. It was a simple machine drawn by a horse, and it did its work most efficiently. The machine dealt with fifteen acres a day, and the yield was between 60 and 70 bushels an acre. My wage is 5s a day as long as harvesting continues, and later £1 a week. Mr Stoyle is a bachelor, and hails from Devonshire in England. He has scores of tons of potatoes in pits which are quite unsaleable now at any price.

Hundreds of harvest men are waiting in the neighbourhood for the harvest to begin, but the rain has come.

After three weeks on this farm the cry of 'Harvest Home' goes up, so I must take up my swag tomorrow.

February *Suspects the fire raisers*

No prospect of work. I applied to join the 'threshers', but there are no vacancies. Dozens of men offer themselves for this job daily.

I journey in the direction of Kingston, and arrived at Mr Glendenning's farm where I worked from January to September last year. I received a welcome from the children and the others.

There are many Bush fires in the neighbourhood. It is known that farmers insure their properties heavily against such fires. Then, it will be reported that a swagman in moleskin trousers was seen in the vicinity of the fire some two hours before. The farmers then proceed to draw the insurance money.

A small Bush fire has just started near Glendenning's farm, so the Master is busy ploughing round his paddocks in case the fire reaches his farm.

March *His week's rations*

The customary St David's Day (1st March) eisteddfod is held at Ballarat. There is too much singing at the meetings, and not enough literary contests in the form of poetry and compositions. It is too much like a concert.

I stay at the labourer's cottage, and I work without a wage, and in lieu of my board and lodgings. I have every comfort except useful work. Work is life's principal form of comfort. I owe a great debt to my parents for compelling me to work when I was young, and to appreciate its value.

The country is in debt to the tune of £25 million, and it needs half that amount to support Melbourne alone.

I have no reading material except the Bible, but I can have none better than this, and that other compassion book — Nature.

I was given notice to move from the cottage, because it has been rented to a bricklayer and his family for 3s a week, so I took up my pack, and found a job, digging potatoes at 1s a bag, at Seven Hills Farm, near Kingston and at the foot of Kangaroo Hill. I had to provide my own food. The name of my present employer is Thomas Carr Morrish. The h at the end of his surname is inserted in order to make it more English-like, more stylish. I went into Kingston to purchase rations for the week, and some odd things — soap, 6d; tobacco, 1s; sugar (3 lb), 1s; tea, 6d; salt (1 lb), 1d; meat, 1s 6d; bread (3 loaves), 1s 3d; candles (1 lb), 6d; onions (14 lb), 1s 2d; frying pan, 2s; potato boiler, 1s 6d; water pot, 1s; pint of beer, 6d; tool for digging potatoes, 4s; 'The Leader' paper; cheese (2 lb), 1s 6d.

The Tzar of Russia has died. He and I were the same age. I am the better off now.

The farmer has just informed me that he is unable to sell the potatoes I dig for him, so poor Joe is out of work again. The potatoes here now fetch only £2 a ton, although they are a good variety and they cook in ten minutes.

I shared both my supper and breakfast with two other swagmen who were hard up and hungry. I had my seventh narrow escape from death since I arrived at the Colony. A stack of hay weighing four tons fell over and I was only just able to move away a few yards before it came hurtling down. It would have crushed the strongest bullock.

April *Melbourne's Great Exhibition*

I have filled up my census form for the second time since coming to the Colony. The Master has sent me into the potato paddock once more. He has reduced the pay from 1s a bag to 10d. On an average I pick six bags a day, making a daily wage of 5s. Out of this I have to provide my own food, but I am well pleased with the arrangement because I can cook better and cheaper for myself than anyone else. My teeth are bad and my taste is rather out of the common. I like broth or soup better than tea, and prefer cheese to butter. I am very fond of sugar.

The rain interferes with my potato-picking, but I have built a temporary hut, which the natives call a mia-mia, in the paddock, and roofed it with potato stalks. It gives shelter from the occasional showers, but should the day be very wet I need not move out of my hut. When I am in doubt whether I go to work in the rain after a good dinner, I follow the advice of the great philosopher Zorvaster, who said that when a man is in doubt whether he should do this or that thing, the safest plan is to leave it undone.

I am saddened when I look at the exhausted land all round me. Should the population of the world continue to increase, a bread famine will inevitably emerge. This will not take place during my lifetime, as I have not many more years to run, but it will in years to come unless the land is properly cultivated and remunerated for the crops it produces. Ploughing, sowing, and harvesting, are simple processes in farming, but no one can farm well without judgment and plenty of good labourers. This farm consists of fertile land, and the tenant has been here four years, but during this time the manure has been allowed to lie in heaps around the yard, some nine of them average sixty tons each, while the paddocks close by are exhausted for the want of manure.

I read in 'The Leader' that the statesman, Lord Beaconsfield (Disraeli) died on the 19th of April. *He writes an englyn on the occasion, in which he attributes his greatness to his intense ambition.*

I was up earlier than usual, and prepared my breakfast and put on my best clothes, for I am bound for the International Exhibition at Melbourne. I walked to Creswick, a distance of six miles, and entrained for Melbourne, the single fare being 13s. Arrived at Melbourne at 4 p.m. Walked miles before finding a suitable lodging house near the Exhibition. It was called The Family Hotel, and was kept by an Englishman named Smart, who fully justified his name. Pickpockets are everywhere, and I walked more care-free in the streets of London, Birmingham and Liverpool than here. Admission to the Exhibition only cost 1s, and I paid another 1s for a guide book. I considered that the grounds were superior to those of the Crystal Palace Exhibition in London. *He describes the different sections in some detail, and compares the merits of the exhibits of the separate nations.* The steel-works shown by a manufacturer from Leeds, England, drew my notice more than anything else. Yet, I came out thoroughly disappointed for not finding even a model of the most essential implement needed at the present time, namely an improved dung cart and dung spreader. None of the kind did I find in any section.

The diarist's vision is exampled here, for such an implement was seldom seen on the farms of his native country before some eighty years had rolled by.

May and June *In the potato paddock*

The main impression which I gained from my short stay in Melbourne, amounting to astonishment, was the pride exhibited by the people there, and the ornate and costly dresses which they wore. Watching the people parading along the beautiful walks in the grounds of the Exhibition, I composed the following englyn:

Gair fy Nuw agor fy neall, — i ffoi	*God, give me understanding, — to flee*
Rhag ffyrdd y balch cibddall;	*From the ways of the proud and*
Waith fi ddaw i'r baw heb ball,	*purblind,*
I orwedd fel tlawd arall.	*Whose certain path leads each to rest*
	In dust like any other mortal.

I came back tired and with sore feet after so much walking, and resumed work in the potato patch. There are now five of us in the cottage, four Irishmen and myself; it is not always peaceful. The soil was working well, having dried after the heavy rain. I never was more comfortable at my work than today, although the potatoes were far between as the Scotsman would say.

The farmers are harrowing and sowing for another crop in the already exhausted land, which is badly infested with weeds of all sorts, French thistles, mother maw, cockspurs, docks, sorrel, wild oats, spear grass, sow thistles, water grass, and many other kinds whose names I know not.

I use the American cramp to dig potatoes, while my mates use short forks. The tubers in some patches are underwater for the past forty-eight hours, so that they are useless for storage in pits or for the market. They are not aware of this truth in the district, and they will not listen to those who know from experience.

I was up very early and saw the new comet (11th of June) in the southern sky, about 9^0 south of the Morning Star. The comet was travelling northwards. Its 'tail' was bigger and more brilliant than the one appearing in the evening above the Western horizon.

The potato field is very wet, and the Master was obliged to employ six pairs of bullocks to draw half a load out of the paddock. The potato harvest is now completed on this farm, and I have dug 360½ bags of them.

I have been asked to dig potatoes for a neighbour, a Mr Dwyer, an Irishman. I can remain in Mr Morrish's cottage because the farm is only 1½ miles away. The pay is 8s a ton; fourteen bags make a ton. I filled seven bags today, so my wage is only 4s. Anyhow, it is better than nothing.

Mr Morrish has to surrender this cottage to his landlord, so I left for Mr Dwyer's farm, where I continue to dig potatoes for ten more days. The prospect of finding work in the middle of winter is bleak.

July *Litigation*

Began to prepare my swag for a start tomorrow to seek work in the country, but to stop a few days in Creswick where I intend to sue for wages owing to me in respect of work done in that district last year.

I arrived at Kingston where I searched for work throughout the day, but without success. Staying the night at the Royal Hotel.

Was up early and took a coach to Creswick, where I took out a summons against Mr Henry Glendenning, and left by train for Castlemaine, and took a cab to Wesley Hill, sleeping at the Albion Hotel in Duke Street. In the morning, my friend, William Davies the shoemaker, drove me by buggy to John Lewis at Ravenswoood. There I applied for the £38 which I had lent him from my hard-earned money enabling him to pay his rent. The loan was made in 1877 and he has paid no interest in the meantime. He said he had not a farthing and asked me to delay legal proceedings for a fortnight. I returned to Castlemaine and thence to Creswick.

I read in the papers that the Black Death Plague is mowing down wholesale the residents of St Petersburgh in Russia.

Attended the magistrate's court and presented my case, claiming nine months' wages from Henry Glendennning. I was cross-examined and left the box to cross-examine the defendant, who denied on oath that he had at any time any dispute with his employees, although his name appeared as defendant on three previous occasions on like charges in the same court. I presented to the court my minute notes which I had kept during the whole time I was employed by the defendant, but even these did not satisfy the 'Geese and Turkey' magistrates who dismissed the case without costs. I intend to refer this matter of grave perjury to the next county court.

I took my heavy swag on my journey to my friend, David Evans at Rheola. There I learnt that the old diggers could find no gold, and there was no work for labourers on the farms. Evans was tending his vine. Grapes and wine pay better than his dairy.

Severe white frost during the night, and there is thick ice on the water pools. I started towards Tarnagulla, thence to Lanakoori Bridge, twenty-two miles on, where I slept the night. The cattle are looking poorly and on the verge of starvation for the want of grass and winter fodder. They would eat straw, but this the farmers burn; in fact they are eating each other's dung, in their struggle to survive.

I intend to go and stay with my creditor, John Lewis. If he will not pay me the money he owes me I will claim it on board and lodgings. Now that Mrs Lewis is dead, it will at least be more peaceful there.

August *Splitting Bush timber*

Stayed the night at the Kangaroo Hotel at Maldon, and then walked to Ravenswood, to the farm of John Lewis and his youngest son, Evan.

On Sunday I took a walk into the Bush to look at the timber and visit the wood cutters. I do not think that I could earn my rations at splitting tough timber at 2s a ton as they do, but I intend trying rather than starve again this year. My health and strength are not bad for my age. The cutters work hard for a low wage. They sell the timber they split, and treat for several purposes; the bark goes to the blacksmith to heat the cartwheel tires, felloes for cartwheels, burnt wood for charcoal which sells at 2d a bag, naves for wheels at 1s 8d a pair, fencing posts, and as firewood for engines in the claims and private houses.

I applied for a licence to cut timber and got it. It cost me 5s for three months. The white box tree provides very tough timber. I cut down six of them, three of which were over two feet in diameter, and I split them. Farmers are cutting, splitting and carting trees away from the Common, and yet they have thousands of acres of land growing good timber, which should be removed by paid labour, so that the land could be used for cultivation and pastures.

I was going on with ease cutting and splitting timber when Evan Lewis turned up with his gun and two dogs. The dogs disturbed a big bear which came my way and I only had an axe to defend myself. Fortunately, the ferocious creature charged after the dogs, but before I was really aware of a contest and the danger, Evan shot him and took him home where he skinned the animal.

Came upon Walter D. Jones of Penwern, Cardiganshire. He too is out of work. Other cutters without a licence mark the trees in front of me and cut them down. They have stolen my axe. Three youths are now felling trees across the ones I have cut down. I must just bear these insults.

Cattle dying from want of food. Selectors brand the ones that stray on to the Common, for which grazing the owners pay 2s a head. John Lewis has just sold a fine two-year-old bull for £1.

I felled eleven small trees. Four gents with guns and greyhounds have just passed by. They started twenty hares, but none was killed!

September *In the name of the Pope*

Now, my cross-cutter saw has been stolen in addition to my axe. I had built a hut for myself. This has been burnt down. It was my only 'house and castle'. I do not feel pleased, because I am living among thieves. The natives or Aborigines would teach them to be civil and generous. I accused an Irishman and his three sons of setting my hut on fire. He became abusive, so I told him my revolver was loaded and at the ready, so he left directly. They claim the land and its produce in the name of the Pope.

No one has come for the firewood I have cut so far, but I am not in a hurry. If I cannot sell it, it will be labour in vain, but it has been enjoyable labour. I took home with me two barked trees with which I am going to make a wheelbarrow. A lot of the timber I cut and split is being pilfered.

Last night I dreamt of the poet Iolo Morganwg. It is strange, for although I am most fond of his verses, and knew him well through his poetical works, I never met him. *This information surprises me also,* because Iolo's chair resided at the diarist's home at Tregaron in Cardiganshire. He had purchased it at a sale and treasured it as a memento of one he held in such high esteem.

October
Unequal pay

A hurricane last night did not bring the much needed rain. The surface soil is very dry and the corn blades turn yellow. Although busy at work, felling trees and splitting them only brings a small wage. I must look sharp or else I will involve myself in debt this winter again. Work is not to be got in the whole of Victoria. Pride, vanity and idleness mixed with dishonesty and swindling, spoil the Colony.

John Lewis and his able-bodied son, aided by a good horse, cut and carry timber to customers for a pittance of 7s 6d a day, while young irresponsible boys, working for the Government, get 6s to 10s a day of public money. They will ruin the Colony within a few years.

I am slow in recovering from a bad cold and suffer from headache and a bad cough. I only managed to split half a ton of timber today which is equal to a 6d wage, while I have to pay 2s for my board and lodgings.

Weak from his recent cold, and trying to split the tough timber, he composes four verses each of eight lines, and a sonnet of twenty lines, in praise of a Mrs Harding, who has newly married, and leaves the neighbourhood where she had served for many years as the school's headmistress.

November *Tenants of a thousand acres rationed*

Splitting timber which had lain on the ground for many scores of years, but were as tough as the recently felled ones. I made two new axe handles. John Lewis took a load of bones to the crushers today, and was paid 2s a hundredweight. The bones were collected from the carcasses of animals which had perished during the drought, and which were strewn over the Common of many thousands of acres, which are now so bare that a few scores of geese would quickly devour all its grass.

It rains heavily and continuously, the creeks begin to run strong, and the water-holes are filling fast. We all joined to keep the day a holiday to celebrate the late, but very welcome, arrival of the rain.

A neighbour's son came here and requested me to go to his father's farm to examine a disordered fine two-year-old colt. I found it in a helpless and hopeless state, but I could not make out the cause of the illness, unless it was a snake-bite.

I received a paper from home, in which I read that my brother Jenkin had won several prizes at the agricultural show for cattle, butter and cheese.

Timber-splitting interrupted for a few days when I went to help two neighbours, the one to bind wheaten hay, and the other to reap and thresh peas.

December *Neither*
Bookies nor
Totalizator

I took time off from farm-work to visit the timber-splitting site, and there met a Mr Francis Owens who bought my consignment and paid me for it, so that has eased my mind on that account.

Harvesting operations hindered by heavy rain and frequent severe thunderstorms, during which many people were killed by the lightning. The wheat crops are not heavy, and in a short time wheat is likely to be both scarce and dear. The exhausted land will simply not produce unless it is heavily, not artificially, remunerated. To plough, sow, harrow, and reap corn whilst the straw is either burnt or carted to market, is not cultivation to advantage.

Two visitors came here today. Both were born long years before the time of Waterloo. They walked over the farm, but they appeared to be more interested in mining than farming. They agreed with my employer to sink a hole in one of his corn fields. When the hole was 'bottomed', 'colour' was found, but it was very fine and small in quantity. They intend to dig another.

I got the 'Sandy Blight' on one of my eyes. It is caused by a very small fly, but its bite is very poisonous, so that my eye was closed by swelling in less than two hours. In spite of this I am as contented as a parrot on a fine morning glorifying over a paddock of ripened wheat.

Although harvesting is now in full swing, not many labourers are employed, because the process of stripping the corn excludes the use of binders, while farmers help one another and do not hire labourers, maintaining that it is too expensive, and that a wage of 2½d an hour is too high!

It is hot and sultry this Christmas day, yet there was goose and plenty of plum pudding for dinner. I took a walk to the race course. Although this is Sunday, three races were run, but both bookmakers and the totalizator were absent. (*The mention of totalizator in 1881 has caused surprise.*)

I met a few Welshmen, but only one acquaintance. There are many Welshmen among the moneyed class in Maldon, but as they are mostly hot Methodists, they oppose racing, especially of course on a Sunday.

1882

January *Curriculum for early education*

No user of my diaries can profit from reading about my simple movements, my whereabouts, what time I rise in the mornings, and what I and others do during the day, but he may appreciate the care and labour taken under great disadvantages, to write down such details each day, and that it is no common thing for a hard toiling man to do.

The present system of compulsive education would be more complete if the Government were to provide a blank diary for every boy and girl, to be filled up regularly. It would lessen neglect and crime in the Colony, which now costs the Government an enormous sum of money each year. Few of the young Colonials take advantage of the education and schooling they receive between the ages of 6 and 16 years, but writing regularly in a diary would nurse their learning throughout life.

I am back at William David's Farm at Porcupine, near Maldon. It is hot and sultry. The harvest work only lasted six days for me, drawing a wage of 4s to 5s 6d a day. I only made £12 last year, and I cannot save money to keep myself during the winter. It is time I considered my position at my advanced age. In this part of the world I have no friend or acquaintance who would give me a meal without being fully remunerated for it.

John Lewis has just reported to me that people are stealing the timber which I cut on the Common, and taking them away wholesale in drays and waggons. Such habits!

The thresher has arrived on the farm, 'The pride of Bungaree'. It was fully manned, and each attendant gets 6d an hour. I handled the bags of grain and there were forty-four of them.

This farm is well provided with water, not from springs, but from dams and underground tanks.

The average yield of corn grown on virgin soil is thirty bushels to the acre. Through ploughing and harrowing in the absence of farmyard manure, the yield has already fallen to six bushels an acre. I am no prophet, but I do foresee that there will be a dearth of bread, butter and cheese in the Colony.

I am up at dawn, and this is the most pleasant part of the day this time of the year. Yet, 90 out of every 100 in the state of Victoria do not rise from their beds to enjoy it.

My employer here is a miner, and he has to be at the Golden Reef at 7 a.m. There he works underground for eight hours daily for a weekly wage of £2 5s, which is nearly 1s an hour, whereas he employs able-bodied men on his farm for a wage of 2½d an hour. My wages for fifteen days at 2s 6d a day came to £1 17s 6d, but he would only pay me £1 10s, saying I would get the 7s 6d later. (*He never paid the amount.*)

The thermometer registers 103⁰ F in the shade. I am engaged on Mr Matthew's farm, threshing wheat with a flail, for which I am paid 8d a bushel.

February *They steal his timber*

After forty-eight hours of hard practice in the use of the flail, I am more proficient at the job, so I threshed twice my usual quantity today. In spite of working so hard, the wage I earn only covers the rations I buy.

It is very hot and the thermometer registers 115⁰ F in the shade. There are many Bush fires, and these spread at the rate of fifteen miles an hour. Water is scarce for man and beast. The big dams and the underground tanks are empty. Many farms fetch their supplies of water from distances of 14 to 16 miles. As the period of drought extends, cattle are dying for want of fodder as well as water.

Part of the Russian fleet visits Melbourne and its senior officers are shown the most renowned places. They may not be spies, but they are not likely to go around with their eyes closed.

The Master has difficulty in hiring a winnowing machine. At last a wreck of a thing arrives which does its work very indifferently and I was only able to fill ten bags during the whole day. This reduces my wage still further. I have finished threshing the wheat and now treat the rye in the same way.

John Lewis called on me and said that tons of the timber I had split are being stolen. I visited the Bush and found that forty-seven tons had been taken away by different wood-carters. It means a loss of £4 14s. It is not fair to rob an old man in this way. I am remaining in the Bush, and gloat over my losses, but mean to carry on with wood-splitting, so I have paid 5s for a licence for a further quarter.

I am tired of going from place to place, and I think I shall build a hut or house for myself.

March *Salute to the young Princes*

The customary eisteddfod is held this St David's Day at Ballarat. A prize has been offered for the best englyn to hail the visit of the two Royal Princes to Ballarat. I have submitted four, but since they were composed hurriedly at the end of a hard-working day, I expect more censure than praise from the judges. (*The following day he was informed that he had been awarded the first prize.*)

Thousands of thirsty cattle travel to the water reserve which is close by that part of the Bush where I have re-started splitting timber. They travel as much as seven miles to gain water. This particular water reserve is also drying up fast.

Today I split a ton of firewood, but 2s won't purchase my daily rations. I had to give up work for two hours midday because of the unbearable heat. I felled one tree whose diameter was six feet. When it lay on the ground, the trunk was taller than I am. Having got it down, I found it too tough to split.

Today I caught a carter in the act of taking away some of the timber I had cut. I was unable to carry on with my wood-cutting because of rheumatism. Indeed, I can scarcely wield my quill-pen because of the rheumatism affecting my right arm above the elbow.

April *Unusual cattle fodder*

Today, hundreds of cattle came for water to the adjoining dam. All are so weak and lean that they can hardly move. They crowd around me bellowing as if begging me to help them. They are so eager that given half a chance they would snatch my coat off my back. In fact, yesterday I left my waistcoat on a tree stump. Before I could retrieve it, they had devoured it. It contained a needle-case, knife, tobacco, and my licence for splitting wood on the Common. People should be prevented from keeping cattle which they allow to starve. They blame the weather and of course, its Author. I agree with the Bishop of Melbourne who maintains that it is wiser to build more dams to conserve waste water than to hold prayer-meetings.

A very respected neighbour, Edward Williams, has died. He was a man in every sense of the word. As Robert Burns said of a friend:

If there is another world, he lives in bliss.
If there is none, he made his best in this.

I wrote four verses on his passing to the local paper. Two days later, his wife died, so I wrote two more. *The verses have considerable merit, but they are too lengthy for publication here because each verse has eight lines.*

Heavy rain fell during the night. Is the long drought at an end? John Lewis snatched a reward job today from the Council, namely to burn the carcasses of dead cattle on the Common at 5s a head. Lewis took out his greyhounds to hunt hares. He raised thirty-five of them, but he got no fur because of the dense undergrowth in the Bush.

The drought continues. Not a blade of green grass anywhere. Butter sells at 2s 6d a pound. The four-pound loaf is 8d, and bran is 2s 6d a bushel, while hay costs £8 a ton.

Although I earn no wages because I am unable to work because of the pain in my right arm, I am remarkably happy, wandering by myself in the Bush. The book of Nature is a large volume, and I feast, as every man under the sun can do, on every page as I turn over the leaves.

The rain has come again after a fortnight's extension of the drought following the previous shower. I received three newspapers from my daughter Nell of Tyndomen in Cardiganshire.

Too wet to go to the Bush, so I stay at the farm making another wheelbarrow. The green grass begins to appear. They will never make farming pay in these parts until they have a system of irrigation.

May and June
A catalogue of complaints

The 'pound keeper' came by here today to brand the cattle that graze on the Common, but the severe and prolonged drought had already branded many of them.

I went into the Bush and piled up ten tons of split timber. I manage to keep in good humour in spite of many complaints which include, toothache, rheumatism, sore eyes, whitlow on my finger, and abscess in my armpit. I have to desist from working.

A horse at the farm died from lack of fodder consequent on the drought. I composed an englyn in his honour, for he had worked hard, in the face of starvation. I drew up the farmer's will, and we took it to a neighbouring farmer to get it witnessed.

Lovely weather. The grass is growing well even on poor soil. The whitlow and the armpit abscess are better, and so is the toothache, but the rheumatism persists, and I am still unable to work. I have finished the Bush-barrow, and also a three-legged stool.

Evan, the son of John Lewis, died of Bright's Disease in Melbourne. *He composed twelve meritorious verses in Welsh to mark the occasion. It appears that he was a blameless character, and so different from his father who persistently evades repaying the diarist the considerable sum of money which he owes him.*

July *A pig fells a cow and sucks her blood*

I read in the 'Aberystwyth Observer' that John Evans late of Clwtpatrwn has died. He was my sister's second husband. I helped my sister at this farm in 1840 before she married John Evans.

I managed to split a tough log which weighed half a ton, but I was unlucky enough to break two axes. There is now nine tons of split wood in my pile, and I dare not cut more because my license has lapsed, so I am without work of any kind and live on what I had earned some years back. Joined a party with guns and greyhounds to course hares; most of them got away.

According to the newspapers England has anchored her fleet in Alexandria, as a retaliation on her inhabitants of some 200,000 Egyptians for annoying a handful of Europeans, who may have been swindlers and fortune hunters. 'John Bull', your time is nearly up! (*What prophetic words!*)

Still tormented by toothache. I do no work at present, and just shepherd the timber that I have split, and await a buyer for the firewood.

A strong black sow, half-starved, was chasing a weak cow. The sow caught her by the hind leg and felled her, and began to eat the poor cow alive. When I intervened, the fierce creature stood up on her hind legs and challenged me. I had nothing in my hand, so I retreated for a piece of tough wood. The poor cow was bellowing and the other cattle were encircling her. Having armed myself with a strong branch, I succeeded in driving the ferocious beast away, but I was unable to keep up with her as she renewed her chase after another cow.

The Sunday paper reports that Mr John Bright has resigned from the British Cabinet. He was a Quaker, so he opposed wars and marchers. Very likely, Mr Gladstone can find a substitute.

Three inches of rain has fallen, but it has come too late to save the starving cattle which continue to die by the score around here as a result of the long drought.

August *Starts to build his hermitage*

I think I shall build a cottage or hut, and I have chosen a spot where water and firewood are accessible, so I have begun to cut the foundations for my little house. There is plenty of timber to hand, and as much land as I wish to possess, but it is not of the best quality. It is too dry and sandy for a vegetable garden. I must take it easy as a man of my age should do.

John Lewis maintained that he had already paid what he owed me in the way of board and lodgings. I informed him that over £30 was far too much for thirty-eight weeks of rough, plain, and unwholesome tucker. I had stopped there at his request and at 5s a week.

I mean the building to be a temporary hut, and I shall build it at my leisure. I must stay here till I sell my split-timber. It looks gloomy for an old man in this Colony, unless he has stored some money when young. I was too late coming here. In the Bush I feel happy because here I feel the presence of the Author of Nature. What more could one wish for?

I have nearly completed thatching the roof of the hut with leaves which I used as an experiment. Already it is proof against wind and rain. I have begun the foundations for a chimney. I wish I had a job with wages sufficient to keep me in food. I lit a fire in order to dry the mortar in the chimney. I want to raise it higher.

Cattle continue to die by the score. I saw six cows in one group on the point of dying; they were too weak to stand. No butter available in the market for any price. It's a fine mild day; everything grows except the tree-stumps in the Bush, and the old man (*referring to himself*) in the Bush. The chimney in the hut draws well.

I hear there is a rush for land in the district. It is rumoured that this Common or Reserve has been taken up, or selected, today. If so I shall sell about 200 tons of cut and split timber, as well as my little house. It is a long time since I earned 6d, for there is no work of any kind to be had. I made a bedstead today. My hut will be ready to sleep in soon.

September *Names his hermitage*

I made a new door for my hut out of bark which I first steamed over the fire. It was in one piece. The stringy bark will last for thirty years as a thatch, or as a partition between rooms.

I walked the ground which I had pegged out for my own use. Under the Miners Rights Act, I claim one acre, a roadway, and the permanent springs which I myself opened, but I do not want to monopolize the water for my own use alone. In fact, springs are better for being drawn several times a day.

A certain Francis Owens has applied for 320 acres of this land under Section 19 of the Land Act of 1869. If he gets it, I will have to forfeit £30's worth of split timber.

I have given my hut a name, so that my present address, is, Ants' Mole Cottage, Ravenswood, North Walmer P.O. Victoria, Australia. I walked twenty-five miles to Castlemaine, and registered my Miners' Rights in order to protect my home and garden.

Engaged in fencing in my new garden, and I sowed onion and leek seed. At 5.30 a.m. I saw a brilliant comet in the eastern sky. The illumination from its 'tail' caused my shadow to appear on the ground. The majority of people lay in their beds and did not enjoy this beautiful spectacle in Nature.

John Lewis handed me a statement to the effect that I owed him £14 for board and lodgings. I will have to take him to court soon.

I dug a plot for potatoes. They say that they will not grow here. The Chinamen grow good crops in their gardens. Crops may thrive in the Welshman's garden too.

They have started work on the railway between Castlemaine and Maldon. Able bodied men who can use the pick and shovel are paid 7s 6d a day, but there is no work for old men.

I cut a good deal of timber for burning so that I may have the ash for improving the soil in the garden. I also burn granite stone sand which has good manural value.

October *Strike followed by victimization*

I have sold 100 tons of my split timber for 2s 2d a ton to a Mr Guyman. The pile was measured but not paid for.

I rose before daylight to witness the glory of the comet. Its 'tail', or rather the rays of the rising sun upon the object were so brilliant over a great distance in length and width, that it was both a mystery and a treat for me. I admire the knowledge of the astronomers, and I regret that in earlier years I was unable to gain introduction to books on the subject. The Divines on the other hand, are at variance in their opinions, and they talk at random about things which they know not a lot more than I do. The world does not improve from their deliberations, but conversely it worsens:

School-rooms and Colleges are no use
To hinder power to abuse.
Ambition, selfishness, pride and grudge
Rule from the Serf, the Pope, and Judge.

From two Home-papers I learn that Daniel Lloyd, Pant, Llanddewi brefi had died at the age of 62. He was my brother-in-law and the husband of my beloved sister, Jane. I composed an englyn faster than the time it took me to read the newsprint.

The potatoes and onions are showing above ground, so I water them because there has been no rain for sometime. I placed a lock on the door. I walked eight miles to Maldon to purchase some necessities. I spent the night at Porcupine because it was getting late in the day and I do not care to walk through the Bush in the dark by myself, for they are not particular here if a man has a few shillings and a good watch on him. It is hot and sultry. Numerous snakes about this year, and there are reports that they have killed several dogs and a farmer.

The Guymers are here today. They are strong and good cutters and splitters. They are used to work and they work hard all day, and as if this day is the last day. Why, race-horses are not allowed to run every day and every hour!

I was up at 4 a.m. and prepared to walk to Castlemaine which is twelve miles away. I went to the Land Board to petition against Francis Owen taking over the land on which my split-timber now rests.

It is warm and the rain falls. The grass grows, the cattle eat their fill, and there is plenty to spare. Before long, the grass will dry, go to seed and wither. The animals once more will die of hunger. Why don't the farmers cut their meadows of young hay and harvest it? They simply won't employ labour to do this. Penny-wise and pound-foolish!

I extended my chimney at Ants' Mole Cottage upwards because the strong south wind blows down it at times. I have written a long letter to the Mining Board respecting my humble residence which is coveted by a tyrant.

The men working on the railway have gone on strike to obtain higher pay. They have succeeded in their object, but those who organized the strike were paid off.

November
Life is sweet

Farmers are collecting their cattle from the Common to be branded by the Beedle. They pay 2s a head for grazing rights. There is no work to be had in the locality, and I cannot be employed on the railway for they don't want grey-haired men.

I watered my garden before breakfast, stayed in my 'castle' till noon, and split timber later. Today (9th of November) is the Prince of Wales' birthday. I drank his health several times in oatmeal and spring water.

In need of rain again. The cereal crops are suffering. This auriferous soil is very acid. It is natural that we should not expect good and rich surface soil covering a rich base where the precious metal is found. I went to deepen a well and to water the garden. I helped John Lewis to split timber, and got just 1s for it. This won't buy my food for the day.

Afflicted by toothache again. I cannot find any good reason why I do not get tired of this world. Yet, I want to live and bear the full share of its afflictions. I am harassed by the worms, ants and flies, but I do not object to them. Alas, I am bossed by proud and ignorant men who do not know one-hundredth part of what I have learnt through practice and experience.

December   'A Queen visits Ants' Mole Cottage'

I was promised 12s for mowing and cocking two acres of wheaten hay, and then went to split wood for the baker.

Was one of five binders following the reaper at David Davies's farm and subsequently stooking the sheaves. Undertook this on twelve-acre paddocks on three consecutive days working on each from 7 a.m. to 7 p.m. I am tired and believe that I am too old for the job.

Having finished with the harvest, there is no other work around here, apart from wood-splitting, and this is unremunerative, so I shall probably have to move my quarters before long.

I dreamt last night that the Queen of England and her attendants came to visit me at Ants' Mole Cottage, and the Queen herself presented me with half a dozen ripe and delicious apples. My brothers, Griffith and John in their smart buttoned overcoats, passed by, but of course they did not stop, nor interrupt my conversation with the Queen. What curious things dreams are! They defy all interpretation.

On Christmas day things are quiet in the Bush, neither fat goose nor plum pudding, but ample contemplation:

Through five and sixty Christmas days
I've run my race through life.
O'er ups and downs in many ways
Through times of peace and strife.

I can't perceive my winning post,
It can't be far ahead.
The race for life was never lost,
Whichever way we tread.

Sad disappointments, ails and want,
Are spurs to speed us on
Along the course, and so we can't
But follow those long gone.

It is very hot. I have never experienced such heat. All the cereals are withering. After my great labour and care for my potato patch and watering it daily, it is a complete failure, for the soil is so dry, acid, and arid. The cattle are bound to suffer this summer like the last unless the rain comes soon. The farmers never prepare straw for them. They never seem to consider the cruelty that they incur through such neglect. Repeated experience may eventually teach them.

Arthur Owens came to the door, wanting to buy my split timber for 2s a ton, but I would not sell at that price.

The year is about to close. All the troubles and comforts which I experienced during it, have passed out of my reach. The present moment appears more lasting than the past or the future. It is of course essential to be forewarned about the future and prepare for the morrow, but to be compact, complete, and comfortable in mind and body during the present time is one's best fortune. When a person harbours the illusion that he will be successful one day, it is probably a comfort to the mind at that moment, but such illusions are generally drowned in the waterholes of disappointments, so that such forboding is never a real comfort.

Life rolls on through months and years,
Sometimes glad and oft with tears.
Life is grand, and a treasure too
When there is something good to do.

Here in Victoria, faith and belief by themselves, are held to be the essentials of religion, but visionaries in the United Kingdom favour practical religion. In France too, the majority believe that Voltaire's views best define the Christian. I have given close thought to the words, 'true Christian', since coming to this Colony, and I have concluded that he who adores God 'in spirit and in truth' has no need to shift his stand. He sees God everywhere, especially in quiet places like the Australian Bush, where neither pride nor ambition interferes with his thoughts, while he joins the feathered tribes in natural and spiritual adoration.

1883

January *The braes aye get steeper*

On Christmas Day the heat was unbearable. On New Year's Day I cannot keep myself warm. The harvest is in full swing, but I cannot any longer do field-work, nor can I walk far carrying my heavy swag of clothing, blankets, utensils, books etc.

Toothache is harassing me. I am thankful, however, that it is one-sided, and I am able to masticate my food on the other side. I realize that I would not be grateful for the freedom from pain on the one side, had I no pain on the other side.

This place, eight miles north-east of Walmer, is a poor spot, the poorest in Victoria in respect of people and the land. The former are quarrelsome, and the latter is acid and auriferous, so that it is no use for agriculture. There might be gold underneath, certainly there is none on the surface.

Cutting thistles in a forty-acre paddock. I finished it because they were not too numerous. Threshing oats with a flail; on my way back through the Bush I composed an epitaph to myself in Welsh. I have composed scores of them since I came to Australia. I cannot remember whether I have written them down somewhere.

I cut a load of firewood for 2s, just enough to provide my tucker for the day. I think of those days when I worked seventeen hours a day in intense heat among the the heavy corn crops of Bullarook, Bunggaree, Warrenheip, and the Black Hills. My arms are still strong, but I cannot now walk far, nor quickly. I take an hour to walk two miles.

Winnowing the corn I had threshed and passing it through a riddle. As a boy, I watched my mother and the servant girls doing the same thing on my father's farm.

I fear that the Bush fires may reach here, and burn down my cottage and the hundred tons of timber which I have split and piled. A neighbouring farmer set out at midnight to drive his cattle to maarket at Sandhurst, seventeen miles away. One cow went wild and she was lost in the Bush. He sold two cows and a year-old calf for £4 13s.

February *The Prince Consort slept here*

I wrote a letter to the 'Courier'. *He does not disclose the subject matter.* I kept today (10th of February) as a private holiday, because it is the anniversary of the marriage of the Queen to the Prince Consort. I once stayed at the Royal Railway Hotel in Birmingham at a time when the Prince was also a resident there.

A thunderstorm has broken out, accompanied by heavy rain. Parliament has been dissolved, and polling takes place on the 22nd of this month. It will be a fight between the Catholics and the Dissenters. The former are waxing strong. Zealots rule the day in spite of education.

Close to my hut there is an ant mole or hill, and I cannot keep them away from my store of meat, sugar and honey. Their nest is deep underground, and when I go too near to their burrow, they forgather to attack me. I am obliged to retreat quickly, for they can kill a man.

A waggon has just taken away seven tons of my split timber, so I was able to buy 7 pounds of cheese at 8d a pound, and 56 pounds of onions for 3s 6d. On a fine moonlight night I hear the report of guns from a party who are shooting opposums. These are innocent creatures with valuable skins.

I wrote a letter to the election committee at Castlemaine to say that I am unable to walk to the voting booth, so that they must arrange to convey me there if they require me to vote. *Evidently they did not respond to his request, for he records later that he proceeded to Castlemaine by foot and train.*

With the approach of the eisteddfod on St David's Day at Ballarat, he mentions that he has been awarded the prize for the englyn during thirteen consecutive years.

I have toothache again. My teeth are decaying fast. It is very hot, and the temperature is 110° F in the shade. This is my birthday (27th February). I was born late on a Friday. If I happen to be reborn, I hope it will be on a more lucky day, and under a brighter star. Yet, when I meditate, I seldom find myself without a contented mind.

March *Tit for tat*

At a recent magistrate's court, an Irish farmer named Michael Owen was charged with assault on a lady, when he bit her thumb, almost amputating it. He was acquitted on payment of expenses amounting to £2 12s. At the same court, three youths, aged 14 to 16 years, were charged with taking ten potatoes from a paddock, and which they had cooked directly to appease their hunger. They were committed to jail for three months. Michael Owen is a good customer at the provision store owned by the senior magistrate, and regularly purchases ducks and turkeys there.

Cattle crave for dry straw because there is no grass. Poor agricultural soil around here, while the district is very liable to suffer from an early severe white frost which kills the grass. Michael Owen has a team of wood cutters and carters which supply timber from the Bush to the Claims, except when engaged in sowing and harvesting crops.

April *I'll pay tomorrow*

I split twelve rails for fencing which should fetch 3d each, if anyone required them. Even then I would have to wait twelve months for the money should it be forthcoming. 'I'll pay you tomorrow' is the usual saying, and that tomorrow never comes. This Colony will never thrive as long as gambling, selfishness, and other forms of dishonesty, prevail. A waggon to cart timber for the threshing engine came today, and was drawn by fourteen bullocks.

I was up at dawn and prepared breakfast; no one apart from myself can lodge a complaint against the cook here! Some gentle rain has come and the grass begins to grow.

I hear the whistle from the woollen factory at Castlemaine which is twelve miles away! Before the break of day I listened in my bed to the dawn chorus in the Bush. That songster the magpie stood out. What melody! An instance of bad farming and mismanagement has come to my notice. A neighbouring farmer who cares for 200 acres of land goes to Walmer for a load of chaff for his one horse, and has no cattle. Robert Burns's words, 'Let him take who has the power, and let him keep who can', are often misinterpreted. My construction of them, and which applies here, is 'Let the farmer keep his farm if he can manage it properly'.

My wood-cutting licence costing 5s a quarter, expired today. My miner's licence only costs 5s for the year. A waggon took away seven tons of my cut timber today, but I did not get paid. Some of it had been cut twenty-eight months ago. Up at 4 a.m. I do not know the number of hours I must toil during the day, or how many jobs I shall tackle. The so-called unskilled labourer is classed lower than the skilled labourer, but I believe that the man who is able to do scores of different kinds of work by rule of thumb is much more skilful than say the bricklayer and tailor who only have a single skill.

Michael Owens called, and warned me not to cut much wood as his son would be licensed soon to run the area.

May *He writes to the Queen*

No remunerative work in view. Grey hairs and rectitude are dishonoured here. I planted onions in the garden for I like onions. It rains heavily. No sale for split timber. Sowing thirty-five acres of corn for a neighbouring farmer, at the rate of one bushel to the acre. I have followed this exercise for about fifty years, and I have never been excelled in the work by any, even the two-handed sower.

Fencing round the well as ordered by the surveyor. News has come that Queensland is going to annex the half-civilized New Guinea. Mr Holles, the surveyor, has inspected the fencing round the well, and is satisfied with it.

No job in view. It seems wrong to have to beg for a job in a new country, where remunerative work could be found for 20 million people if there was proper organization. Nearly one third of the population of Maldon is affected by typhoid fever.

I wrote to Queen Victoria condoling with her on the death of her faithful servant and her intimate friend, John Brown.

I agreed to sell my split timber at 2s 3d a ton, but I have some doubt whether this bargain will be honoured (*Three weeks later the deal was called off.*)

June *Robbed again*

I now burn kerosine in my lamp, because it is cheaper than using candles. I eat meat three times a day. I received £3 from the Council for fencing around the well.

A waggon carted away my split timber during two days, but I have not yet been paid for them. (*He was never paid for the consignment, so that he had been robbed again.*) I take up my swag and travel to Mr Mathews's farm near Porcupine Flat, five miles from here, to thatch two stacks, one of rye and the other of straw. It's a long way to go for four or five days' work. I have to cook and fend for myself in a swell house where most of the rooms are crammed with bags of wheat and oats.

Heavy rain fell continually all day, the wind having shifted from the north to north-west, which is a showery quarter, so that no work is possible today. The wet weather will reduce my wage to less than 4s a day. After completing both stacks, I returned to my comfortable hut.

July *His favourite daughter dies*

I received thirty-seven home-papers which had been kept week by week by the post office. One contained the bad news that my eldest daughter Margaret had died on Sunday the 29th of April, at the age of 32. When I left Wales I placed my books and accounts in her custody. *He is very grieved at her passing and dwells on the tragedy for days. He extols her virtues, writing a verse and a suitable epitaph in her memory.*

There is a general complaint throughout the Colony that there has been too much rain, but man for ever growls about something or other in spite of the daily proof that everything ordained by Nature is for good. Lately, I have felt and seen the perfect beauty of Nature, which makes me more content with my lot and being, than when I was in the prime of life. The more I study Nature, the more contented I become even when under the discomfort of bodily pain and affliction.

On Sunday I read 'The Leader'. It always has a good sermon, one adjudicated by the editor as the best delivered by the popular preachers of the day, but none can equal the 'Sermon on the Mount', one which cannot be read and comprehended too often.

I feel very happy in my residence with plenty of firewood and water, but the soil is so poor that my little garden won't grow a thing, although I am going to try onion seeds once more.

The 'George Roper' was wrecked on the reefs in a gale. It was a fine new ship and cost £28,000 to build. Its cargo was valued at £50,000. The complete wreck was sold by the insurance company for £3,600. It happened through a mistake by the pilot. It might have been a wilful act, in order to bring benefit to certain people. Many such stratagems take place in the world nowadays.

I went into the Bush to cut a tree suitable for clog-soles. The trees here are not the best to make clogs from, being too hard and heavy. The white box tree is so hard and heavy that it sinks in water whether dry or green. The bark of the wattle tree is superior to that of the oak for tanning leather.

Hard frost last night, the severest that I have so far witnessed in the Colony. Those who possess a thermometer testify that it was 14^0 below zero. Had a letter from my daughter Mary. I wish I had not received it. (*He does not explain why.*)

I went to see the council surveyor and pleaded for work. I said that the roads were in a bad state, and suggested they could be improved through drainage, and that I would only need a trifle in the way of wages. He said that no funds had been allocated for such work. Back home, I turned to mend my old clogs which I had made myself. They are more comfortable than the new ones which I bought for 9s.

At present, I am living with three worries, I have no remunerative work, no one wants to buy my split timber, and I fear that both my timber and cottage will be impounded by the new selector when he takes possession of the area.

August *Silent clogs and impervious roof*

The papers report favourably on the state of the Colony in regard to grass, cereal crops, and the lambing season. Shearing is about to commence and in the colder parts it will continue till November. The new selectors overcrowd every sheep-station so that the ordinary labourer has no chance to gain employment there.

I have nailed leather under my clogs to silence my tread as I enter some of the smart houses in the neighbourhood which have timber flooring and similar roofs which let in the rain. The roof of my residence is proof against rain, for it is thatched with wheat straw over leaves; it was proof against rain even before I covered it with straw.

I read that the English soldiers are still falling in Egypt, but Nature is now showing her hand, for the Egyptian army is bedevilled by cholera. The Italians too are in a state of terror for within an hour 3,000 were buried during an earthquake. Nature does not give quarters; before it we fall to rise no more. Remained indoors to examine my accounts. I am unwilling to let people rob me of my hard and honest earnings.

I received a postal order for £1 10s 6d; it should have been drawn for £2 2s, being two prizes of a guinea each which I had won at Ballarat eisteddfod on St David's Day.

The surveyor drove by today, and as he is fond of poetry, I quoted to him four lines from Robert Burns's poem, 'man was made to mourn'. The lines and the sentiment fell on deaf ears for he offered me no work.

At night the moon looked foul and watery. Next day it rained incessantly, causing severe flooding, the severest I have seen in the Colony.

Two shirts cost me £1 7s 9d. Wool sells for only 9½d a pound, and the two shirts together weigh less than 2½ pounds, so that some workers earn better wages than the farm labourer.

I met a swagman who was travelling up-country for the shearing. I cannot do anything at that job as I tried it when I was much younger, yet I have seen much older men, who had never used shears, make the journey, for it was thought that every squatter would give tea, sugar, bread and meat to all travellers gratis, but when I went, I did not find it to be so.

I devoted the day to modifying my fireplace. I had to carry stones in my wheelbarrow a distance of half a mile. The chimney is so well made that it will draw the smoke from any point of my solitary castle. In fact the draw is so great that it takes away too much heat, and I am going to stop that. Toothache bothers me again. I am satisfied with the food I take; and with the cooking. The only addition I would like would be a quart of skimmed milk each day. Four big farmers are near neighbours, but none can provide me with a pint of milk for money. Two of them come from Cardiganshire, one from Carmarthenshire, and the fourth is a cockney; he is by far the best farmer of the four. He is a sheep-farmer and is a very industrious and compact man. His garden and homestead are good to look upon.

The swallows begin to build their nests. When my door is open they fly in and begin to build with the same materials as they used at home. The feather tribe throughout the Bush show great activity as a sign that Spring is at the door.

I was on my withered pins long before daylight, and relished an early breakfast. Another cold, calm and bright frosty morning. Ice covers the water holes which both in this country and Britain they call 'black frost'. It always looks white to me and never black. Even when the water is muddy and copper-coloured, the surface ice looks silvery white.

I have just made a ladder of sixteen rungs which will enable me to extend the chimney higher, for the outlet now is too near the thatch, constituting a fire danger in hot weather.

A gaming party called on me, and invited me to join them. They were a disorderly lot, and their shouts forewarned the hares of our coming a long way off, so that few of the sixty-seven hares were seen by the greyhounds. The young blades of corn are stripped in field upon field by these magnificent creatures. Their number increases because of the dearth of dogs on account of the dog-tax which should be rescinded for the benefit of the farmer.

While out coursing, I composed an englyn which appeared in the local paper, 'Mount Alexander Mail', together with an accompanying letter. *He used 'Wood Cutter' as his nom-de-plume.*

I was engaged in limiting the opening at the top of the chimney for it was drawing too vigorously, taking all the heat up along with the sparks. It is a long time since the renowned Dr Franklin and Dr Dick issued accurate instructions on the proper design of chimneys which would effectively draw smoke. More than half the chimneys nowadays are smoky. Their plan ensured that the entrance to the chimney below should be as narrow or narrower than its mouth at the top.

I must go out to look for work. A job won't come my way here where I am surrounded by farmers who take on odd jobs instead of confining their activities to improving their lands. Unless the land is cleared and cultivated, labour is not wanted and men go idle. The interior of Victoria cannot be judged by the standards of Melbourne, Ballarat, and a few other go-ahead towns. Rural toiling men especially, have their part to play in a new country. A nation was never formed without them, nor ever will.

September
The transgressor favoured

I walked to Maldon and back, a journey of sixteen miles. It is a dull place nowadays because the precious metal is no longer plentiful in the rocks. The old experienced reefers say that they don't tunnel deep enough. They have no money to pay the wood splitters. The labour market in Victoria is at a standstill except for reefing and shearing. Employers will not even give a meal for a good day's work.

I went over to see Mr Byrne who owes me £2 for firewood. I was given a good dinner of roast beef and plum pudding. They live rich there, but I was not paid a penny.

I tendered to the council for a job which is only a mile from here, but it will probably go to the farmers who are so eager for such work that they tender so low that they scarcely earn their provisions while carrying it out. In that they are also in arrears with their rates, their applications are favoured by the Council. Thus, the labourer is excluded from taking part in any public or private work.

My tender of £2 9s 6d was, however, the lowest, but only by 6d, so I was awarded the contract to cut a drain one foot deep, 5 feet wide at the top, and 2 feet at the bottom. I had also to clear the dead trees and burn the rubbish. The rate of pay is small, 1s 10d a chain compared with 5s a chain in Wales, but I prefer to be occupied at any kind of work rather than be idle.

I planned the track of the drain, cleared and burnt the roots and the stumps, and started picking. It was hard where it had been trodden down by drays, buggies and waggons.

Lost a valuable pocket knife. Something undesirable often happens to me on a Friday. I was born late on a Friday when the moon was nearly full. I wrote a long letter to 'The Leader' on 'farm labourers', and it appeared in full today.

I work hard on the track, and I am thankful that I am able to enjoy my work. I also relish my meals, and bless my sleep, and easy rest.

I did not make such satisfactory progress on the track today as yesterday. I cannot explain why, unless it be that this is Friday. The drain looks more like a boat-canal than a road-side drain. I have finished it and take a day's rest, having removed 307 cubic yards of soil at a rate of 22 cubic yards a day. I hope it will bear examination by the shire council surveyor, Mr Campbell.

October *Another tender accepted*

I walked to Maldon again and tendered for another contract, namely to clear thirty chains of road, which is three miles from my residence. My tender of 3s 4d a chain was accepted, and the work has to be completed in a month.

Found that a walk of six miles a day, additional to the job, was too much for me, so I loaded my swag on to the wheelbarrow in order to be near my contract. I sleep in a stable belonging to a Mr Rowe who is a farmer and butcher.

The timber is green and hard and is difficult to burn, and each trunk has to be burnt for a distance of one foot below the surface of the road.

The surveyor inspected the work, and later Thomas James, a councillor spoke to me. Two other surveyors drove to the site in a buggy. They all appeared well pleased with my work.

I was obliged to get assistance today to bring down a tree. He was a boy whom I hired for three hours at 1s an hour. I am only paid at the rate of 2½d an hour myself. The whole length of the road is ablaze with burning stumps.

November *Admonished by a babe*

Mr Rowe in whose stable I sleep appeared in court at Castlemaine, sued by his brother, a neighbouring farmer, for damage to trees through burning, to the value of £58. It was a case of revenge rather than claiming damage, and the case was dismissed with costs.

It has been very wet, and this has hindered the burning of my avenue of trees. When engaged in piece-work, I make it a rule to eat when I have relish for it, and to rest when I feel inclined to retreat. My last obstacle on this job is a big tree which I have to burn down, along with several other smaller ones. I read in one of my home-papers that my brother Jenkin had been a successful exhibitor at both Aberystwyth and Lampeter agricultural shows.

A boy not quite 7 years old entered my sleeping quarters at 4 a.m. and blamed me for staying in bed so late. He told me it was time I stirred, so I got up to a beautiful morning.

December *Dentures from nowhere*

I received the 'Cambrian News' from home, and I am fond of reading it. Its editor, Mr Wilson, writes sound sense, and is forthright in his criticism of the world's ill-habits. His writings are both harmonious and poetical.

The law in regard to lighting fires is very strict in the Colony at this time of the year. The fine is £50 for lighting a fire in the Bush or six months' imprisonment. Splitting wood is heavy and unrewarding work, and I should have ventured up-country for the harvest, work which would be more to my liking and within my competence. I wish I could dispose of the timber back in the Bush which I have already split.

Miss Mary Rowe, daughter of the farmer who had allowed me to

127

sleep in his stable while doing the council's job, is to be married tomorrow to William Williams, a nearby farmer. I composed four verses on the occasion.

Binding corn on William Williams's farm. I was in good spirits, and was able to stoop as readily as when I was 18 years old. This is my fifty-fourth year of binding corn. I remember clearly the day my grandfather showed me how to bind a sheaf. Hand-binding is nearly out of date. The combined reaper and binders are numerous in Victoria and they work efficiently. *This machine did not make its appearance in the cornfields of Wales till twenty-five years later.*

Then comes the remarkable statement, 'I had a new set of teeth', because there is no word about frequenting a dentist, and during this time he was leading a Bush life.

I have been at the harvest in different farms for the past week, working really hard and enjoying it. I went to the council office at Maldon and was paid for the drain and road work.

Returning home to my Ants' Hill Hermitage, having collected the implements I had used in the road construction, I came across a party of some 150 young people out for a picnic. They invited me to join them, and presently asked me to compose a song for the occasion, so I tried to oblige. *A lyric of forty-two lines is included in his diary!!*

I regard 1883 as my most unfortunate year since my arrival in Australia, not in respect of health, but because I was unable to get remunerative work, and worse, for one-half of the year I was without any settled work. The people shout, 'Advance Victoria', but it advances only towards all sorts of inequities. The rich surface of the country's soil, properly managed, would supply the whole of Europe with their necessities in respect of meat and bread. Instead of that, the best of its land is monopolized by the few, and left in its natural uncultivated state. No labourers are employed except for bark-ringing the Colony's fine trees here and there. The selectors in general avoid the further clearance of the land, and they exhaust the little that they have cleared of scrub, so they become too poor to improve what they have. O Victoria! You cannot boast of your advancement.

1884

January
The Justices escape justice

Binding and stooking corn for a local farmer. During the night great damage was done to the sheaves in an eight-acre field by kangaroos, hares and rabbits. The last two vermin are very numerous. The landowners have distributed notices that trespassers in pursuit of game will be prosecuted, so the selectors are unable to be rid of the furry scavengers. The grass begins to wither and Bush fires rage.

The harvest around here is concluded. I should move south where the farmers are in the midst of it, but I dare not leave my split timber, in case some carter will mistake them for his own. Two trees have fallen across the road and the surveyor has asked me to remove them. There is no market for split timber, for the reefs at Maldon are not producing the precious metal any longer.

The papers report an earthquake at 11.15 last night at Castlemaine, Walmer, Maldon and Ravenswood. I was in the centre of this area from 9 p.m. to 10 a.m. because I was shepherding the burning of long grass around my abode in case it spread into the Bush. I can swear that no such thing happened. There was neither noise nor disturbance of the ground. What a curious earthquake!

No less than five Justices of the Peace were summoned last week for cattle stealing, drunkenness, rioting, and other breaches of the law, but they got away from it when judged by their equals.

The hot weather has been interrupted by unexpected rain. Many farmers have been caught out. They had expected the threshers to call soon, so they had not carted the corn into stacks, but had just left it in the yard. The damage from the rain will have cost them thousands of pounds, all because they grudged paying a good stacker to give the corn proper cover.

William Hagarth has taken away seven loads of my timber, but he did not pay me today, *nor did he later.*

February *Another comet appears*

A comet has appeared above the western horizon. It is not as bright as the one seen last year. The magenta and red sky is brilliant. The colour encircles the horizon, and it first made its appearance towards the end of August. The astronomers are unable to explain the cause of this unusual colour, and it remains a glorious mystery.

The rate collector called, and I paid rates for the first time since I came to the Colony. Threshing oats, and thatching a straw stack, at Mr Byrne's farm. I was paid £1 10s for ten days' work, a wage of 3s a day.

This (27th of February) is my sixty-sixth birthday:

I cannot just foretell the future,
And must obey the rules of Nature.
Man is just a lump of clay,
To flourish once and then decay.

The Ballarat eisteddfod approaches. There is only one competition for poetry, namely an englyn to a Methodist Minister, but as I never met him I am unable to compete.

March *Respect for the worms*

There has been severe flooding of a creek on the way to Maldon, for the big nearby water dam had broken its banks. Horses drawing a timber waggon in which I was riding had to swim across. I had not witnessed such a flood before in the Colony, but it was not as severe as the flood I witnessed in Wales in 1846 when Dr Rogers and his servant were drowned when crossing the river Aeron in a trap.

Many parties hunt the hares and rabbits with greyhounds and guns. Like farm labourers, hares and rabbits are too plentiful. The law of supply and demand takes it course:

Scarcity of gold makes it dearer
Than either brass, iron or silver.

It's a general holiday on this St Patrick's Day (17th of March), and I joined a party to course the hares and rabbits. We travelled far and were very tired at the end of the day, so we walked home in single file like the Chinamen do. They never walk two abreast in order not to tramp on too many innocent worms. It was a fine Spring day, and I returned thanks in this way:

This is a gift from Nature,
Bequeathed by God above.
Sweet kiss for every creature
To prove His endless love.

I went to Maldon and called to see the surveyor at the Shire Hall, but there was no job for me. It is delightful weather enabling the farmers to plough for another crop, but they don't employ dung carts. A small farmer nearby has grown twenty-five tons of hay on four acres of land through manuring it well, while the so-called big farmers in the neighbourhood do not grow as much on forty acres because they do not add manure. Their land is not half the value now than when they bought it from the thieves who stole it from the natives. The timber has been sold and the soil has been deplorably exhausted. That is the general rule throughout the Colony, and the bankers do not advance money as readily as in former times.

April *His gift to Australian husbandry*

I turn my hand to ploughing once more. I have done it in due season for the past forty-seven years. I have ploughed over 1,000 acres in the Colony. The two horses I plough with are named 'Bob' and 'Charlie', and we plod on slowly. Bob is lame from a dislocated hip, but he pulls better than Charlie who is weak from ageing and ill-feeding. I limp along with them, for I have rheumatism in my knees and arms, the handicap of old age:

The Trinity is denied
By the Unitarians.
The Trinity is defied
By all the Deists and Arians.
I'll contradict such creed,
And can let them know
That there is Unity indeed
In Charlie, Bob and Joe.

I witnessed a total eclipse of the moon at 9.20 p.m. It was the time predicted by the astronomers, so they must know the tracks of the planets, although one is inclined to doubt their estimate of the distance between them and the earth. Their calculation, that the sun is 93 million miles from the earth, is probably correct.

The ground is too hard for the plough-share to penetrate. In turn it is hard for the aged ploughman and the crippled horses.

A party of seven men drove to this neighbourhood with greyhounds and guns. They went into the Bush at dawn, and returned at noon with sixty-five head of game, mostly hares and rabbits. There soon followed another party from Sandhurst (Victoria) with about fifty guns, mostly breech-loaders, and camped near Ravenswood railway station. They had with them well trained ferrets which soon chased the rabbits from their burrows to face the guns. Three other parties were operating in another sector. I was told by a nearby farmer, who is a religious man so I believed him, that one party had accounted for so many that three drays were used to carry them away. Yet another party left half their game behind them to rot in the Bush. Four years ago a jugged hare was a delicacy, but now they are so numerous to be unwanted, and no one will skin them, so they are just boiled to feed the greyhounds which are kept for the sport of coursing. In fact, hares and rabbits are now in such large numbers as to be regarded a serious pest which destroy whole paddocks of cereal crops while in the blade-stage, and devour grass pastures, causing famine among cattle, and depleting the Colony's larders.

May *The Queen in mourning*

Sowing wheat and oats and harrowing; the hares will have a treat when the blades appear. Some farmers boast that they have taken twenty-seven crops from the land without giving it a shovelful of manure in return. I wrote a letter home to my daughter Mary.

Delightful afternoon. Ploughed nearly an acre today. I did it with ten times more pleasure than labour. Such is the vantage gained from toil, namely to toil with pleasure and a contented mind. John Lewis is back at his old trade, selling firewood in Maldon. He has no interest in his farm of 180 acres.

I was sowing a mixture of wheat and oats. The crop is cut and harvested as hay when it is green, and before the head matures.

The Queen does not wish her birthday to be a holiday this year, her twenty-third year of widowhood. *In May of the previous year, the diarist had written to the Queen sympathizing with her on the death of her faithful servant and intimate friend, John Brown.*

June *Opening of Castlemaine-Maldon railway*

Ploughing all day. The land on this farm (John Lewis's) is exhausted. Six months ago one load of dung was brought to the corner of a fifteen-acre paddock, and today he distributed a load on the very same spot. The ignorance of this man is unbelievable. The horses are kept working in harness for 10½ hours each day. It is downright cruelty. About fifty fowls pick up the newly sown corn seed, and scratch at the harrowed ground. Every creature on this farm is starving.

I was present at the opening of the railway line between Castlemaine and Maldon. The weather has been generally wet with frosty nights.

Although the items chronicled from the diary for June, as also for some other months, are brief, the reader must not assume that the diarist's account for the month is also brief. Nothing of the kind; he devotes the same space to each day, but the events recorded might be mundane and repetitive, and for this reason are purposely omitted. Even for the months more fully recorded, only a fraction of the original is represented. Being the poet that he is, he frequently breaks out into verse, especially in englynion, and these too have to be laid on one side, for they are in Welsh and do not lend themselves to translation as do traditional verses.

July *Mud walls and straw roofs*

Several parties are out shooting hares and rabbits. Reports from the guns from dawn to dusk. The vermin are now feeding on the new blades of corn.

The horses are dead-beat. The farmer, John Lewis, came to the field and blamed me for not driving them fast enough in the harrow, so I handed him the reins and the whip, and left the field. I was only paid £3 on account, and he already owes me £25 which I had loaned to him. I fear he has neither the money nor the principle to settle it; pride and poverty.

What glorious colours are to be seen at sunset in the western skies, the same that appeared in August last year, and which have puzzled the astronomers.

Being out of work again I pick up my swag and walk to Porcupine Flat, where I am to thatch a shed, twenty yards long, for a Mr E. W. Brown of 'Forresters Arms'. He carries on a butcher's trade as well as a farm. I am well pleased with my comfortable quarters and with the good food and prompt meals.

I was told several times by my employer to make a good and permanent job of the thatching for his fine shed which shelters his buggies and spring-carts. A thatch-roof will keep them in a better condition than a galvanized roof which generates too much heat from the sun in summer. The best dairies in the Colony are built of mud walls with thatch roofs, but since they are mostly underground, the cheese and butter which they hold get stale and mouldy.

Mr Brown employs about a dozen men and women, and each have a specific job. He has eight horses at work daily. A two-horse power engine grinds meat for sausages. I keep away from the busy bar.

I began to lay the comb on the ridge of the shed. My hands are sore, but I finished the thatch in three days, and began to trim the ewes. Afterwards, I cleaned up, which is the final duty of the thatcher.

Up early and proceeded to Maldon in search of another job. I entered the Shire Hall, and found seven specifications for tenders on the table. Only one involved manual labour, namely to grub and clean 143½ chains of road, 32 feet wide. I inspected the road in question and submitted my tender for the job. In that I was out of work, I had to mention a very low figure, namely £15 and deposited £1. I was given the contract because my tender was the lowest; the others had varied between £16 and £21.

In that my present abode is three miles away from my work, I shall have to build a hut in the Bush.

August *Builds a mia mia*

I prepare my tools for the job, and in between times I read Alexander Pope's translation of Homer's Iliad. Its composition is so good, I wish I could read it in the original Greek.

Started to build my new hut in the Bush, a 'mia mia' as the natives call it. I nearly had it ready to thatch before the end of the day, and I expect to complete it tomorrow. I doubt whether I shall earn more than 2s a day at the job.

I shall call my new hut, Hermitage No. 2. There, I shall now cook, eat and sleep. I can see the work is to be tough and will last a long time. In my favour is the fact that the weather has changed so that the ground is wet and easier to grub. On the other hand it will be more difficult to burn the old tree stumps. Continuous rain has already tested my roof, and it is water-tight.

I have a nice neighbour living by himself and caring for a big garden. He is a musician, and I am near enough to his house to enjoy his playing on the fiddle after supper. I only enjoy music when it is played at a distance.

I have never seen so many hares. They run about the Bush like a flock of sheep. Corn-growing for that reason is out of the question in this district. I have cleared one chain of the road which grew forty-five trees, some of them eight inches in diameter. I have to burn the big stumps, but will leave the scrub to be disposed of later.

September *Pleasure from the fall of a tree*

They are very kind to me in this neighbourhood. Mr Brown's son brings me bread from Porcupine. There is not much profit from selling me bread. The stumps burn with difficulty because the soil is wet. The ground is gritty and arid, and looks auriferous, full of quartz. I am not digging deep enough for the precious metal. A small nugget would be welcomed by the old man.

I now call the new hut, 'Joe's cabin'. Most Sundays I return to Ants' Hill Hermitage but this Sunday I rested quietly here, reading Spurgeon's sermon in 'The Leader'. He is a faithful child of John Calvin who made martyrs of many honest men beside the sage Servitus and his valuable manuscript.

It is the first day of Spring (25th September) and everything is growing. The flies are beginning to tantalize me, and I must find my fly-net. My breath is getting short, and in this job the pleasure I get from looking at a tall tree comes only when it is falling. The surveyor came by today, and I was highly commended.

October *A passengerless train will not pay*

I went to Maldon, and called at the Shire Hall where I was given £5 as a progress payment.

John Lewis has again cheated me over my loan to him. He had agreed to repay me, but now refuses. He is the most deceitful person I have ever met. He is now an ill man otherwise I would sue him.

I have said before that the grass here remains green and plentiful till Christmas time, and is then three times more than the cattle can eat. Afterwards, and throughout the Summer, it withers away. It is not half as good a country in this respect as Britain.

The papers report bad feelings are rising between Germany, Prussia, Russia, Austria and France. United against England, any one of these powers would warm the tough hide of 'John Bull'. He must be conquered one day!

Still burning tree stumps, one of them being seven feet in girth. Continually feeding the fires when they begin to dwindle. It is a very hot and smoky job. If the dry weather lasts, I will finish the contract in four or five days; not bad for an old man. Should I finish next week it will mean £15 for fifty-four days. I fill the holes where the stumps are burnt out.

Went to Castlemaine to invite the road inspector to pass my completed road-contract. I was the only passenger to take a ticket from Muckleford station today. Railways without passengers won't pay!

The inspector called as promised and passed the road job with commendation, so I am out of work again, and I will soon eat away the proceeds of the last contract. Bullocks are cheap, but meat is dear. Wheat is only 3s a bushel, but the 4 lb loaf is 6d and is under-weight at that. The baker takes £2 12s 6d for baking 200 lbs of flour. The producer, namely the farmer, gets a poor deal. In turn he cannot afford to apply labour in order to farm efficiently, so the Colony is poor.

I have been paid for the road contract. Having purchased clothes and some provisions, I was only able to deposit £5 in the Savings Bank. I kept another £5 in reserve when without a job.

The gold digger is not much better off. Before starting on his job, he pays the owner of the surface land £2. The experienced digger cannot make more than 15s a week, while he has to pay for his board and lodgings.

November
Mountains of dough

I find the day long and weary. I am perfectly well in both mind and body when at work. Within 100 yards of 'Joe's cabin', lives a Mr Moore. He used to hold a fine farm in the neighbourhood. His young wife was in the habit of leaving him from time to time, but not without causing great annoyance before departing. On one occasion, she made dough of all the flour in the house, three sackfuls of it, and left it in that state.

I have derived great enjoyment from reading Pope's tranlation of Homer's Iliad. It is a masterpiece!

I went to see the surveyor. He gave me a small job, but not an easy one. It was to dig a big drain through a thick plantation of red gum saplings, some of them twelve inches in circumference. It is very warm and sultry. I do not feel like work, but I must if I am to finish this job before hay-making time. The corn crops are poor because of the havoc wrought by the hares and rabbits.

The drain is nearly as big as a canal, and I have not enjoyed this job as much as the previous one, while the wages are to be far less. I finished the drain at last. I tendered for the construction of a new water dam, but was not successful.

December *Spilt ink*

The hay harvest has begun. This is an easy harvest in Australia because it is seldom disturbed by rain. On the other hand, thousands upon thousands of pounds' worth of hay is made useless as a fodder every year, through exposing it for too long a time to the sun. I am unable to persuade the farmers of this Colony that too much sun and dry weather lessens the value of hay.

Heavy rain has prevented a start of the harvest, so it is another idle day for me. *He rests on his bed and composes an excellent englyn on the comfort it brings to a tired body.*

Flies and fleas torment me in the Bush, and I spend a shilling each month on Kruse insect powder. Several picnic parties visit this neighbourhood, and they appear to have great fun.

Through my awkwardness, and the fact that I have to carry my diary and ink bottle in the same pocket, the cork came loose, and the ink was spilt as had happened several times in the past. Those who have a permanent home cannot imagine the inconveniences of a swagman in this Colony. There are over 200,000 of us in Victoria, while the total inhabitants number under 1,000,000.

Started reaping and binding a paddock of mixed oats and hay, continuing from 6 a.m. to 7.30 p.m. We were well fed during this time, and the horses were changed every three hours.

A carpet snake, six feet long, crawled from under my bed. There was only a thin stick within reach, and a blow from this failed to kill it, so that it dived back into the hole beneath my bed. I poured boiling water directly into the hole, but with what result I know not.

I am back with Mr Brown of the Forresters Hotel at Porcupine to thatch a stack of hay. Started carting hay from another paddock which nine years ago yielded eight tons of hay to the acre, but which now has only yielded three tons, because of the hares and rabbits.

I tendered for a contract to clean the water channels at Maldon daily, and to keep the pavements in repair for twelve months with the exception of Sundays and public holidays, the council supplying tools and materials.

The labour market is depressed, and the Government promise to build 1,100 miles of railway, for which they have to borrow £4 million.

My tender for the Council contract was accepted, being the lowest of four. *In the local paper, the 'Tarangower Times' for the 19th of December, 1884, the following entry appears:*

A Facetious Tender

Mr J. Jenkins of Hermitage, Ravenswood, who is the successful tenderer for the work of keeping the water drains clear during the year 1885, put the following poetic addendum to his tender: —

I'll pave and curb to your command,
If good materials are at hand.
The man who shouts is silly ape,
That he can do what he can't shape.
He is doubly silly who can't tell
What he can do, and do it well.

One pound a week, or 3s 4d a day, without board and lodgings!! Well done, Walmer poet, there is a good deal of truth in your sentiments.

The sentiments expressed in the diarist's verse, were born of an incident which is recorded inside the front cover of this his 1884 diary, and reads as follows:

When swagging the Colony I once worked with a mate who would tell the farmers that he could tackle and shape any sort of work that was needed on the farm, and further, that he could do mason's, blacksmith's, and carpenter's work if required. We were engaged at last, he to plough at £1 a week, and I to 'knock about the place' at 14s a week. We made ready our beds, and he began to question me about ploughing, admitting that he had never done any, and that he had never harnessed a horse, but he thought he could do it. We went in for breakfast, and afterwards he ran away. In regard to our separate agreements just contracted with the farmer, I characterized my mate in the two lines:

The man who shouts, is silly ape,
That he can do what he can't shape.

and myself in the next two lines:

He's doubly silly who can't tell
What he can do, and do it well.

1885

January
Scotch leeks

I was interviewed by the clerk of works to the Maldon Council. I expected to commence work there today, but the clerk said that the job was to be tendered for again. They still hold my deposit, and I came away disappointed.

I again applied to John Lewis for money in respect of loans and wages. He only gave me £2 10s. He maintained that my agreed wage was 17s and not £1 a week. A loss of 3s a week for eleven weeks, meant a loss of £1 13s to me.

I walked from Porcupine Flat to Maldon to receive the further decision of the councillors regarding my job to look after the town's drains for twelve months. They awarded me the job at a salary of £1 a week. I was advised by many acquaintances not to accept it, but I decided to stick to my own judgment, and to accept it.

Rented a cottage in the town for 1s a week. Firewood will cost me 5s a month. I determined to visit my good friend David Evans at Rheola, thirty-eight miles away, for many of my books and possessions are in his care. I have not seen him for two years, and my new job will not allow me to visit him for another year. Started my long walk which I mean to complete in stages. Walking past many farms I perceived in the distance two big fields which looked like two beds of leeks in Wales. It was a cheerful sight, because all grassland is now brown and withered, so I walked up to examine them. I was greatly disappointed, for instead of Irish shamrock or Welsh white clover, I discovered both paddocks to be thickly and evenly covered with tall and strong Scotch thistles.

Walked twenty-six miles the first day, I was at Rheola at noon of the next day after covering the remaining twelve miles. My friend has a small compact farm and vineyard. It was very hot, and 104° F in the shade. I enjoyed the company of many visitors and the wine prepared from Evans's own crop of grapes.

Evans drove me twelve miles to meet the train at Inglewood. Travelled forty-four miles by train, and walked another seven miles to 'Joe's cabin'.

I prepared for the move. All my things were ready to be loaded into a dray, but the man arrived in a spring-cart, so I was unable to take firewood which costs 12s a load in Maldon.

Commenced work for the council. The water channels are foul with Scotch thistles, docks, hogweed, sorrel and native grass. Their roots are fast between the paving stones.

The heavy rain that fell yesterday had little effect on the water dams which are nearly empty. I had to walk half a mile to fetch two bucketfuls of brackish water for my domestic use this morning. Tremendous quantity of water runs waste in the town. The water supply is brought by iron pipes from a distance of thirty miles. The council has borrowed £17,000 at an interest rate of six per cent to lay new pipes.

I came under notice of all passers-by. The inhabitants of the town number 1,800. I work from 7 to 5 with an hour for dinner. I have taken out a miner's right today in order to keep possession of Ants' Hill Hermitage.

When a gale blows the dust rises in clouds in Maldon. When it rains the dust turns into mud. Whichever state presides, the ladies complain of soiled dresses. I learn that the original name for Maldon was Tarangower.

Against my inclination I have wheeled over six tons of the best sort of muck for the use of gardeners or farmers, and tipped it where it cannot any more be extracted, into a deep digger's hole. Manure is not valued here, and the council will not allow me to tip it into anybody's garden.

I have not had a letter from home for three months. It would be acceptable now as I have time to read. I am forgotten!

February *Black Thursday*

I walk a mile and a half for water for my tea and even this water is unfit to drink unboiled. Any amount of water runs waste by the doors of the moneyed people. It is very hot, and over 100° F in the shade.

This, the 6th of February, is the anniversary of 'Black Thursday' of 1851, when one half of the state of Victoria was on fire. Several Bush fires were visible last night, but at some distance from the town.

The letter-box is within 200 yards of my cottage which I rent for £2 12s a year, and which is expensive enough for one smoky room without water or fuel. I wrote a lengthy letter to the editor of the 'Tarangower Times', for he had made an unnecessary attack on Unitarians and their creed.

News has just come that General Gordon has been killed in Khartoum by the Arabs under the command of Madhi, or 'False Prophet' as he is known. His prophesy was right this time. Bought a small Bible (revised version) for 3s, and a pair of woollen socks for 2s. No money to spare for a glass of beer. Received eight home-papers, some of them dated for early November. Australia is to send men to assist the English at Khartoum. They may as well remain where they are, because the Arabs have never been conquered. I purchased a small bellows for 3s. The rain has come.

March *Maldon is like London*

Working today in the main streets. I had not to heed any passer-by. The clerk of works was with me, and he wanted some special jobs done.

At work in the hilly part of the town. In the outskirts there are many fine residences owned by storekeepers and magistrates who are known as independents. They prospered from the profits of the gold reefs. Maldon is like London in one respect, few are very wealthy, and the majority are very poor, and are oppressed.

I am very happy in my work, for which I am grateful to the Author of every good cause, for this gift. Every Wednesday afternoon is a half-holiday here, but not for the gutter-man.

I have been for my month's wages, and have squared accounts with all my creditors, leaving me only a few shillings for papers, stamps etc. I cannot live as cheaply here as in the Bush, rent and firewood costs me 2s 6d a week.

This is St Patrick's day (17th of March), and in deference to the Irish, I took my half holiday, and toasted the late Dan O'Connell, Tom Moore the poet, and Dean Swift the jester. Rheumatism has set in in my right thigh, I hope it will not go chronic. I have been told that there is no compulsion to work the full eight hours, and that some days I need only work three hours. I am advised by some of the councillors to do that.

It has rained all night, and I have found that my rented cottage is not fit to harbour an otter when it rains heavily. One shilling a week for a hovel like this makes me wish that some other country had dominion over this Colony, and which would not require the working man to dwell in such a place for such small wages.

Working on the main streets today while the channels in the outskirts are neglected. A gentleman from the town called on me. We had a friendly chat about religion. He is a Universalist or fair thinker.

Working about the middle of the town. Two other men there making foot-bridges across the side-walks. They were getting 7s a day. The boss was also there the whole of the day. Those who have the highest wages have it more easy than the folk who are obliged to work at low wages. I had proof of this today.

April *Someone steals his bread*

Followed my routine work, namely up at dawn, lit the fire, made tea, fried meat, prepared dinner to take with me, washed myself, ate breakfast, swept my floor, shut the door and locked it after me, and walked to my work station by 7 a.m.

It is Good Friday and I turned to make a new water hole nearer to the cottage, but I did not finish it. On Easter Monday, I wheeled four barrowfuls of bricks and stones in order to cure the most non-drawing smoky chimney I have ever met. I visited the Fair-ground with its 'Merry-go-Rounds' and all sorts of amusements. All the profits are to go to the hospital.

I have cured my smoky chimney. My landlord ought to give me a pound for the job. I have called my newer abode, 'Four Trees Cottage'.

On Sunday, I had a chat with my neighbour who is a Swiss. He is like myself rather backward in the English language, but a good neighbour for all that.

This is the first time since my arrival in the Colony that it has rained with the wind blowing south-south-east.

My grocer, Edwin John, who hailed from Glamorgan in South Wales, has died. He was highly respected in the town, as shown by the large attendance of between 900 and 1,000 people, at his funeral. *The occasion caused him to compose six Welsh verses, each of eight lines, as well as two englynion which portrayed a dialogue with death. Both have great merit which is lost in any translation to English. One only is given here:*

O angau pa'm y cwympaist ti	*O death why fellest thou a tree*
Bren llawn o dwf a ffrwythau,	*Sturdy in both growth and fruits,*
A gadael boncyff crin fel fi	*And leave a rotten stump like me*
I wywo hyd ei wreiddiau?	*Stand to wither to its roots?*

While preparing to go to the funeral I hung my parcel of four small loaves of bread and three newspapers on the fence for ten minutes. When I went to collect them they had gone. I was obliged to buy them anew. May someone enjoy the others.

The working classes have a holiday (21st of April) which they call the 'Eight-Hours' anniversary. The bankers, lawyers and postmasters joined in. The day shortens. It is pitch-dark at 6 p.m. It dawns at about 3 a.m., but the sun does not appear before 6.15 a.m. The weather is most agreeable for April. O what a lovely life to be at work and in good health!

May *The Absentees are in the majority*

The clerk of works paid me a visit. He was well pleased with my work and my dispatch of it.

The churches and chapels are well attended on a Sunday, but the 'Stay at Homians' are numerous.

It would appear that Russia and England are not so quarrelsome at present, but like the farmers they may be preparing their hooks and knives for harvest-time. Some of the town's drains have not been cleared for eight years. News has just come in that England and Russia are at peace once more. Well done, the great peace-maker and friend of the people, Mr W. E. Gladstone!

I will never become proficient in speaking English here, because half the time I converse in Welsh. I was invited to dinner to the home of Mr Rees Jones from Ponterwyd (Mrs Jones is from Penrhiw Pal near Newcastle Emlyn). They have a family and live well.

Today (May 24th) is the birthday of H.M. Queen Victoria. I am older than she is by three months and three days. I am no prophet, but I believe that the Prince of Wales will have a thorny job, should he survive her and ascend to the throne. Being a general holiday, I went for a barrowful of sand to make mortar so as to mend my fireplace, and plaster the walls all at my own expense. I could build a house for myself here on crown land, and pay 6s a year rent, but should my health and strength permit, my next job could be 200 miles away from here.

June *Friend to little children*

Dogs and little children are very fond of me. The children play with my tools, but the parents call them away. The older children, on their way to and from school, use abusive language as they pass me, but I appear to take no notice, in the belief that this is the wisest course to take.

I spend most of my time in Main Street, High Street, and the very dirty Chapel Street. I paid 10s for firewood, and that in a Bush country. The shortest day of the year according to the Australian calendar is the 21st of June.

July *The purest spring of education*

It is raining consistently. Received sad news that the University of Wales at Aberystwyth was completely burnt down on the 9th of July. It was a fine new building, and was one of the purest springs of education.

Frosty morning and the water holes are covered with ice. The waterholes are numerous here and are the remnants of the gold-digging operations.

My brush has been taken. It belonged to the council, so I will have to replace it at a cost of 5s, which represents a day and a half wages.

August *Good manure wasted*

Nearly all the cottages in this scattered place have an acre, more or less, of land adjoining them, but one-tenth of them are neither manured nor properly cultivated. I believe that I have wheeled over fifty tons of good manure and tipped it into old diggers'-holes where it can never be retrieved. I do not have a square yard of land adjoining my rented cottage.

In the town council elections, a Mr Way was elected. He obtained 145 votes, while my favourite got 116 votes, so that now I have 4 instead of 3 that are against me on the board that governs me.

I have just seen the first swallow this year. This bird may be seen in some part of the country in all seasons.

I went to a lecture in the Catholic church. The building was overcrowded by people of all creeds. The subject was, 'The effect of Religion on Civilization'. The lecturer described the Irish as the best and most religious nation in the known world!!

I cleaned ten chains of water channels in two days. It is a lovely day for outdoor work. All the almond trees are beautifully covered with white sheets of blossom. I am fond of almond nuts, although they are not as tasty as the filberts and the ordinary fruit of the hazel tree.

September
Excursion to Melbourne

On Sundays I rest and read my books, especially the Bible and the beautiful psalms of the Druid bard, Iolo Morganwg, which give me a better understanding of uprightness and truth.

While working in front of the state school, the boys and girls come out into the playground to drill. They number about 250 and are from 5 to 14 years old. Altogether, some 600 children attend the school.

I have a bad cold and incessant cough. This 19th day of September is the last day this year to obtain a railway excursion ticket to Melbourne and back for 6s, with the option of staying in Melbourne for three weeks. Some 300 passengers boarded the train. The usual fare is £1. They call it the Farmers' excursion, and they entice the poor dupes to spend three weeks in Melbourne.

I am unable to obtain a drop of skimmed milk, as very few milch cows are kept in the vicinity, while the farmers' kine are so lean and weak that they scarcely survive.

October *The scavenger's sermon*

There follows here a dialogue between a Captain of the Salvation Army and the diarist. It is recorded verbatim as it took place in the streets of Maldon on the 3rd of October in 1885.

A Captain in the Salvation Army stopped to speak to me. He said to me, 'Good day my man, I see that you are cleaning the gutter; is your heart clean, that is the main thing?' I replied, 'Yes sir, and with a guiltless and free conscience, but regretting one course which I took in life. I have devoted the best part of it listening to men of different denominations, and I was obliged to fall back on my own initiative, which led me to read the New Testament in order to find the truth in the enlightened religion of Jesus Christ.

I have read the expositions of scores of different expounders and interpreters of the inspired scriptures. All of them held different opinions, and the present day preachers of religion have no authority to compel their fellow-creatures to believe these separate opinions. I started reading the New Testament without bias, and I came upon that plain and magnificent verse, the 12th in the 7th chapter of the gospel according to St Matthew, being the last portion of that unequalled and authoritative Sermon on the Mount, delivered by the great exponent of truth, and who was authorized to do so by God. The verse runs like this: "therefore all things whatsoever ye would that men should do to you, do ye even so to them, for this is the law and the prophets." It should be for the director of education to have this verse printed in capital letters on the inside of every school book. If this verse does not truly interpret the gospel in respect of the duty of man both towards his fellow creatures and his God, where else can it be found, and who has the authority to proclaim it? I acknowledge Jesus Christ as the head of the true church of the living God, whether in the Bush, on top of a mountain, or inside an ornamental and costly building, the handiwork of man.'

The Captain politely agreed with my humble observations, and we parted amicably, but to my sorrow he left without asking any more questions.

I drew my month's wages, and went to square my accounts with the butcher, grocer, my landlord, draper, and wood-carter. There were only a few shillings left. Had I been in my own hut in the Bush, I could save 10s a week, but it cannot happen here.

I am not troubled in body or in mind, and appreciate the beauty and goodness of Nature. I have no grounds to growl at anything.

November
A bad man dies

A goat sale was held here today connected with non-payment of grazing rights.

I visited my old hut, Ants' Mole Hermitage, in order to get my cross-cut saw, and many other things. I walked the sixteen miles.

Mr Campbell visited me today and told me that I was working outside my boundary. It was good news for it meant less work for me. I cleaned two miles of drains today in addition to clearing out two cesspools which took me two hours.

I went to the hospital reserve, and listened to a good sermon by Mr Angus. A congregation of some 2,000 attended. A collection was taken at the gate on the way out, and I gave my 2s.

John Lewis has died. He was a native of Llanon, Cardiganshire. He had bought a selection of land of 190 acres near Walmer. He was a bad farmer and he borrowed money from many people. I was foolish enough to lend him £10 towards building his home, and later £29 to help him pay for the land. I also built for him a big mud-walled dairy with a straw roof. I shall never get my money back because I learn that his farm is heavily mortgaged. I found he was not only dishonest, but a mean rogue and a liar, and worse he was cruel to man and beast. He abused his horses, cattle, his dogs, and his cats. *In a Welsh verse of ten lines, he praised a merciful God for removing him from further acts of evil-doing.*

An epidemic has been current during the past nine months which is not Colonial fever, not influenza, and not malaria, but it has some of the characteristics of each. By some it is called 'fog fever'.

It is very hot. I am sorry for the cattle. They have no grass, and no dried feed has been prepared for them. Rain would be very acceptable.

I paid another visit to my old hut at Ravenswood, and on this occasion I had hired a dray and horse to bring back all my belongings.

December
Melbourne gets lion-share

I cleaned three miles of channels today, but tomorrow they may be foul again. My work is endless. Too many dry storms happen here.

Today I worked for eleven hours. Too much for an aged man. There was no compulsion; it was my own fancy. I am doing some of the drains for the first time. It will come easier for me later, and likely for somebody else. Every house in the main street now has a tap in the house.

On Sunday I took a walk to Mount Tarangower, involving a climb of two miles. It was very steep for the last 500 yards to the top. The view was superb. I could see thirteen towns, and many hills in the distance. On the road down I passed the butts where the volunteers are practising rifle-shooting.

Up at dawn and prepared for a day's work in order to do justice to my employers. Having employed labour myself, I should be able to judge what is justice and duty between men.

Very heavy rain has produced flooding, so that many of the water channels are filled with mud and gravel. The flood has also submerged the foot bridges.

This Christmas day, the train has brought in a large number of people from Melbourne. They are Maldonians who earn a living in Melbourne. The heart of this Colony is neglected. The railway was constructed in order to bring the squatters' wool to the ports once a year. There will be an uproar one day when the cockney will want his loan repaid. The railway will never pay a dividend as long as no passengers travel by train. No nation can survive unless it improves the surface of its soil through proper cultivation, employing labour at fair wages.

What of the £60 million that remains as mortgage on the land in the state of Victoria, when the land is carelessly neglected and does not improve in value? One-third of the squatters have bark-ringed their trees and caused them to wither. All mortgages bear interest rates of between 7 and 12 per cent. For how long can things go on in this way only time will tell, but the day of reckoning cannot be far off. Nearly two-thirds of the hard cash borrowed in London is spent in Melbourne and its immediate environment. When I arrived in the Colony in 1869, my share in the public debt was £4 13s 4d, but it is now £32.

I have spent a most pleasant year. When young I was for ever longing for something in the future. Man is never contented with the present. My health has been reasonably good, and I have been in constant work, although at low wages.

1886

January *Re-engaged*

It is very hot and the strong wind from the west blows the thick smoke from numerous Bush fires. It rained a little from the south in the afternoon. I have never known it to be heavy when coming from this quarter in this country. *Next day, however, it rained heavily.*

A German engine-driver at the Cymru Claim, has met with a fatal accident. He left several thousand pounds to his widow. There was no child to mourn his loss. He had a large funeral and two-thirds of those attending were Germans. All nationalists in this Colony stick together selfishly. The Welsh are quite to the contrary. They do not heed a man's colour, or nationality as long as he acts straightforwardly. I do believe that they prove the best colonists of any nation.

My contract ended today. I was engaged for another year at the same wages of £1 a week. The council would not give me more. My advanced age cannot demand higher wages, so I must be satisfied. My work will be lighter this year than last year, for the water channels were in a very bad order when I began.

After a spell of hot weather followed by rain, the drains grow hay, weeds, sorrel, docks, thistles and marsh mallow, which greatly add to my labour.

February *Becomes a property owner*

A small house, 'North Railway Gate Lodge' was put up for sale. I bought it for £15. Unable to sleep last night because of the noise created by the Chinamen who were celebrating their New Year (3rd of February). Their camp is only 500 yards from here. Reports from their guns and crackers lasted throughout the night.

I worked hard today removing seven barrowloads of objectionable contents of two cesspools, which are situated in a conspicuous place in the main thoroughfare. It constitutes a danger to health, and should one or two die of a contagious fever, the authorities will have to pay dearly. The tradesmen throw all sorts of refuse into the gutters at night, and are over-particular to have them clean and tidy during the day — they are 'the poor would-be gentlemen' of the town.

This year, the goats and the geese graze on the Common, for there is plenty of fodder there, whereas last year they foraged for food in the gutters.

The Colony's scavengers have gained their demand to work eight hours a day for 7s, while poor Joe works nine hours a day on average, for a wage of 3s 4d. No one in the Colony tries to work at my age. All have some influence to be accepted inside hospitals or such places.

Gold is again a topic of conversation, even on Sundays. Some of the reefs are yielding over 100 ounces of the precious metal to a ton of earth. The Claims' shares are rising on the market.

March, April and August

The diary leaves for these months are missing, and a later note explains what happened. Some children broke into his cottage when he was at work, and destroyed some of his papers, books, part of his diary, and stole much of his property.

May *The beehive yields golden honey*

The Beehive Reefs are very productive nowadays. This afternoon they retrieved one piece of quartz which contained gold worth over £300. It is beautiful to look at, and they should send it to the Indian and Colonial Exhibition, recently opened by Queen Victoria and the Prince of Wales.

Today I was at the cesspools or cesspits, and discharged many barrow-loads into a disused pit. No one seems to value it as good rich manure, which should feed the exhausted land. The two cesspools are in a prominent place in the main street, and are close to three banks and a food store. This is against the regulations issued by the central Board of Health, and is a punishable offence.

Rain is awaited. My cottage has an iron roof and there is an underground water tank. A friend has brought me a book on medicine written by four doctors.

June *Fast horses need fast shoeing*

I have a good fire which is a great comfort this time of the year. I am able to get good firewood, but am obliged to pay 12s for two loads. The dry white box is as good as Welsh coal. The steam engines use this kind as do the blacksmiths. They burn charcoal from different sorts of timber, and find this better than the coal obtained from New South Wales.

There are good craftsmen here. I wonder what the blacksmiths of Cardiganshire would say if they saw a young Maldonian nailing four shoes to a horse in 1 minute 22 seconds!!

I have a square mile of streets to clean and look after. The water channels or sewers are nearly twenty-seven miles in length, or two days' walking for me at my advanced age.

I am obliged to run over about 2½ miles of main streets on three and sometimes four days each week. The council admit that the channels were never kept in such good order, and at a cost now one-third of what it used to be. I am satisfied and do the work with ease.

The following are among the streets I care for: Main, High, Franklin, Thomas, Ireland, Hornsby, Reef, School, Adair, Stappleton, Parker, Tobin or Zig-Zag, Templeton, Webster, Fountain, Church and Spring.

I have had a bad cold and have a severe constant cough. An old Saxon saying in the case of an old man is:

'Every cough is a nail in one's coffin'
If that be so, I'll be fast within.

It is very cold with a fifth of an inch of ice on the waterpools. I have seldom met with such a severe frost. It is very dry too and no rain has fallen for some time. Cattle are dying by the scores for the want of fodder. The farmers have stored no hay to save them from starving. Butter is 2s a pound and cheese 10d a pound. It is curious that I can get better Colonial meat in London at the same price as I pay here for inferior meat. I cannot understand it. Wool has advanced to 4d a pound recently, and I fear that this forebodes war in Europe.

July
Rain does his work

There has been a serious train accident in Tasmania. Many passengers have been injured and killed. The driver of the engine and the stoker were among the dead. There were many important people as passengers, but no women.

A little rain has fallen, but not enough to fill the water hole which I had dug, and which receives the water from the eaves. I am not at all well with bronchitis which causes me to cough persistently. My appetite is poor, and I have chronic dysentery which at my age is a fatal complaint as a rule. I took a glass of medicine at the Albion Hotel and three glasses at the Shearers.

Heavy rain has come and it has washed clean my drains. I find work a pleasure and I value life, the good world and its natural beauty. *He writes fourteen lines of poetry to his ill-health.*

I was down in the town too early this morning, and before the junior clerks had brushed the rubbish from shops and offices into the water channels.

September *Was it the first Zeppelin?*

News has come from America of an earthquake with great loss of life and property, together with a description of a new invention whereby a balloon is steered like a ship.

Much troubled by dysentery. The complaint causes me annoyance rather than pain, yet they say that the condition is mortal.

I am now able to get fresh milk daily and pay 1s a week for it. Milk and firewood will cost me £6 a year. In this dry part of the country, milk, cheese and butter are very dear, for all the best grazing lands are in the hands of squatters who keep sheep and store cattle, and no dairy cows. The world is wide and full of beings, but human beings are the very beings that don't enjoy the laws of Nature, and the world's natural fruits.

From my humble cottage I hear the church-bells in different parts of the town inviting sinners to attend, but the young men pass here with their well-reared greyhounds to chase the hares in the Bush.

In front of my cottage there is an area of level ground of some twenty acres over which men follow their separate pursuits of training dogs or horses, but most of these attend churches or chapels in the afternoon.

The railway commissioners from Melbourne arrived here to decide upon an extension of the railway track. I was on the platform when they arrived:

Welcome to our railway kings,
They deserve our credit.
Through them our railway system brings
Our comfort, speed and profit.

The gardens and orchards are looking well and promising, and the fields and hills are green with grass, but frost may come to retard it. This country would be a paradise for man and beast, if late frosts stayed away, and more rain visited us.

I do not feel well. No relish for food. Getting gradually weaker. I am low-spirited. *Composes an englyn of considerable merit on the occasion.*

Home at noon for dinner. An hour to cook a meal and eat it, is too short a time for an aged man whose grinders are not sharp-edged.

Senior members of the Congregational church intend to hold a prayer meeting to return thanks for the recent rain. They had better look sharp before the need arises for another meeting to pray for the return of the rain. How long will people presume to know how to rule Nature better than the Author of Nature Himself?

The dust is most annoying in the Colony. It drifts like snow in some places. Travellers have been known to lie prostrate on the ground to avoid thick clouds of dust. Should the rain come before the wind subsides, the rain becomes muddy. Many times when travelling the country at harvest time, I have been obliged to lie on the ground to avoid a thick cloud of locusts, some of them as big as sparrows.

October *Sunday's panorama*

Wheeled two tons of good manure into old mining shafts 170 feet deep. When I was farming in Wales, I would have paid 5s a ton for it. The land must always be remunerated for what it produces. This lack of cultivation of land in Australia will bring the country to insolvency before long. With proper cultivation of the soil in Victoria and the other states, it would produce more from cereals in one year than the income derived from the gold found by the diggers.

The Miners' Association have held their annual gala at Maldon. Those attending are well-dressed. They took part in games, and received £32 in gate-money.

I went to the council offices for my monthly pay of £4, and then to settle my debts with the tradesmen — grocer, £1; butcher, 7s 6d; shoe shop, 7s 6d; baker, 4s; draper, 6s 6d; wood-carter, £1; news-vendor, 4s 6d; stamps, etc., 4s 9d; charity donations, 4s 9d. Not a shilling left, poor Joe! Most of the stores have a combined barometer and thermometer outside their shops.

Looking through the window of my little cottage on Sundays, I see the world go by. Young men are making for the Bush with greyhounds and guns. Others walk with a well-dressed girl at their sides. Others play cards and dice on the platform benches of the railway station. Some go to church or chapel. The Salvation Army keeps on drumming till midnight, and disturbs the sleep of those who take their rest before joining a midnight shift of work.

November *The naughty Prince*

The Chinamen are the best gardeners here. They carry every variety of vegetables from door to door in two big baskets suspended from a pole across their shoulders. The contents of each basket weigh about eighty pounds when they start their round. They travel at the trot, and the spring of the pole helps them, for they keep in step with it.

The Prince of Wales is in the news again, as having an affair with Mrs Campbell. Naughty boy!

I have not witnessed such a nice Spring since I arrived in the Colony. There is plenty of grass. The cows and the team-bullocks make beef rapidly, and the other animals look well. The paddocks of corn look splendid and the crop is in full-ear.

I intended dressing up in my best clothes for the service tomorrow at the hospital, but discovered that my suit of colonial tweed had been ruined by moths.

December *Time was before chaos*

I have read Charles Dickens's novel, 'David Copperfield' again, and I spent two hours in the evening reading Shakespeare's works, having had the loan of his complete writings from a friend. I do believe that many readers applaud his plays because they are beyond their comprehension and understanding.

I enjoy my Sundays when I can rest my withering limbs, wash my clothing, trim my beard which is the only part of my body which grows, and read. My appetite is much impaired. My favourite meal is oatmeal in milk, or bread in boiled milk. I eat great quantities of eggs which are sold for 1s 2d to 2s a dozen. I am tired of meat and potatoes. I often drink beef tea which I find is nourishing. Beef is 6d a pound and beef steak 8d. Australia sells its best beef in the London market for 4¼d after a cost of 1½d for transporting it. Such methods of trading puzzles me. Again, the butchers melt their beef fat and mutton tallow to sell in Melbourne at 2½d a pound, but the working man here has to pay 6d a pound for it in the raw state.

I was invited by a William Skinner to join his family for Christmas dinner, which consisted of a goose, roast beef, plum pudding, etc., etc., with plenty of drink with which to wash it down. It was too hot to do justice to such a magnificent feast. Skinner farmed in Yorkshire before coming to this Colony. He came here in time to 'make his pile' as they term it. Those who came over in 1851 had a good chance to find gold, but less than one-tenth of them could care for it. Some kept the wealth they accrued through speculation, but others squandered it. Thousands returned to their native lands with the gold. Those who prospered and stayed here, should recognize the duty they have towards their unlucky fellow-creatures, and know that property begets duty towards those who do not happily possess it.

The wheat harvest is in full swing, but the yield is unlikely to be good, because the soil round here has not been properly cultivated or managed. Self-binding machines are numerous where the acreage is large, but when the machine starts in a twenty-acre paddock, with one or two boys in charge, it often goes out of order at the first round. It then goes to the blacksmith who does not understand its mechanism, but will tinker with it, ending in great frustration. The machines cost £75 each. They need to be simplified and improved greatly before they become dependable.

When I farewell with another year, I am mindful that it is *we* that are on the wing, not *time*. Time is a standard element in Nature. Time was before chaos. It was divided by man into years, seasons, months and hours. Devices like clocks and watches dot or measure time; they move as they record, but time does not move. *These sentiments are in line with ones expressed by Henry A. Dobson, in his 'The Paradox of Time'*:

Time goes, You say? Ah No!
Alas, Time stays, We go.

1887

January *Soliloquy before the camera*

He commences this, his forty-eighth diary, and his eighteenth in Australia, with the preamble that should he die, his friend David Evans, farmer of Rheola near Inglewood, should be informed, so that he might be buried without trespass on public money.

The weather continues warm, and the cattle begin to suffer from the absence of green grass. Crowds travel to the Tarangower races. The horses enjoy it as much as the spectators provided the whip and the spurs are not used.

For breakfast I now take a pint of fresh milk with oatmeal, both items costing 4s a month. I am heavy on sugar and devour 3 lbs a week.

Very warm and sultry last night in my single bed. I do pity those who are obliged to sleep in a double bed. The thermometer registers 103^0 F in the shade and 156^0 (*sic*) in the sun. These have been the hottest three days in Australia for nine years. People die from sunstroke. There are many Bush fires. The withered grass ignites from the heat rays of the sun impinging on a broken piece of glass. The air is foul with smoke from the fires.

Disappointed on rising to find my water-hole dry. I cleaned it out, and had to walk 150 yards for drinkable water. A comet appears above the W-S-W horizon; I stay up late at night to gaze at its grand bright tail.

The State has borrowed £3 m from London. Speculators have invested £120,000 to work the Claims at Maldon. This is in addition to £30 m previously borrowed from the Government. The country is going headlong into ruin!

Had my photograph taken. I composed the following lines on the occasion, and they appeared in 'The Age' newspaper:

Here you may draw my ugly shell,
And to the world describe it well.
Your art how'er is somewhat blind,
Can't show my principles, heart and mind,
Those shining pearls that make the man
Above the monkey and his clan.
The monkey can be spry and bold,

Well dressed in diamond and gold.
The man pretends to know and tell
His future state in heaven or hell.
If monkeys have no soul or sense,
They make the best of present tense.
They do in Nature keep their place,
And may in time be fav'rite race.
O man, O man, do see thyself,
Shun being proud and selfish elf.
Face you must a change of station,
The planet earth has strong attraction.
The mother earth gave birth to all,
And every object back must fall.
Go by the tide as sailors say,
When one is dead and thrown away.
Please draw my carcass as I am,
All pearls and gems are lifeless sham.

February
Look before you sit

Instinctively I made to sit on my customary chair, but found that I had moved it. I fell heavily and awkwardly, and hurt my side badly. It is painful to breathe and I fear that I have broken two ribs. The doctor affixed a plaster to my side and said I must not work for a long time. *He went to work the next day.*

The roads are very dusty, and the dust lies three inches thick in places. The wind increased and the dust rises in clouds. I use the brush and rake, but my painful side does not allow me to use the pick and shovel.

A man from the council joined me today. He gets a wage of 7s a day and I get 3s 4d, although I do three times as much work as he does. Influence and partiality are the world's curses, especially in the state of Victoria.

I had a long letter from my daughter Nell. It was as easily read as if it had been printed.

A public holiday has been proclaimed to encourage everybody to go into the Bush in order to reduce the rabbit population. Everybody appears to be carrying a gun, and many of them have not carried one before. It is really dangerous. They were conveyed to the Bush in buggies and coaches. They returned at dusk singing merrily because they had consumed barrels of beer. One party alone had killed 450 rabbits, and had left the carcasses in the Bush, but the ears were brought back as evidence when they claim an award from the Government, which had already paid out £7,000 for destroying the hares and rabbits. More money is to be voted for the destruction of foxes and sparrows, but vermin cannot be overcome as long as land remains uncultivated, and as long as those who possess it are allowed to retain it in its natural state as a wilderness.

I have sent a post order for £10 to my friend David Evans who has bought an additional piece of land for his farm.

March
Looking back

After settling with my tradesmen, and contributing to charitable causes, I had nothing left of my monthly wage of £4 to take me to the agricultural show next week.

The sun sets at 6 p.m. The astronomers say that the sun sets at this time in all parts of the world on the 21st of March. I cannot comprehend it.

I have written to my nephew, William Lloyd of Trefynor, Gartheli, Cardiganshire (*to whom he had intended bequeathing his diaries*), to correct a detail I had mentioned in my previous letter to him, and which referred to my voyage to Australia. In 1868 I had part of the Christmas goose in the tropics when crossing the 'Line'. The voyage had been a most pleasant passage, except for its start when we were knocked about in the Irish Sea by a gale for nine days. The ship had failed to return to Liverpool, nor could it reach Queenstown in Ireland. The Captain then tried to enter Milford Haven in Wales, but the south-westerly wind was too strong for the tired ship. Eventually, we got underway, and arrived in Melbourne on the 22nd of March, 1869.

Maldon is quiet and dull. Many people are selling up and leaving the place. Only young boys work the air drills underground nowadays. Their wages are 12s to 15s a week, while the miners get £2 5s. Although there are places in Victoria where blue-stone reefs are rich in gold, the mining of gold decreases annually. Last year the yield was 30,000 ounces less than in the previous year. Paper money is replacing gold, and bank notes for £1 to £1,000 are now available, while cheques are used more frequently than bank notes in business dealings.

Rain and warmth causes everything to grow, especially thistles and docks in the water channels.

Few take notice of St Patrick's day in Maldon, although some were locked up for drunkenness and fighting, during which two men sustained broken arms.

The rain has come, and with it flooding. More work on the gutters.

April
In praise of charity

I asked the boss for a day's holiday on Good Friday. He told me to mind the gutters of the township.

This Easter Monday, there were military parades with bands marching through the streets in the morning and sports were held in the afternoon, when £150 were given away in prizes. Each year a goodly sum of money is collected for the hospital, asylum and the fire brigade. Some acquaintances on the sports' ground asked me to compose a few lines to mark the occasion. I wrote down the following:

Give kings and queens their jubilee.
Give charity the same.
And let the Queen of England be
Remembered for her fame.
But charity's the queen of all,

The strength of every nation.
Her forts and castles never fall,
They're built on God's foundation.

I could not sleep because of the sound of heavy rain on the roof, so I went down into the town at 5 a.m. to attend to the blocked drains. I cleared the obstruction before returning to breakfast. Went out again to continue the work at 8 a.m. It is the biggest flood I have experienced in Maldon. Footpaths have been ploughed up. It will take me a fortnight to clear the mud and sand from the gutters which have no fall.

I intended to go to Sunday school, but remained indoors, and read my Bible aloud when alone, so there was none about to dispute any verse of it.

The town's allotments each measure an acre or less. The owners are busy, ploughing, harrowing and seeding them. They sow wheat, oats or barley. These paddocks yield well because they are well manured.

May
Anthem-building

I attended a service at the Welsh church. The congregation consisted mostly of children who sang melodiously. The majority of the Welsh community in Maldon attend English churches. They don't keep together like the other nationals do. The main reason is that they wish to be well versed in the English language. Many of them are managers in the Claims. They are generally good miners. News has just come of the collision of two trains in Melbourne with many killed and many more injured.

This, the 24th of May, is the birthday of H.M. the Queen, and is kept as a general holiday here. They keep as many as fifteen public holidays a year in the Colony. I have been asked to compose an anthem, suitable for playing by bands on the 21st of June when the Queen celebrates her jubilee in the fiftieth year of her reign. I am under two disadvantages, the metre is strange to me, and I don't understand music which renders it difficult to attune verses to the melody. I shall try. *He composed six verses, and inscribed them to Lady Loch, wife of the Governor. Only two verses are shown here:*

Our Queen Victoria's name,
Epitome of fame,
No king has ever been
For fifty years at peace.
Her subjects all at ease.
Makes every strife to cease.
   God Save the Queen.

Her heir apparent will
The throne of England fill.
Dispel wrong tales.
He has his parents' blood,
He cannot be a dud,
Time will unfold the bud,
   Our Prince of Wales.

I have never seen the sun all day. This is unusual. I do not think I have experienced a dozen days in the Colony when the sun failed to appear. Once in 1870, the sun did not appear during four days of continuous rain which was followed by a destructive flood which swept many bridges away.

June *A field of gold*

John Lewis occupies one of the finest residences in Maldon. It is roofed with Carnarvon slates. His wife hails from Glyn Uchaf, Llangeitho, Cardiganshire. They now live on the interest of £20,000 sterling. He and three of his friends had a field in Maldon, and at the beginning of digging operations in the Colony, they found that the field was rich in gold.

One and a half inches of snow has fallen here on the 6th of June which is most unusual.

A serious railway accident has taken place in New South Wales, with six deaths and over thirty seriously injured.

Heavy rain has fallen in spite of the wind blowing from the south-east, reckoned to be the dry quarter. The Queen's jubilee is celebrated in indifferent weather.

This is a glorious country, but badly managed. Gold, gold, gold is on every tongue while the fine surface soil is shamefully neglected. Each man, myself excepted, appears to have come here to seek his fortune.

The council meets. It is £1,500 in debt. Those who have little work to do receive high wages.

July *A blow on behalf of the under-dog*

This first day of July is declared a general holiday in Victoria, to celebrate its separation from New South Wales. Yet, their chief endeavour at the moment is to federate it along with all the other States in Australia as in New Zealand, so it is surely time to cancel this holiday.

I met an Aborigine. He seemed half-starved. I took him into my cottage, and invited him to share a meal with me, and I shared my blankets with him during the night. He could speak fair English. The railway commissioners from Melbourne were to visit Maldon, and I advised my new friend to meet them at the railway station and to hand them the undermentioned note:

To the railway commissioners.   Maldon
                                                                                                                                28 July 1887.

Gentlemen and Brothers too,

I am the last of the Aborigines tribe in these parts. I do humbly wish you to compare two lots of Title Deeds.

I received mine from the Author of Nature, while the land occupied by all the railways is titled by the white man's lawyers.

Always humble. Praying for your charitable consideration.
                              'Equinhup', but nicknamed by whites —
                                              'Tom Clark'.

The response to the short petition brought him 20s in silver, with a promise of more.

A severe hurricane has just passed, and there is more flooding. This has been an exceptionally wet Winter in this state, and the farmers are complaining and murmuring, 'Too wet! Too wet!'

August *'The Month of Floods'*

A thick sheet of white frost, has caught the early blossom while it was still wet. The cereal crops have suffered in the same way.

This is Election day (the 11th of August). In Maldon there were vacancies for three shire councillors and one auditor. There were eight candidates, and the four presently in office were elected. When the cogs run smoothly it is unwise to disturb the engine, and it is best to leave well alone.

It has been a good spring with good growth. It doubles my work because of the proliferation of weeds and grass in the water drains. The adjoining hills are green and well-stocked. Hundreds of goats feed there. When the hills are bare, the goats come down by the scores at night to forage on the grass which grows in the channels. Cattle are not allowed to do this. The hills are open as common land. The young corn flourishes, but thousands of acres are covered by the sludge which remained when the floods receded.

After a restful night I said my morning prayer as usual. This morning it ran thus:

Diolch O Dad, hâd pob hedd,	*I thank thee Lord, who givest peace,*
Cysurus iawn ces orwedd.	*For rest this night, and perfect ease.*
Dan gwsg, a breiddwydio'n gu	*Midst gentle dreams, and safe from harm,*
A gŵn nos i gynesu.	*With woolly gown to keep me warm.*

After my Sunday dinner, I set out to visit my old abode, Ants' Hill Hermitage, where I once lived while splitting firewood in the Bush. The journey should have measured seventeen miles, but I lost my way and this added another four miles, so I was very tired when I arrived back.

I am still stiff after yesterday's walk. It was too much for an old man to undertake.

This month will be long remembered in Australia as 'The Month of the Floods'. Every tank, reservoir, and water-hole, has been well filled for the coming dry Spring and Summer.

September *Some lose. Some win*

I read in the 'Cambrian News' that my youngest daughter had won a prize at her school in Kensington, London. Well done, Anne!

I enjoy my Sundays, resting, reading, mending, washing and writing. If I have callers, I do not find their conversation very stimulating, as they talk mostly about the gold reefs. Once I was foolish enough to invest £40 in the business. I only received one dividend of 10s, and that was a sham payment intended to induce fools to re-invest. *On this occasion the sprat did not tempt the bitten whale.*

Many people, especially farmers, proceed by excursion train to visit the great Exhibition at Adelaide. They will change into sleeping carriages in Melbourne. Many of them only go so far as Melbourne, but take advantage of the cheap fare. The return ticket to Melbourne, permitting a stay of fourteen days there, is 6s 3d. The distance between Maldon and Melbourne is 100 miles.

Clearing the clogged drains near the premises of Mr N. Oswald, Maldon's gold king. His weekly and free income from his own Claim is £1,000, and there are indications that this will be doubled soon. He also has shares in all the profitable claims in Australia, as well as in coal and silver mines.

Took a short walk of eighty yards from my abode on Sunday evening to inspect the engine house where twenty-nine tons of firewood is burnt each day in an attempt to pump water out of the deep shafts of a Claim which has been water-logged and unusable for two years.

I now take 'The Age', a daily paper, in addition to the weekly paper, 'The Leader', which I take in order to send to Wales. The postage is only 1d although at times it weighs a pound. From Wales I have just received the 'Daily News', where I see it reported that my youngest son, John David, has qualified as a doctor.

October *Australia in the van of agricultural machinery*

Throughout the Winter the general complaint has been directed against the mud, and shortly it will be levelled against the dust. O frail humanity, how dare you thus blaspheme Nature in words, and remain unable to improve on it in deeds!

I bought 3½ lbs of neck of lamb for 1s from Mr Way the butcher. I was overcharged by 1½d, but I dare not object, nor buy elsewhere, because he is a member of the council.

The Chinamen have cabbage and green vegetables on sale all the year round. They are good gardeners, and are also very persevering in search of gold. They collect worthwhile gold in soil which has evaded the most up-to-date machinery, and even from water that runs from the Claims. They have the knack of capturing the precious metal through using quicksilver. The Government impose a poll tax on each Chinaman entering the Colony, and they propose to raise it to £100. Should the Chinese progress as they do at present, China will soon be the strongest nation in the world.

Reapers and binders arrive by train from Melbourne ready for the harvest. As my cottage is only twenty-five yards from the station, I have the opportunity to examine the complicated machinery. I would have no idea how to assemble them, nor do the farmers who buy them. I have not seen a dung cart and distributor among the machinery.

A letter box stands only sixty yards from my house, and I have posted a letter home which will be included in the mail bag which was placed in the van of the 6.30 a.m. train leaving Maldon and arriving in Melbourne at 10 a.m., where it will be placed in the 'Lusitania', the fastest steamer afloat, and which will be well out to sea in the early afternoon.

I got great enjoyment from reading about the Welsh national eisteddfod held in London, in the 'Cambrian News'. The editor, Mr Wilson, is a man of great ability, and he ought to be a member of Mr Gladstone's ministry.

The combined reaper-and-binders have been arriving by the dozens, and so have the mechanical shears, annd one-fifth of the sheep will be shorn by machines this season. *This did not become universal practice in the United Kingdom for another sixty years!*

He then composed fourteen lines of poetry as quickly as he could write them down. He apologises for its poor quality, although he admits that the rhyme is 'middling good'.

There was a severe storm yesterday in Ballarat, Bendigo and Sandhurst, where there was an earthquake, and which was felt by miners working in solid rock, 2,000 feet below the surface.

I understand that the steam pumps which I recently visited, are gaining fast on the flooding at the 'Old Alliance' gold claim, after being unworkable for two years. £120,000 of London money has been invested to restart the mine.

November
A therapeutic trial for toothache

The big horse races were held at Melbourne, and it is reported that some 84,000 people attended. A young Welsh rider, Williams, was killed. It has been calculated that in the state of Victoria alone with a population not many hundreds above a million, £20 million is spent annually on horse-racing.

I have derived great enjoyment from reading Milton's 'Paradise Regained', and preferred it to his 'Paradise Lost'.

Applied to the surveyor to have a 'day off', not to celebrate the birthday of the Prince of Wales, but for the purpose of mending my chimney. He gave me permission. I wrote to my nephew in Wales and enclosed fifty-six lines of poetry. Paid 3d for a rabbit; the vendor did well because he got 9d from the council for the ears. The Government has already spent £350,000 on schemes to exterminate the rabbit, but with little effect.

I have many miles of drains to look after. The Medical Officer of Health is particular about keeping them clean, because there is typhoid in the Colony, but none in Maldon. Tobin Street has the dirtiest drains because the sludge from two butchers' shops run into them. Both men are on the council and when their colleagues complain they turn to blame me.

Cheese costs 10d a pound at the grocer's, but the farmer gets no more than 6d for it. The tradesmen here form a 'ring' or union, so they are able to charge the customer what they like. I could buy Australian cheese in London cheaper than here.

Toothache troubles me again. I have been advised to adopt a certain remedy, namely to insert a few drops of the best brandy in each ear, and having soaked a plug of cotton wool in the brandy to place it in the ear on the side of the painful tooth. It would please me better if I were to take the brandy in my mouth, and allow it to flow down my throat. It is likely that it would do me most good.

For £1, I bought four waggon-loads of timber which had been left over by contractors from a building in the High Street. I will have to pay for cartage again.

December *Unity with Nature is prelude to happiness*

I predict a change in the weather because my knees ache, and this is a certain sign. The old folk back in Wales used to notice the same thing, but I laughed at such a suggestion. Young people are heedless of the wisdom of old age. I believe that young men and the women suffrage movement will turn this world upside down.

Generally, I have my midday snack in a private room at the baker's where no one bothers me. I am also welcome to read any of his books, for he has a library full of poetical and philosophical tomes of the very best kind.

There are seven different kinds of thistles in the Colony, but the farmers do not cut them at the proper time, namely when they are fully grown, in flower, and before they ripen and seed.

I received a post order for a pound as Christmas gift from my daughter and son-in-law. I acknowledged it in this way:

Fe welodd plant haelfrydig,
Wir angen tad methiedig,
Ac i'r hen wr Cysurus fydd,
Cael gwledd ar ddydd Nadolig.

Boed llwyddiant yn Tyndomen,
A'r plant yn iach a llawen.
In peace and love, and always well,
Y byddo Nel ac Eben.

A certain tinman or tinker in the town, annoys and insults me whenever we pass. He has opposed me unsuccessfully for the job I now hold. Today, he riled me with the ditty:

Taffy was a Welshman,
Taffy was a thief,
He came to my house
And stole a leg of beef.

I informed him that he was misquoting the true version, and I handed him a slip of paper on which I said was written the correct version:

Taffy was a Welshman,
But never was a thief.
It was the Tinker Satan
That stole the leg of beef
And cooked it for his dinner
On a rusty piece of tin.
And stole a pound of solder
To buy a glass of gin.*

*The Tinman was very fond of his beer and gin. I do not think he will tantalize me again.

Mr Ware of the Oriental Hotel moved this morning to a new hotel which he calls 'The Grand', omitting the word, hotel. *The diarist writes a poem of twelve lines, which he heads 'The Grand Trap', thus supplying the missing word and exposing the subterfuge.*

Over at Thomas Street this morning cutting thistles, cape broom, and gorse. The last variety spreads into the fields and roads from the hedges. The shrub is heavily loaded with blossom and seed. The white thorn forms the best hedge in this locality. Gooseberry bushes flourish, but they are spoilt by the children when collecting the fruit.

I spotted a few scouting locusts, and soon the swarms arrived. They were passing over Sandhurst, twenty miles away, three and two days ago. They devour every blade of grass, and the leaves off the fruit trees. This swarm today is the thickest I have seen. Some of them drown in the water pools. They lay their eggs on the bare patches, and scratch the earth to cover them.

I took down my old chimney, and commenced building a new one. The mortar must not be allowed to stand, and has to be used directly. Lime is expensive and costs 4s 6d a hundredweight. I cleaned 500 bricks before relaying them. There are still three feet to add at the top, and the whole has to be plastered. A friend said he would help me, but he failed to turn up. I do not blame him because he is over 80 years and suffers from rheumatism.

Flies and mosquitoes are troublesome, and I wear a veil to protect my eyes. I busy myself clearing the evergreens which were used for decoration at Christmas. Natural indigenous trees are plentiful here. European trees grow well, and all of them cast their leaves in the Autumn, that is during the months of July, August and September.

A heavy thunderstorm broke out. The foot bridges were carried away by the flood which entered stores, cellars and houses. There has been great havoc. I was knee deep in water, and the current was very strong with a fall of 1 in 9. It is all the fault of the council and neglectful engineering. They cannot blame me because I have warned them many a time of the likelihood of such a catastrophe happening.

On this last day of the year when I look back on my pains and my troubles, and on my joy and contentment, they seem of no importance. It is the present moment that matters, for it is the only period of time in the possession of every living creature. The past and the future are out of our reach, the former has passed out of our control, and the latter is uncertain, but the one may be remembered, and the other can build up our hopes.

I have never been so contented in the pursuit of my work as in 1887. It is my sincere opinion that it is sinning against Nature that brings discontentment, while to be in unity with it in doing good, brings lasting bliss. Goodbye 1887, I am loathe to leave you.

1888

The diarist opens with the statement that this is his forty-ninth diary, having recorded his first at the age of 21 when working on his Aunt's farm at Clwtypatrwn, Llanfair, Cardiganshire, and that this is his nineteenth diary in Australia.

January *The unequalled sermon*

I find it best not to make my bed in the morning here, for at bed-time in the evening I may find a black or tiger snake coiled between the blankets.

The clerk of works to the council should be a trained engineer, but ours is only a weaver from the north of Scotland who has weaved himself into the job through influence.

There is no twilight here. As soon as the sun goes down, it is dark, but in the mornings we have two hours of dawning.

My Sundays are spent in cooking, cleaning, mending, resting, reading and writing. I have plenty of reading material, the Bible, Iolo's Psalms, the week's 'Leader', and the works of Milton, Dryden and Butler. Of these three, John Dryden is my favourite. Some of my Sundays are disturbed by casual visitors who talk about nothing other than gold reefs and racing. The floods have left over twenty tons of mud and gravel to cart away from the gutters. I do it with ease. Nothing pleases me better than work when I am able to do it without undue tiredness.

The mail trains now leave Maldon every day, but I have no time for letter-writing except on Sundays.

I attended three church services today (Sunday), and listened to two sermons. It would have been better had I stayed in my cottage and re-read the 'Sermon on the Mount'.

Water is brought to Maldon by pipes from Castlemaine, a distance of thirty-three miles. It cost £18,000. The money came as a loan from London, and the ratepayers are responsible for the six per cent interest. A tap has now been installed in each dwelling in the town, and households pay an annual water-rate of between £1 and £2.

In the town I found hundreds of young girls dressed in thin white muslin and satin gowns. On inquiry I found that the daughter of our 'mining king', Mr Oswald, was to be married. The bride and bridegroom rode in a carriage drawn by four greys which had been brought from Melbourne. Flags were hoisted everywhere. A friend asked me to compose four lines. These came as fast as he could write them down:

Fair success to the wealthy pair,
Without much pain or bother.
Their honeymoon be bright and fair,
And last an endless summer.

I had my breakfast at 6 a.m. It consisted of preserved salmon from America, tea from China, and sugar from Fiji. The salmon was expensive, 1s for a tin which was insufficient for a meal.

There are twelve separate denominations in this small place. Each Minister preaches different precepts, but none touch that golden sermon, 'The Sermon on the Mount'. Young and old can understand it. It is sufficient guide for all men and women to live by, and to die by.

February *A dual internment*

From my monthly wage of £4, I was left with £1 after settling with all the tradesmen. Most of this will go on some new underclothing, so I must go carefully with my spending, and follow my late father's advice, 'Gochel dafarn; Na ochel dalu', which I would translate as under:

Avoid all hotels, escape another way.
If you should go in, never shun to pay.

The chief clerk of the New South Wales Bank requested me to remove and bury a fierce dog which had been destroyed by poison the night before. The dog belonged to a doctor in the town. Soon after, I was approached by a man to take away a dead cat, I went to collect it in my barrow. The owner of the cat gave me a shilling for my trouble. I took both animals and buried them together in a three foot grave. I composed the following lines, and placed them where the head stone should be:

Here lies the savage dog and cat
In one grave together.
Can anyone be sure that
They won't fight each other.
None has returned who knows their fate
After evolution.
What will be our future state,
Peace or revolution.

It is reported that General Booth of the Salvation Army has accumulated a fortune of £45,000.

My near supervisor, Mr G. Piper, asked me to help him hose the dusty streets, but the water inspector soon stopped the wasteful venture.

I recorded my vote in the election of two new members on the Mining Board. There were five candidates. The one that headed the poll was a poor cripple with a large family, and he was my choice. The office brings £50 a year from the Government. They attend a Board meeting once a month to talk nonsense together for a few hours. Only those with Miners' Rights are eligible to vote, and we number some 500.

This is my birthday (27th of February), and I enter on my 70th year. I am reminded that my father died at the age of 70. I celebrated with a nobler (*sic*) of brandy at the end of my day's work, and composed a verse of ten lines on the occasion.

March *The epidemiology of typhoid accurately predicted*

My neighbour and close friend, Robert Ogle, was taken from me suddenly with heart trouble at the age of 63. He was a German and an upright open-hearted man.

Up before 6 a.m. and I hurried over the cooking of my breakfast which consisted of bread in boiled milk to which was added two tablespoonfuls of sugar, together with cheese and two boiled eggs. I have not taken any butter since I came to the Colony. In the afternoon I attended the funeral of my friend, Joseph Thomas, who was 65, and had suffered great pain for the past two years. His body was taken to the cemetery in a hearse drawn by two black horses, and was followed by fifteen carriages. At the request of the relatives I composed a verse on the occasion before I left the cemetery.

The Emperor of Germany and King of Prussia has died (9th of March) at the age of 91. He was a peaceful monarch, and had led his army successfully against the French under Napoleon III who was responsible for the quarrel. Flags were hoisted at half-mast. I composd an englyn to mark the occasion.

It's St Patrick's Day and the town is celebrating, for one-third of its inhabitants are Irish. Mr John McIntyre, along with an engineer from the ministry and his staff, were here today to discuss an increase of the sewers. They were a jolly crowd, and fully enjoyed the hospitality and entertainment given them at the expense of the ratepayers. When will these realize that they are being duped by the hangers-on?

The authorities are getting daily more particular about the water channels or sewers. They fear typhoid and other fevers, which are mowing down the young Colonials by the dozens each week. I consider what they eat and drink to be the most likely cause of their ailments, and not dust, gravel and smells from the water-channels. The clerk of works should not call me away so often from my duties connected with keeping these clean.

April *The bard triumphs again*

Large fair with all sorts of entertainment arranged by the fair committee was held on Easter Monday. The proceeds are donated to the hospital and other charities. Among the competitions was the Greasy Pole on which was fixed a bank-note thirty-five feet up, which was the award for anyone who reached it. There were scores of failures, but towards dusk a boy of 16, Jack Llewellyn, managed to reach it. I composed appropriate verses on the day's happenings and gave them to an official for reading. He never returned them and they were lost. I received a telegram informing me of the death of my great friend, David Evans of Rheola. I sought permission to attend the funeral. I journeyed by coach and train, a distance of 100 miles, and arrived there at 4 p.m. It was a very large funeral, and those attending trailed for a mile behind the cortege. The next day, along with a local magistrate, I valued the estate, and at the widow's request I drew up her will, and then departed for Maldon. On the journey back I composed six verses to his memory, for my grief at his death has been very great. Trade is very dull at Maldon. Storekeepers and hoteliers have just grievances. Only one man has found worthwhile gold here in two years. Cattle are suffering froom want of fodder, and even the inhabitants for the want of drinkable water.

An eisteddfod is to be held on the 24th of May at Williamstown where a prize is given for the best two verses in praise of the piano. *Later he mentions that he was awarded the prize.*

I owe letters to my three dear married daughters, but I get too tired for letter-writing after my heavy day's work.

May *Burdening the unborn*

I carted a large quantity of leaf mould and manure, and tipped it into the diggers' holes. When farming in Wales I would have gladly paid 2s for each load to spread it on my land. Here, where farms and gardens are hungry for manure, they deprecate it. All attention is directed to the gold reefs, and the majority of these are on the way out. The managers try to persuade the shareholders to hold on and they seem to say, 'a good time is coming, so wait a little longer'. In fact these managers do not know more than I do where the gold lies, and they are surprised when they meet with it.

The council has borrowed £5,000. They were already in debt for the sum of £1,000. This is a fine to be borne by the children and posterity. There are in the Shire 260 square miles of land, and two-thirds of this is good cultivated land, but it is not being improved, and is again growing timber.

On Sundays I am happier should I be alone, for the casual callers only talk about the two gold reefs, and this in spite of the fact that no gold comes to the surface nowadays. Some of the alluvial diggers are unable to enjoy even one meal a day.

June *A daring suicide*

There has taken place here an ugly tragedy. Mrs Woodward, a greatly respected lady, left her home on Sunday, apparently to attend chapel.

Instead she went into the Bush and took with her a box of matches. She set fire to her clothing. All that was found of her that night was a heap of ashes. Apparently she had mentioned that she would do this one day.

Returning from my work, I stopped to watch a digger breaking up a piece of white quartz in search of gold with a sledge hammer. A piece of it flew and struck the forefinger of my right hand, and injured it badly. I believe I shall lose the use of it. I should not have stayed to watch the performance. Had it been all gold I could not have claimed one grain of it. It was as well that the metal did not hit me where my brain is supposed to be.

They have metalled six chains of Main Street. The metal is finely broken, and laid to a thickness of eight inches. It should last as a good road for a very long time.

July *A rejected suitor*

I was aroused at midnight by a drunken man knocking on my door, and seeking admission. I recognized his voice as that of a young farmer living not far from Maldon. He blamed his condition on the fact that he had been jilted by a young lady. He remained with me till breakfast time when he was sober enough to go home to his mother.

My finger is so mutilated and painful that I can hardly hold the pen and writing is a most difficult task.

August *The writing finger inactivated*

Exciting day at Melbourne where the great Exhibition is being held. The building has been enlarged at a cost to the Government of over £1 million. It stands on an area of fourteen acres. England's Crystal Palace occupies twelve acres of ground.

My two friends, Davies and Gibbs visited me on Sunday. As usual their conversation turned to gold, and I was glad when they left.

I am now unable to straighten two of my fingers. They are very painful, and I fear that I will end up with two stiff joints. *His writing has deteriorated markedly, and his account of his daily movements is greatly abbreviated.*

September *Ill at ease*

I feel ill from rheumatism in my left knee and right arm, pain from my injured fingers, and sore eyelids. I was forced to see the doctor who advised me to give up reading and writing by candle or any other kind of artificial light. This is difficult for one who has to work during every minute of daylight.

In the course of my work I happened to pass the clerk of works with his two devotees. They were levelling a certain footpath, and spent several hours at it, expending about £3 5s of public money. I would have finished it in ten minutes.

Disturbed on the third consecutive Sunday by a farmer who wished me to draw up his will. My fingers will never come right, and writing has been more trouble than pleasure for five months.

My fingers now are very bad,
Cause pain and disappointment.
Five months now since I have had
The unexpected torment.
They are coming by degrees,
Much as lawyers' march to heaven.
I have saved the doctor's fees,
Which in pounds, be six or seven.

October
Farthing a mile

The Annual Sports are held in the Reserve. I asked for leave from work for the afternoon, and this was granted. There was a large attendance. The miners earn £2 5s a week in wages, so they can afford to be merry once a year without worry. There were keen races, and Maldon boys took most of the prizes. The highest prize was £20; not bad payment for running just 300 yards downhill.

To write I have to tie my middle finger to the stiff forefinger. Even then the ritual is both difficult and painful.

I grubbed a big tree near the shire hall. A rope was tied to the top, and it was brought down at the very spot where it was intended to fall, between an ornamental tree and the fire brigade's store room. The site is required for a building.

I remained out for two hours in the evening during a heavy thunderstorm, watching the lightning. It was both dreadful and grand. Nature appeared to be out of temper. Some of the oldest inhabitants in the town declare that they had never before witnessed such a splendid sight in the Australian sky. Little rain fell. Another three weeks of this weather will cause a water famine in Maldon.

I feel far from well and I have multiple complaints. I wish I could save £30 in order to be admitted into the benevolent asylum, and be assured of a decent burial.

I have given up speculating in gold claims for it is foolish continuing to pay 'calls' without receiving dividends.

Don't regret and vex for the past.
Bide by the true things to nurture.
Determine to hold to these fast,
And avoid to fear the future.

In July 1889, he gives to this verse a slightly different interpretation.

November
The widow's mite

It has been a dull time in Maldon for the past two years. Among the twenty-five underground claims, only one produces gold in profitable quantity. It belongs to one man, and he gets £5,000 from it each week. Twelve years ago he worked as a plumber and he could not afford a load of firewood, but soon he will be a millionaire. He is a Scotsman, and knows how to keep his money together, but his greed will never be satisfied in this life.

A gale was blowing, and there was a threat of thunder. Heavy clouds were gathering. To a passing gentleman I said that those clouds were mountains of snow which would be churned before reaching the earth. He laughed at my foolishness, but in less than half an hour it commenced to pour down hailstones as large as ordinary marbles until the streets were white.

The papers report a failure of the corn crops, and the wheat crop will be insufficient to feed the country's population of 3,000,000. The water tanks are empty, and I have to walk 200 yards to get water for my own use.

A new neighbour of mine, living alone, and owning his own home as well as many houses in Maldon, always craved to be rich, and speculated heavily in the gold claims. Latterly the 'calls' became too heavy on him. Last Saturday morning he settled all his accounts through taking an overdose of arsenic.

A friend and countrywoman of mine has died at the age of 86. Mrs Elizabeth Davies used to recount to me her earlier days in Wales. She had preserved all her faculties till the very last hour. I attended the funeral at the nuggetty cemetery. At the request of a friend I composed a verse of ten lines in Welsh in her memory.

Today (9th of November) is the Prince of Wales' birthday. I don't care very much for him, but I enjoy the public holiday. I honour his mother, the Queen. If I don't feel drowsy when I get to bed I always read a few of Iolo Morganwg's psalms. It always cheers my heart and my soul.

Mondays are washing days in Maldon. Woollen blankets and woollen underclothing are too heavy for the laundresses to handle. Women charge 5s a day for housework, along with good meals and certain 'perks' besides.

The drought is getting serious, and the summer does not start for another month. The stock cattle and sheep are dying by the millions. Bush fires are raging, and one-third of New South Wales is estimated to be on fire. The loss is tremendous, and the country is already some £35 million in debt. Temperature is 105° F in the shade, and 169° (*sic*) in the sun.

This is Hospital Sunday when an open-air service was held, and attended by some 2,000 people, but the collecting plates at the gate only held £40.

On my way to work I noticed that several stores had only partly removed their shutters, so I concluded that someone of importance had died. On inquiry, it turned out to be my wealthy countryman, John Lewis who lived in the best residence in Maldon. He was exceptionally rich and he left all his wealth to his widow, and on her death it is to go to their housemaid. Mr Lewis was the mainstay of the Welsh Congregational Church at Maldon, and it was mostly through his support that it was built in the years 1862-3. The church stands on a healthy and hilly site within the township, and is surrounded by ornamental trees. The building is of brick and is well built. At the request of his widow I composed three englynion, and 500 lines of prose describing his life in the Colony. I read it over to the widow who appeared to be well pleased with it. She offered me the princely payment of 6d for my trouble!!

December *Fortune easily gained and readily lost*

The drought continues. It has lasted throughout the winter and spring. Corn and potato crops have failed. The price of food is rising. Flour has doubled in price in six weeks. The price of a 4 pound loaf has risen from 5d to 7d. Yet wheat sells at less than 5s a bushel. The effects of this drought will be felt for years. It continues to be unbearably hot, and the early fruits are a complete failure. I have not known anything like it.

On the first day of summer, an equinoxial storm broke through for half an hour, bringing down trees, and ripping off roofs, with hail and rain.

I had an undisturbed Sunday, for no callers came to talk about their lucky gold finds during the period 1851 to 1860, when the alluvial digging started. The luck and its proceeds have now gone. Less than eight per cent of those lucky diggers were wise enough to invest their earnings in safe securities. Instead, in their greed for more, the majority invested it for the prospecting of more gold, and lost their temporary fortunes. Indeed, at the time they considered that gold would soon be as cheap as copper. I was foolish enough to invest in the reefs myself, but having paid 'calls' through the years, I eventually forfeited my shares, for I had received no more than £1 10s in dividends.

Christmas day passed quietly and uneventfully for me, and I had no goose for Christmas dinner. Competitive meetings and all kinds of sporting events have taken place at Maldon, among them horse-racing, pigeon shooting, cricket, football, wrestling, concerts, dancing, billiards, etc. Connected with most events there has been betting and gambling. This is no way for a young country, heavily in debt, to carry on.

I am walking lame today because of rheumatism in my left knee. It's a sure sign of rain, *and so it proved on this occasion at least.*

1889

January
A speck of gold

Serious flooding at Castlemaine some eleven miles from here where twelve people were drowned. Many of the foot bridges here are either clogged or have been washed away, and the water channels are filled with mud and sand.

When sweeping the road in Main Street, I was watched by a small boy aged 12. He picked up a small piece of white quartz in front of my brush and handed it to me. I discovered that attached to it was a small piece, about a pennyweight at least, of gold and probably worth 5s. It was so pretty that I told the boy that many a person would pay £5 for it. Notwithstanding, he offered it to me for 6d. I corrected him for his folly, and advised him to treasure his lucky find.

I was up at 4.30 a.m. to witness the awesome spectacle of the fire ball (*alluding to the red sun*). It became incredibly hot during the day. This sort of weather kills one by inches. Temperature was 114^0 F in the shade, and when at work in the sun it was 45^0 above blood heat. My left knee is very painful from rheumatism. I cannot understand why my right knee is alright because it is the same age as the left knee.

Because of the late rain, the grass is still green, but a few more days of this intense heat will wither it. There is very little green grass here during the months of February, March and April, and often even to the end of June. During such times I am sorry for the beasts of the field, for nothing in the form of dry fodder is prepared for them. In October, the grass should be mowed and kept until it is needed instead of allowing it to ripen and then to wither, and so frequently to perish from Bush fires.

The present year will be trying for the toiling man as everything will be dear. Potatoes, £4 a ton last year are now £18. Onions are £12 a ton, cheese 10d a lb, butter 1s 4d a lb. The 4 lb-loaf is going up from 7d to 8d, and yet wheat is only 4s 7d a bushel. The millers, bakers and brewers are making large profits. Neither wheat nor flour is to be exported this year, and it is likely that Australia will have to import them from either Russia or America.

For breakfast nowadays I have 'pap', which is boiled milk and flour, to which is added two tablespoonfuls of sugar and a pinch of cayenne pepper. For dinner I have cold tea with bread and cheese or meat, and mutton broth to which I add bread and meat, for supper.

Some five miles from Maldon there is a minor gold rush. Scores of men are taking up claims for plots of sixty feet square. In the first three holes they have reached bottom within nine feet. Pipes are being laid to bring gas to Maldon. It is an expensive project because Maldon is a scattered township occuping an area of one square mile. The ratepayers are hesitant about bringing the gas into their homes because the rates will rise.

Too many Welshmen here pretend to understand English better than Welsh and in this way discredit their native tongue.

The Government are borrowing another £3 million so that the national debt will mount to £40 million. The hot weather continues and it is 109° F in the shade.

A new chaff-cutter came by train this morning for a farmer, Mr David Anderson. It feeds, cuts and bags without manual labour. It despatches hay and straw as quickly as the thresher can deliver them, and of course it is driven by steam. It was awarded a prize at the Great Exhibition now taking place in Melbourne. I have been told that a muck-spreader is again missing from the farm-implements' stand. This is a grave omission because good clean crops cannot be grown without manure and good cultivation. Irrigation will not improve cereal crops in the absence of manure, because the soil has to be remunerated for what it produces.

It is cold here today, and yet tomorrow it might be 90° F in the shade. This variable weather puzzles me. With Isaac Newton we can say that 'we came to know that we do not know'.

February *Christian deviationists*

A heavy thunderstorm has visited Maldon and the flooding is the worst ever experienced by the inhabitants here. Water filled every cellar, and poured through doorways and windows. The damage amounts to several thousand pounds. Walking over my territory in the morning, I found work sufficient for scores of workmen for a month, and the rain is continuing. I shall do my utmost to bring some order out of the chaos. The water channels are full of mud and gravel. About twelve tons of gravel and stone have to be removed from the streets. Many of the foot bridges have been swept away. The rain has stopped, and it is now unbearably hot again.

Several cases of typhoid have been reported from Castlemaine. There is none in Maldon. They blame the dirty water channels, but I am convinced that this is not the cause, but that it results from the things we eat and drink. Children eat unripe fruit and those confounded lollies!

I had hung my waistcoat on a fence while moving a barrow-load of debris some 100 yards away. When I returned the waistcoat was on the ground and its pockets had been emptied of my spectacles, needle case, pocket book, and other things.

It is Sunday evening, the church and chapel bells are ringing and the Salvation Army band is playing. This small town is full of religious buildings, Church of England, Church of Rome, two Wesleyan Chapels,

Baptist Church, Bible Christian Church, Scotch Presbyterian Church, the Welsh Methodist Church and the Independent Church, but the 'Stay at Homes' outnumber all the other denominations. Many spend their Sundays with their guns in the Bush.

On his 71st birthday (the 27th of February) he composes another *englyn*.

March *Wales and Australia go to the polls*

The Welsh people in Australia show great indifference to honouring their national day (St David's Day), and to keeping up their language. The Irish on the other hand join together to honour St Patrick, and form their separate societies.

I have read in the 'Cambrian News' of the death on the 20th of February of my grandson Ieuan Evans aged 7 years at Tyndomen, Tregaron. He was the son of my daughter, Elinor.

Government inspectors and engineers visited Maldon today to estimate the damage caused by the recent flood.

Newspapers from home report that my brother Jenkin has been elected a member of Cardigan county council, appointed as its chairman, and created an alderman, while my nephew Jack Jenkins had also been made an alderman.

Today (28th March) was observed as a public holiday on the occasion of a general election. Many new members won at the polls. Each member is paid £300 a year, and I believe that is the only thing they care about.

April *'Tis an ill wind that blows no good*

Last night the dilapidated Phoenix Hotel was burnt down. The small building was insured for £400 and the furniture for £200, so the 'accident' was a great gain for someone!

The last year and the early part of this year have been the driest experienced by the oldest inhabitants of Victoria. It has rained all day and there is a small flood. Although it was Sunday, I put on my oilskin coat and went out to see that the channels were running freely, and that the bridges were alright.

The collectors from the hospital came round and I gave my 2s 6d. I could not afford to give more because they visit me fairly frequently.

I was at John Kent's farm sowing oats before the sun was up. I covered a paddock of five acres, and I was back at my usual work at 9 a.m. so that I will make up this two hours later for the council. Nearly all the children in Maldon, aged 3 to 13 years, are suffering from a mild form of measles.

On Easter Monday a great gathering assembled on the sports ground, where a charge for admission of 1s brought in a goodly sum, and which was donated to various charities. I drank a few glasses of ginger ale. I will never take that stuff again, for I did not feel well afterwards.

May Queen's weather

Walking tires me more than working. My finger still troubles me, and writing continues to be difficult.

I was grieved to read in the 'Cambrian News' that some farmers in Cardiganshire have had scuffles with the police concerning the payment of tithes. I know it is a very unjust tax, but the way to get rid of it is to urge members of Parliament to plead their case in the House of Commons, and not molest the police.

Official holiday throughout the Colony to celebrate the Queen's 70th birthday (the 24th of May). It was a lovely day, which favoured the many sporting events at Maldon.

God bless the English Queen,
I had a day of rest.
Of all the monarchs that have been
She is among the best.

I was asked to hang a gate at the entrance to the Reserve. Afterwards I was asked to hang another gate near the shire hall. Gate-hanging is outside my contract, but it is unlikely that anyone will notice that. I have at least the satisfaction that both gates hang properly.

June The weather misbehaves again

There has been a moderate flood. This assists me because it cleans out the gutters. Mrs Rees requested me to watch over her husband who had been taken very ill, and she raced to call the doctor. The rain continues and floods are widespread involving loss of life. When a north-west gale was blowing, my little cottage was shaking like a gum-leaf. Both May and June have been exceptionally wet. I fear that July will also be a wet month, and this will spoil the newly sown cereal crops. There is already a shortage of grain in Australia, and there is insufficient to support its population till Christmas. Yet, if the soil were properly cultivated, there is no better agricultural land anywhere in the world.

July There are rainbows and rainbows

After a heavy shower of rain, single and double rainbows appeared, but only in the form of half-circles. They were not the same as those I had witnessed when crossing the Equator. There they had appeared as complete circles with both ends spliced on the ship's deck, or occasionally on the sea.

This morning there was thick ice on the water-pools, and the frost has spoilt the young potato stalks and other tender vegetables.

I had a good dinner at William Rees's home for sowing an acre of clover and lucerne seed. Partial eclipse of the moon (13th of July) was grand to watch.

Favourable weather has come to help the farmers. The cereals are coming on so fast that the blades are already two feet high. The sheep have to be turned in to graze the crops, otherwise they are liable to develop rust, or some other disease. Those that cultivate the soil here as elsewhere, should never 'shout haloo before the fox is out of the wood', wood being the fox's sanctuary.

There is again ice on the water pools. This is rather unusual in this part of the world even in winter. So unusual is it that the children bring fragments of the ice into the house to show their mothers.

I did over twenty chains of road today, but daily I fear lest I shall be unable to do my work, and it looks dark ahead, for I am among strangers from whom I cannot expect to get assistance of any kind, but I advise myself:

Don't vex and regret for the past.
Now is the time for good culture.
Determine to hold to it fast,
Avoid the dread of the future.

This differs in a small way from the verse he composed in October, 1888.

Today (28th of July) is a big day in Maldon, for the first sod is being cut of the long awaited rail track of fifteen miles between Maldon and Lanacoori. It was sanctioned by the Government nine years ago, but the selectors could not agree on the surveyed route. Some owners of large tracts of uncultivated land wished to have it pass through these well-wooded terrains so that they might despatch the timber to the sea ports. At last the differences have been resolved.

August *Boys will be boys*

Ordered by the clerk of works, although outside my contract as in the case of gate-hanging, to cut up a large Tasmanian gum tree which had fallen. It was eighteen years old, four feet in diameter, and eighty feet long. It was as straight as a ship's mast.

Election of Maldon's councillors took place today. There are ten of them besides the secretary and the clerk of works, so that there are twelve to overseer me and my work. Mr Pollard, who was president of the council was defeated by twenty-two votes. He was a good man, and I do not know the quality of the elected man.

My cottage has a corrugated roof. It has the advantage that I hear the rain patter on it at night, but it has two disadvantages, namely that it is unbearably hot when the sun directs its strong rays on it, while small boys like casting stones on it deliberately to annoy me. Inside the cottage, the mice disturb me as they tear at my books and papers. Tonight I have placed a little strychnine in their oatmeal; perhaps that will quiet them.

I was told that a ploughing match at Barringheip, some six miles from here, was poorly attended. I was not surprised because some one-half of the so-called farmers round here have sold out lately after exhausting their lands.

Coming home through the square, I found two bands playing, the Salvation Army's and the fire brigade's. The latter is there to spite the former. Whatever the Army stands for, I think this is a mean trick on the part of the brigade.

I was asked to draw out William Rees's will. He is 80 and feels very feeble. I have it ready for his signature tomorrow.

My cottage has been broken in to, and several valuable things have been stolen. Doubtless, someone watched me placing the key in its hiding place. The key had been replaced, but not exactly in its customary position.

Disastrous floods have again been reported in different parts of the Colony, and miles of railway have been washed away.

September
Depression and gloom

I was visited by a young man named Rees, aged 35, from my native village of Tregaron in Cardiganshire.

The weather is boisterous and the rain continues, so I often work in wet clothes; as a result I have a bad cold with a severe cough. I am really out of sorts. *In this depressed mood he breaks into verse:*

For all our troubles, pain and strife
We have strange instinct for long life,
With hope for better day tomorrow,
But cloudy skies may bring more sorrow.
I often think that he is blest
Who's early called for quiet rest.

I did not receive my usual monthly wage today. I do not know the reason for this, but I do know that the council has an overdraft of over £1,250 at the bank. My Sunday's airing of clothes and other domestic jobs were disturbed by a visit from two Welsh friends. I was not pleased with their company, because I need rest on a Sunday to enable me to carry on with my work during the week.

This year of heavy rain and floods is like that of 1870. The inhabitants of Echuca on the River Murray, proceed from house to house in boats. The melting snow on the mountains adds to the volume of water from rain. Crops are ruined and the harvest will be a poor one.

I went to visit William Rees whose will I drew up last week. I found him very ill, so I asked the doctor to visit him. He did, only an hour before he died. I attended his funeral. He had resided thirty-three years in Maldon. He speculated heavily in gold, was never outstandingly successful, but managed to live respectfully till old age.

October *The curse of early frost*

Anniversary (8th of October) of the passing of the eight-hour working day Act. Sports are held on the Reserve ground, and the proceeds go to the fire brigade and the miners' association. I have to work nine hours a day and sometimes twelve. For the past five days I have laboured outside my contract, but I get no extra remuneration for it, simply my low wage of 3s 4d a day.

It rains continuously and there are small floods. It is a remarkably good season for grass. The papers report that it has been a glorious spring for the farmers, but they should not crow too early, for there may come a night of severe frost to destroy the young fruit and cereals, followed by a long drought which will kill the grass. Such a destructive frost, I well remember, visited the Colony on the 9th of November 1876.

In Wales a wet harvest, which happens once in seven years, destroys the mature crops, but this event never takes place in this Colony, although badly made stacks which are seldom thatched, can be ruined here by a heavy shower of rain lasting 3 or 4 hours, for minus its thatch the stack gets sodden-wet down to its foundation, all through man's neglect.

My rheumatic knee is very painful and I walk lame. I get very tired at work, and have to seek my bed early each night in order to be ready for work on the morrow. I shall have to give up, and use my few extra pounds; then to go out into the Bush to starve there. That I believe will be my fate.

Cocking hay all day between the ornamental trees in the Reserve. It was more pleasure than toil. I had my snack under a fine oak tree. It was only planted fifteen years ago as an ornamental tree, and it has grown big with prolific branches. How quickly they grow in this part of the world, and soon they produce a good crop of acorns!

November
The Melbourne Cup

This is Sunday. I have been busy all day, cooking, reading, washing underclothes, and doing other domestic jobs.

Horse-racing at Melbourne during the past six days. Last year's attendance was 130,000. Elaborate gambling takes place, and large sums of money change hands. Some one half of the ladies attending are attired in borrowed dresses for which service they pay dearly, especially if they are returned with stains. Should it be wet and muddy, the charge for the loan of the dresses is trebled. On this annual occasion the maid-servants look as flash and dainty as do the countesses.

This year the Cup was won by a horse named 'Bravo', and he started as third favourite. Over 140,000 saw the race.

It is an excellent spring so far, and the cattle are laden with fat, but they may be lean again before Christmas for want of grass, which is usually the case here.

I attended the memorial service to my friend William Rees. There was a powerful sermon, but in spite of the preachings by Pope, bishops, and quack-diviners, the iniquity of the world increases by seventy per cent, disregarding the increase in population.

This is the birthday of the Prince of Wales (9th of November), and much toasting goes on in the public houses which here are designated, hotels. There are twenty-two of them in this small place of less than 2,000 inhabitants, half of which are children.

It continues warm and sultry, and I am beginning to realize that I cannot work at any job much longer. *He composes a sad and defeatist verse of eight lines in Welsh.*

This is Hospital Sunday. Large gatherings used to frequent Hospital Hill, and collections were liberal, but now the donations are small. Children contribute their threepenny bits, and adults either a florin or half-crown. Subscriptions to the hospital are small considering that the Government subscribes a pound for each pound of voluntary subscription. The collection today was less than £50.

It is so hot that I cannot bear holding the crow-bar. I perspire freely. An old man has not much fat to spare, so he ought to keep easy and quiet. He has no chance of a second life, for Nature gives daily proof of this. The preachers of course say that there is a future existence, one in heaven, and one in hell. I, together with others, must chance it.

The Earl of Hopetoun has been installed as the new Governor at a salary of £15,000 a year.

December
The pipes are too small

There is a meeting in the Temperance Hall this evening at which our Parliamentary member is to give an address. I do not feel well enough to attend, but I composed these few lines to advertise the occasion:

Come join the Ancient Britons
To fill the spacious Hall.
Heed not the Name of Nations,
In God we are brothers all.
So let us pull together,
Unite in Christian life.
Love all and one another,
Avoid all zealot's strife.

I left for a drink of water from a tap which was only a short distance away, when I returned I found that someone had stolen my knife from my waistcoat pocket.

Returning home from work I found a glass-pane had been removed from my window. My belongings inside had been rifled. Lots of things were missing. Two I.O.U.'s had been taken, one for £10 and the other for £30. My diaries had been scattered outside the house. This is the sixth time that I have been robbed in this place during four years.

The death of H. Searle, a young man aged 23 years, has caused great grief in New South Wales. He was a champion rower and oarsmen. *He composed a verse of ten lines on his passing.*

I went to dig in a neighbour's garden, and I was given 3d for 1½ hours' work.

Men today were preparing the footpaths for treatment with asphalt. The council is in deep debt already, and it would be better if the townspeople were to walk on the fine gravel for a little longer. It is curious how the council and the state saddle posterity with these debts unnecessarily.

The fire brigade sports and baby show were held today, and thirty-two babies were entered for competition. Only one prize came to Maldon. Many mothers were disappointed and angered by the results. It is always so on such occasions.

The water inspector watches over the domestic users of water lest they waste it, but they water their lawns and their gardens during the night. The authorities have now discovered that the pipes which they have laid to convey drinking water from the Coliban River over a distance of 100 miles are much too small!

It has given me great pleasure to receive such an interesting letter from my dear cousin the Rev. John Davies who has returned in retirement to Tynrhôs, Llangeitho.

There is much sense and wit in the compositions of my learned uncle, David Davies, Castell Hywel, but he was not very particular about the strict rules of bardism, and not so exact as the old Iolo Morganwg. I have been meaning for a long time to send to Wales for a copy of his 'Telyn Dewi'.

1890

January *Typhoid and discoloured water*

Spent the day cutting thistles along the water channels. It is very hot. Temperature is 101° F in the shade and 136° in the sun. Severe Bush fires are raging. Drinking water is scarce. A short but heavy shower of rain came suddenly, and flooded the street.

I write my letters on Sunday, but since I injured my fingers of the right hand, I write with difficulty because it brings on cramp. I had three such attacks while writing this page. My correspondence, especially to Cardiganshire, has been neglected and a dozen letters remain unanswered. I send them a newspaper now and again to show them that Joseph is still alive.

I was at work at 6.30 a.m. I can turn up as early as I like because I am on contract-work, otherwise they would mob me in this Colony if I turned up too early to do salaried work.

There are a few cases of typhoid in the town, and two have died. Water from the taps and tanks is scarce, warm and discoloured. It is not a pleasant drink to quench one's thirst with. Railway contractors cart water for their workers from a source eight miles away. Much rain has fallen in Queensland and New South Wales, but not in Victoria. The thermometer registers 108° F in the shade. I had to turn my back on a dust storm. Wind blows from the south-east, and I have not seen rain setting in from this quarter since I arrived in the country.

The Police Sergeant called on me today to ask whether I knew a certain man who had taken £2 from another man, but I could not supply him with any evidence.

February *Air foul from forest fire*

Water for domestic use is scarce. I get mine from the tank which feeds the railway engine, about 200 yards from my cottage, but this source has now dried up, and the engine gets its water from Castlemaine, eleven miles away. The heat is intense. There are many Bush fires. It could be another 'Black Thursday' tomorrow like the one that took place on the 6th of February, 1851. Another unbearably hot day, so that after returning from work I had a nap under a shady oak tree, and later composed the following lines:

Tan bren derwen mi orweddais,	Under the oak my bed I made,
Un tewfrig a changhenog iawn.	Its spreading branches gave me shade,
Tan ei chysgod yno cysgais	Beneath the fierce scorching sun
Heibio haner y prydnawn.	There I slept till day was done.
Fel pe buaswn yn y gladdfa	O how lovely it would be
Tan bren Iwen wyrdd ei wedd.	To lie beneath the old yew tree.
O mor hyfryd yw goyphwysfa	There to enjoy a blissful rest,
Y mwyafrif yn y bedd!	Safe in one's grave with those so blest.

The atmosphere is foul from smoke arriving from the Bush fires.

At last a thunderstorm arrives with heavy rain, so I hurry around to clear the obstructed drains as the flood rises. Many foot bridges are dislodged. A hundred yards from my cottage, a cow in the middle of a field, with no tree near, was killed by the lightning. I saw it happen.

I brought home fifteen pounds of cheese. I eat five pounds each week. My knee is really bad. I can hardly walk. I may have to give up work. What then? I must eat to live. The small amount of rain has made little impression in the water tanks.

The election of two members on the mining board took place today. They have little to do now that the alluvial diggings have been exhausted. All the members got £1 a week from the Government, and there are 300,000 of them in the Colony.

On Sunday I spent four hours at the Cemetery reading inscriptions on the tombstones. It is warm and sultry again. In certain parts of the town, the dust in the street is four inches deep. It will be most unpleasant should high wind precede the rain.

The fires have been extensive and destructive. They have been attributed to incendiarism by swagmen in order to gain employment through bringing the fires under control, but I believe that it has been the work of selectors providing an excuse for insolvency!

March
The lone invalid

I accidentally poured hot water over my foot. I had to visit the doctor, so now a sore foot has been added to a sore knee. The foot is very swollen and oozes fluid. Blisters break, and open wounds appear. It cannot bear my weight. I try to bathe it. I am unable to fetch water. I cannot walk to the doctor. No one calls. The toes cannot be separated. I try poulticing it with linseed oil. At last Mrs Rees has called on me, and has gone to summon the doctor.

Three weeks after the accident I hobbled to work. I was lame, and the foot was extremely painful. *There is no mention of a visit from any official of the council.*

April
Writes his epitaph

On the 1st of April, as I was limping to work, a small boy of about 10 years old shouted to me, 'Hey Mister, look what's beneath your foot'. I did so instinctively, and to my surprise I found a shilling there, and I picked it up. The boy was equally surprised, and said that he would not again try to make an 'April Fool' of anybody. I had never before found any coin on the streets of Maldon.

The council kept back even my small pay for the month of March. My foot is still swollen and painful, but I hop along doing my customary work. I am going to try to get my boot on. I failed in the attempt, so I shall have to keep to the slipper.

My painful foot prevented sleep. As I lay awake I composed a suitable epitaph for myself:

Marw sydd raid, nis gwyddom pryd,
Pa fodd, pa fan, yn hyn o fyd.
Ac os yw bywyd i ni'n rhodd,
Mae marw hefyd yr un modd.
Can's beth fo'n rhan, mae'n eithaf eglur.
Cawn chwareu teg gan Awdwr Natur.

The translation of the epitaph as under, although not as rhythmically expressed as in the Welsh version, does convey the meaning, and portrays a philosophy which calls for a willing acceptance of whatever may be our fate hereafter:

Die we must, and cast aside this
  mortal shell.
How, or when, and in what place, we
  cannot tell.
If we assign to life a gift so rare,
Then death itself claims equal share.
Whate'er our fate, it is quite clear,
We'll get fair-play from Earth's
  Creator.

This is Sunday and I mean to rest my foot today, because it is getting worse and shows no sign of healing. My friend John Davies paid me a visit, and he helped me so that I might rest my foot. It is the first help I have had. I do wish one of my daughters could be at hand, especially the one who has died, and one whom I assisted when her arm was dreadfully scalded from a boiling starch mixture.

Although generally, there is a scarcity of water in Australia, New South Wales and Queensland have experienced the most severe floods ever recorded, and thousands of families have been made homeless, because they build their houses too near the big rivers.

There have been no frosty mornings recently, the grass grows well, the cattle improve in condition, and the farmers are ploughing and harrowing, providing a suitable bed for the seed.

My foot still aches and swells, and I am still unable to wear a boot. It looks as if I will have to rest it again.

May
No work. No pay

Many Maldon residents are suffering from what the Yankees call influenza. I had thought it was a severe cold. We have had a long spell of fine weather, and the older residents cannot remember such a long one.

Now, I feel very ill with influenza. I should stay indoors, but I must try and go to work. On the way home I walked like a drunken man and presently I fell backwards like a loose gate-post. I was helped to my feet by two passers-by. They wanted to take me to hospital, but I insisted on going to my little home where I managed to light a fire, and a kind neighbour made me some mutton broth. I feel queer and chilly all over.

My friend John Davies called on me on Sunday. He has the same trouble. We sat in front of the fire and coughed and coughed. In fact we had a regular coughing match.

On Monday I went into the streets to work, feeling ill, weak and giddy. No wages for the past nine weeks. How can I live?

Failed to go to work and had to remain indoors. Severe dysentery has set in. No proper meal for ten days. No appetite. It is now unlikely that my diaries will ever be returned to Wales.

It is the Queen's birthday (the 24th of May). I am fifteen months older than she is.

I am too ill to go to hospital in this state. I would be too much of a nuisance to them. I have unbolted the door, so that some one can come in to find me dead.

The recently widowed, Mrs Rees aged 77, came to see me today. She wishes me to be buried inside their burial plot in the Cemetery. I am unable to fetch water or cut firewood. No one to assist me, but Mrs Rees helped me to go and see the doctor. He sent me into hospital.

June *Hospital diet sweetens his discharge*

Visited by Mr and Mrs Hopkins of Walmer. I was glad to see them. Some visitors have the effect of mellowing the attitude of certain hospital officials towards their patients.

The doctor has informed me that I am fit enough to leave the hospital soon. I was glad to leave after a scrumptious dinner consisting of one pint of thin broth without bread or anything else, and I was charged £2 a week for my stay. It is a crying shame!!!

I do not have much in the way of provisions here in the cottage, but I can keep myself warmer than in the hospital, and it is more restful.

On Sunday half a dozen people visit me to inquire about my health, but none can improve it.

I have gone back to struggle with my work. I have received word that my nephew Jenkin Jenkins (Aeronian) of Felincoed has lost his wife. They have ten children, nine girls and one boy.

July and August *Gradual rehabilitation*

I sleep most of the night if I can count dreaming as sleep, but this I doubt in that I remember them in the morning and could recite them.

There is snow on the hills, and a quarter inch of ice on the water pools. *He composes a verse of seventy-four lines in memory of his friend, William Rees of Parkin Road, Maldon, and sixty-two lines on the occasion of the death of the Rev. Charles Jones, Sunny Hill, Tregaron, and incumbent of the Welsh church, Cardiff.*

The rain has now turned the dust into mud, and this fills the drains. Today, I was working in Church Street opposite the fine residence of Mr Rees Jones. He was a miner from Cwmystwyth, Cardiganshire. He is now the manager of the Beehive Golden Claim, the largest of the twenty-two claims in Maldon. He gets his £4 a week, and has a swarm of well-behaved children of varying ages from 20 down to the baby.

Election for a member to the council today. The one I supported was ahead by thirty-five votes. The streets are very muddy after more rain. Pedestrians complain they are ankle-deep in muck.

The gold diggers John Davies and William Williams called to see me on Sunday. They talk of nothing else except the luck that is going to be theirs, but one cannot live on expectations, although they do.

The papers report strikes throughout the civilized world, that is if one regards the world as civilized. I don't. Twenty-three big ships lie idle in Melbourne harbour alone, for want of hands to man them. The price of every commodity rises steeply. Even the price of bread soars when plenty of wheat and flour are obtainable inside the country. Vegetable prices are up. Coal is 45s a ton, and sugar 10s a ton. How the middle-man takes advantage of the consumer on these occasions!

September *Hard boiled eggs for dysentery*

The strike still goes on. The shipowners will not employ any Union men. I bought two dozen fresh eggs, and boiled them hard. They keep in good condition for weeks, and they keep away my threatening dysentery. Eggs are cheap now and are only 1s a dozen.

From the 'Cambrian News' I learn that David Davies of Llandinam died in July at the age of 71. When 25 he was poor and was employed as a top sawyer, but when he died, he owned several collieries, was the biggest landowner in his county, and a millionaire. The wheel of fortune turned in his favour, but alas!

The whistles at the Claims and the fire bell sounded at midnight. An empty cottage only thirty chains away from mine was completely destroyed by fire. It had been sold recently for £60 and insured for £100. People say that insurances are of no use except for this kind of stratagem!

Arriving home from work I found a good load of firewood at my door. I had paid 10s for it some ten days ago, so that I had feared it would not be delivered, for this is not unusual in the case of pre-payments.

At sunset I climbed up a nearby hill to watch the sun go down, and the moon and stars appear. I lay on my back to study the night-sky.

October *Not a drum nor funeral note*

Better in health than for years, although I do not feel active, and my advanced age tells on me at the end of my day's work.

I was at work opposite the London Chartered Bank, the largest building in the town. The other two banks appear puny when compared with it. I heard a report inside, but I thought little of it. Some twenty minutes later I was told that the manager had shot himself dead. He was 36 years old and married with one child. His young wife had left him to join her own family. He was buried the next day like a pauper. His wife was not present, and no one mourned him.

A few days after, on the way to work I had to pass a water dam. People had collected on its banks. Presently the police dragged out a body. It was one known as the 'silver king', for he made a fortune in the silver mines. He had spent this fortune on drink. He drowned in two feet of water, so presumably he was drunk at the time. His waistcoat carrying his watch and his gold chain were missing.

I am given to understand that Danish law decrees that all drunken persons shall be taken home in spring carriages, and wholly at the expense of the landlord who sold them the last drink.

Attended a lecture on total abstinence by a Mr Good from London. His remarks on the subject were extravagant. I went in with a few shillings in my pocket, but it was empty when I came out. It is a trade to delude fools.

November *I drop my florin*

I had to decline an offer today to mow hay with a scythe. I could do it when I was 13, but that time will never return.

A letter from my daughter Nell tells of her small son Ieuan's death, and she mentions that my brother Benjamin has been ill in bed with consumption for the past two months.

On Hospital Sunday, about 1,000 attended in the hospital's grounds. We had a sweet and short sermon on the Samaritan attending to the wounded man. The collection only amounted to £36. I dropped my florin in the collecting box; 1,000 florins would have made £100.

I assisted William Rees's widow to place her hay in fifteen cocks. Wind blows from the north-north-west and is usually a prelude to rain.

Received a paper-cutting from home which reported the death of my youngest brother Benjamin on the 15th of October. He was a solicitor aged 51 and the youngest of my parents' twelve children. There was a large attendance at the funeral, and 111 carriages followed the cortege.

Although a long distance from the scene, I confess to shedding a few tears because I was very fond of Benjamin.

December
Locusts halt a train

My health is better than it has been for many weeks. On Sunday, my three friends Williams, Davies and South paid me a visit. They talked about nothing else but gold, and none of us held any of the precious metal.

I posted letters to my two brothers, John and Jenkin in Wales. It is reported that the locusts will pass through here tomorrow.

The locusts have arrived. The train was unable to run through a swarm. They were so thick as to cover the rails which became so greasy that the revolving engine wheels failed to grip the rails.

A big fire broke out at Mr Oswald's claim. The damage is estimated at £7,000. It was insured for £3,000. Of course Mr Oswald is able to afford it. At times his private claim produced £10,000 a week.

On Boxing Day I took a train at 6 a.m. to Castlemaine, and from there to Sandhurst. On the way to Inglewood we met a swarm of locusts and they entered all the carriages. From Inglewood I took a rough coach-journey through the Bush to Rheola where I arrived at 5 p.m. I inspected the farm and vineyard and found that all was well. At 4 a.m. I rose quietly and walked to the cemetery to visit the grave of my friend David Evans. I was disappointed at the verse inscribed on the headstone which alluded to death as a thief. Death is anything but a thief. I then commenced the journey back to Maldon.

The object of my visit was to retrieve my eleven earlier diaries written in Australia, and add them to the ten which I have here. If I do not return to Wales, my intention is to send the diaries there so that someone will have the chance to know how I fared as an antipodean.

1891

January *Home is a dangerous place*

Russell, the engine driver at the claim which is only 100 yards from my cottage, paid me a visit today. The claim owned by a company with representatives from London, Argentina and Australia, has produced no gold yet, and the sum of £45,000 invested in it is fast running out.

The heavy rain has been a boon because it has drowned many of the locusts. I cut my finger when slicing bread. I almost severed the tendon completely. I am a clumsy fellow at these household duties!

A telegram arrived from Lily, David Evans's adopted daughter, to say that her foster mother had died at Rheola. I was not aware she was ailing, and she was well when I visited her just four weeks ago. I wrote three letters, one to Lily, one to the magistrate William Johns who was co-executor with me, and one to a close friend of the family, Mr W. Bonar.

Water is scarce again. The railway tank is empty so I was up at 4 a.m. to draw water from the spring before it became fouled up by the geese and ducks; I got there before them. Residents pay £1 annually for taps at their doors, but these are only allowed to run at intervals.

While preparing firewood, a splinter penetrated deeply under my thumb nail. I fear it will turn into a whitlow. It is aching and beating like a drum.

February *Unexpected journeys*

A Bush fire is raging some sixteen miles away. The fruit trees are suffering; the fruits are dropping and many of the trees are withering. The wind increases, and the dust is so thick that one cannot see clearly the face of the one you are talking to.

I journeyed to Rheola to attend the Evans's sale. There were no bids for fourteen hogshead of old wine, so the auctioneer bought it at 2s a gallon, which was half its value, and he made £50 profit from that deal. The cattle sold well, but the good young horses realized only half their value. In all, the sale realized £500. Evan Evans, who had travelled 700 miles from New South Wales, bought the land, vineyard, and the house, for £775. After the sale there was no food left in the house and no furniture. Evan Evans had been wise enough to buy a bedstead and some bed-clothes. Lily, her sister, and uncle, left with friends. I intended staying in a hotel, but William Johns, J.P. drove me in his carriage to his fine residence, and both he and his wife treated me as if I were the Governor of Victoria. I started for Maldon in the morning. My journey had cost me £1 10s 6d. Eight years ago, I had walked the distance, and my expenses then amounted to 6s.

There may be a water famine here soon. David Roberts, a storekeeper, tried to commit suicide through slashing his wrists. Two doctors saved his life for which he was sorry.

I received a letter from Thomas Thomas on the ship, 'Star Bengal', which is presently docked at Melbourne. He states that he was with my brother Benjamin on the day before he died, and that he attended his funeral. Thomas invited me to visit him on the ship, of which he was the steward. I went by excursion train and I was well entertained, but I was very tired when I returned to my cottage. The journey had cost me £1 6s.

Interleaved in his February diary is the certificate entitling him to 'Miner's Right'.

March *Fires in Bush and town*

A big fire broke out in Maldon. Four premises, namely a drapery shop, a shoe shop, a grocery shop, and a book shop, were burnt down to their foundations. The fire brigade had no access to a good water supply. The origin of the fire of course remains a mystery. All were insured to the full value. It is reported that the loss amounts to £7,000, and that the insurance companies will not pay in excess of £5,000.

From here I am able to see three Bush fires, and two of them are not far from Maldon.

The Maldon to Lanacoori railway was opened today in the absence of any special ceremony. I went on board the engine, 'Eastern Ho'. The engineers were testing the line, and the engine driver was worse for drink.

The barometer is falling, and heavy rain has come at last. Heavy flooding has taken place. Water is ankle-deep in the streets, and the foot-bridges are blocked. The Easter sport's meeting is hindered by the flood in spite of the great preparations that had already taken place and in accordance with custom.

April *Age, not work, is burden*

This is census day; there are many questions to answer. The grass grows forward now, and the farmers are speeding the plough. I am now engaged in moving by barrow, the mud, sand, and clay left by the flood, and clearing the gutters running under the foot bridges. The work is

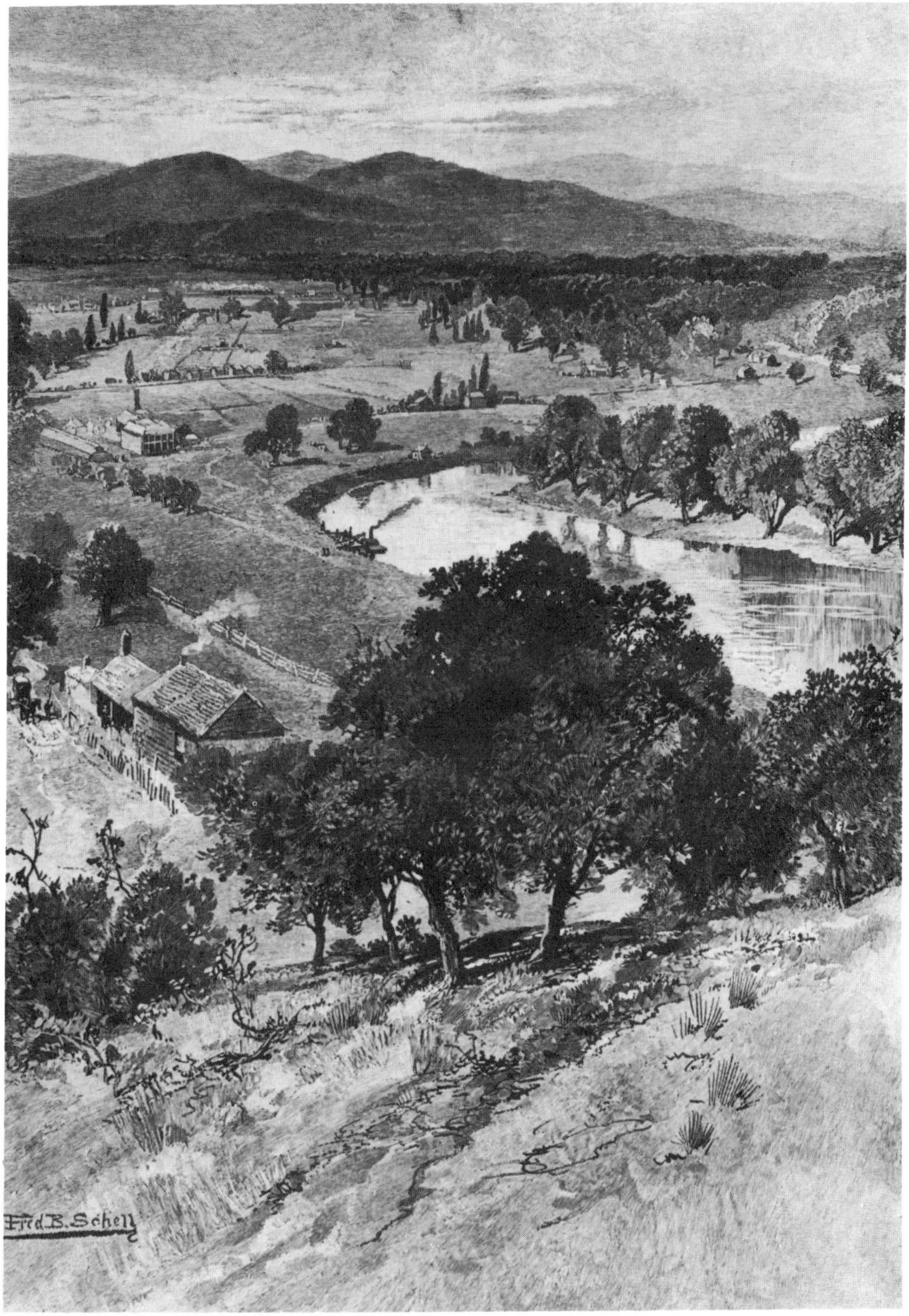
Fred B. Schell

heavy, but to work is pleasurable toil. My legs fail more than my arms.

Mae'm bywyd mewn byd yn bwys-y boreu,	My life below is a burden,
Yn barod i orphwys.	Ready to rest at day's dawning,
A ngamau yn anghymwys,	My steps are short and uncertain,
Ond dyna gaf, mynd dan y gwys.	To an early grave hastening.

Such were the feelings of an ageing man in his eighth decade.

May *Shipwrecks*

While winding up my watch the spring broke. Received a letter from my nephew, 'Aeronian'. There have been two shipwrecks, one on leaving, and the other on entering Melbourne harbour. Both could have been avoided. One of them, an American boat, had on board a cargo valued at £60,000.

A man came to help me paint and whitewash my cottage. I was in good temper, and working was no bother.

Whilst cooking my breakfast I was seized suddenly with lumbago, but I managed to go to work, which was clearing the water channels opposite the fine state school where between 300 and 400 children receive tuition. They have drill and military exercises four times a day, girls and all. I don't see any harm in it.

This is the Queen's birthday (the 24th of May), and the weather is quite beautiful.

Mr Wells, secretary to the shire's council, was thrown from his horse. He developed pneumonia, and died unexpectedly four days later. He was my, and everybody's, friend. I attended the funeral; it was the largest that I have witnessed in Australia.

June *Women, God bless them*

After a moderately restful night I was on the floor by 5 a.m. It was cold and frosty with ice on the water pools. I performed my usual household duties which are too numerous to mention. What a lot women have to do in the mornings. Apart from cooking, there is sweeping, washing, bed-making, dusting, etc., etc. I was at my usual work at 6.45 a.m.

Bricklayers have arrived in Maldon from Melbourne to rebuild the burnt-down houses. The insurance money has been large enought to build substantial ones. It is plain that the fires were started deliberately.

July *What stuff are dreams made of?*

I get vivid dreams which I can describe in detail in the morning. Dreams are a real mystery to me. I do not believe we are asleep when we dream, or as one may put it, 'I sleep as if I am half awake'.

The storm has played havoc around Melbourne. Ships have been lost at sea with loss of life. Three thousand families have been rendered homeless by flooding in the lowlands, and financially the loss is estimated at one million pounds. The Government should prohibit building on low-lying and marshy ground, when there is plenty of high ground available for this purpose close to the City.

It is reported that the eminent preacher, Spurgeon, is seriously ill. I went to see the engine-driver John Lewis. He is in the last stage of consumption. His brother, sister and father died of the same complaint.

I deposited a few pounds in the Government's Savings Bank. I try to put away about 5s a week from my low wages. When I buy a pair of boots and some underclothing, I find myself in debt again.

August
Delayed demise

The storekeeper, Mr Dabb, brought a hundredweight of potatoes to my door, but only the Harbinger of all can tell who will survive to consume them.

Two councillors were elected at the shire hall, one for this Ward and one for Walmer. My two friends on the council, Pollard and Smith, were defeated. Since the treasurer died lately, no one on the council will now have the least interest in my welfare. I have been better in health during the past three months than at any time in the last four years.

My countryman, Rees Jones, has died of consumption. He leaves a widow and nine children, only two of them old enough to work. His life was insured for £500, and the premium in respect of this had been £20. He was a manager of the 'New Beehive' claim, and earned £4 a week. He had worked with his father in the Cardiganshire lead mines when a boy of 13 years of age. It has been a false alarm for Rees Jones is still alive.

There has been a collision between two steamers at the entrance to Melbourne harbour. One sank within three minutes with the loss of twenty-one lives. The accident resulted from deplorable negligence.

Rees Jones is now dead and he had a swell funeral. Twenty-five carriages followed a beautiful hearse drawn by two black horses. The coffin was covered with wreaths; withered flowers over a withered body!

September
Brain saves brawn

I made enough pancakes to last the week. I have them with cold tea at midday when I am out on my work station.

It is very quiet at Maldon. Many of the miners have to leave their fine houses and families, and proceed to the adjoining states in search of work.

I went to the railway station where they were loading a big boiler weighing over twenty-eight tons. Twelve strong and skilful men, moved it from the railway truck on to a strong waggon drawn by eight horses.

They did it quickly and appeared to do it easily. It was obvious that they were using their brains as well as their hands. The horses found it difficult to draw the load along the road. The boiler was destined for Mr Oswald at his payable gold claim. I was told that it will consume thirty tons of firewood in a day.

The incident brought to my mind the occasion when old Mr Price of Pontfaen, Lampeter, moved a waterwheel crank, weighing fourteen tons, from Aberayron to the silver mines at Llanfair. On each hill twenty-eight horses had to be hitched to the waggon. On the journey, the wheels found a wet patch and they sank to the axle. The load had to be abandoned for the night. A number of children collected to view the wreck, and the old Mr Price gave a penny to each child to prevent them running away with the crank during the night!

It is the first day of spring (23rd of September), the day when the New Fleet arrives in Melbourne harbour from England; it is also the day when Mr Vale, the zealous teetotaller, lectures at the Temperance Hall, and of greater importance still for Maldon, it is the day that Denris, the leather merchant moves into his fine new stores erected after his old one had been burnt down. Another visitor to the Colony is General Booth.

Thomas Jones, a prosperous farmer, has died suddenly. Recently he and his wife had moved into Maldon to enjoy retirement. It was not to be, and he was cut down at the age of 60. His son has taken on the farm. One soweth and another reapeth.

October
A strong fielder

The water reserves are low, and a downpour of rain for twelve hours at least is necessary. A dry period would injure the present promising cereal crops. Everything goes up in price. A loaf of bread is 7d, and although the bakers and retailers are legally bound to supply it at a weight of 4 lbs, it sometimes only weighs 3½ lbs.

The desired heavy rain has come. The reservoir and the water tanks are full again, so that Maldon should have an adequate supply of domestic water for the approaching summer.

I was working near the cricket field. A batsman hit the ball over the fence, and I was asked to throw it back. I undertook an underhand throw, and the ball landed the other side of the pitch and farther on the far side than it had been on the near side. Some of the players cursed me, others were laughing, and one shouted, 'Well done, old man'.

Evan Evans of Rheola called on me unexpectedly in regard to his brother's estate. He had travelled the eighty-two miles on horseback. I handed him his brother's will executed on the 23rd of December 1878. He intends staking his claim to some of the estate in spite of his sister-in-law's will in which she left everything to her adopted daughter. Evan Evans finds New South Wales more friendly than Victoria.

They have appointed a new treasurer to the council at a salary of £208 a year, a good wage for little work.

Miners' Association sports' day takes place in the Reserve. I paid my 1s at the entrance gate, but I did not go in. I gave my ticket to someone poorer than myself, if that were possible.

Very busy day at the railway station when an excursion train left for Castlemaine. Twenty big carriages were crammed with school-children and their guardians. The children were neatly clad, but their manners were appalling, and their language foul.

A Mr Handorff of the Commercial Hotel has died of cancer of the stomach. He was a German and was greatly respected. Among the nationals that have colonized Australia, the Germans are acknowledged as the most social and friendly. *He writes an englyn on his passing.*

November *Anti-sunstroke measures*

Over 70,000 saw 'Melvalio' win the Melbourne Cup. In this new country, as yet largely a wilderness needing to be cultivated, gambling, swindling, and defaulting are common practices.

At dusk on this 5th of November, I counted twenty bonfires burning on the adjacent hills. Fireworks displays are everywhere, and the children are burning effigies of poor Guy Fawkes.

Mr Oswald, the 'gold king' of Maldon has died. He was reputed to be a millionaire. *He writes a verse of twenty lines on the occasion.*

This 9th day of November is the birthday of H.R.H. the Prince of Wales, but the flags of Maldon are at half-mast to mourn the departed Mr Oswald.

Voting takes place to decide on licences for the town's public houses, so the contest is between the brewers and hoteliers on the one side, and the optionists and Salvation Army on the other. The former win by fifty-two votes. The legal quota for this small town is six, but it will now have nineteen public houses (*in November 1889 his tally was twenty-two*). The people will have their beer!

It was a very warm day, and I went to help the elderly widow, Mrs William Rees to gather in her hay. I soaked a piece of calico in water and wrapped it round my head, and placed a green cabbage leaf inside my hat, as precautions against sun-stroke.

December *Contented*

Battling with tall Californian thistles in the water channels, so called because the seed came mixed with corn grain from America.

Excursions on the railway are well patronized. I wonder where all the passengers come from. Money difficulties are forgotten because the fares can be borrowed anyway. O Victoria, whither goest thou? Headlong to destruction I believe.

The temperature is 108° F in the shade. I read accounts of many fierce fires in this and other States of the Colony. On windy days, a fire gains at the rate of twenty miles an hour. In its course it destroys sheep, ponies, homesteads and sometimes people. Even when fleeing on horseback, they may not escape. Good crops are burnt up, and it specially advances along the runs or sheep-walks, where the grass is tall, thick and dry. Hares, rabbits, foxes, and all sorts of wild animals, even snakes, go without mercy. At the moment it is dark, and I can see five fires raging. The fires are extinguished by farmers with the help of swagmen.

Large commercial firms are breaking down here, too many of them on account of frauds and forgeries. Food prices are rising and many families suffer, yet games, betting, and gambling, thrive, but pride and poverty have not dissolved partnership. When I arrived in Australia in 1869, the national debt was £4½ m, but now it is £44 m. Victoria used to be called the 'golden state', but now I believe that firms cannot produce more than 3 per cent in hard cash. The banks hold large numbers of mortgages on the uncultivated land. The Bank of New South Wales alone holds 127 sheep-walks under heavy mortgages. The banks pay interest rates of 6½ per cent on deposit accounts, but the depositors cannot legally enforce repayment within four years.

According to the last census there are 270 different creeds or denominations in the country, and each pretends to know what will happen in the hereafter.

Pride and ambition or greed are at the root of most sins like murders, thefts, quarrels, drunkenness, divorces, and national and domestic wars. They are the parents of all sorts of miseries throughout the known world, and they are on the increase every day and year within my memory.

I am alone in my cottage this Christmas day. I cooked some mutton chops for my dinner. I enjoyed it and said grace as follows:

Thanks to him who has the care
To give the toiling man his share.
He trusts in Him again for supper
Equal to his Christmas dinner.
Health and contentment to encompass,
Contributions to a Happy Christmas.

I am easy in my conscience,
Contented in my mind.
I am placid in my patience
No grudge of any kind.

1892

January *Drought once more sears and sours the Colony*

I proceeded by train to Melbourne to try and retrieve £1 which a farmer owed me for past work, but he pleaded similar poverty to my own which is now increased by the rail fare of 2s 6d.

The conduct of children during picnics in the Bush would astonish every decent person. I blame the parents. The school-teachers dare not admonish the children. If they did, the parents would summon them to appear before the magistrates.

Water is scarce. At Broken Hill, muddy water is sold at £3 per 100 gallons. The atmosphere is most uncomfortable on account of dust-clouds blown by high winds, and the smoke which comes from the Bush fires. Temperature is 112° F in the shade, and no rain falls. A severe gale has ripped off part of the cottage roof. I was unable to mend the damage by myself. I got a man to help me. His labour and material cost me 11s. I was too tired to fetch water. My milk has turned sour. Bush fires are causing great havoc throughout the country. Heavy floods in Queensland have swept away dwellings and churches. The cattle are suffering from the drought. The earth is parched and water is scarce. I had to go 400 yards to get water from a water hole. I balanced two kerosine tins containing 7½ gallons on a beam across my shoulders in the manner that Chinamen do. Not bad for an old man in his 74th year! Still no sign of rain. Milk is in short supply, so that butter is scarce and costs 1s 6d a lb.

It is reported that the young Duke of Clarence, and the aged Cardinal Manning, have died.

February *Calvinism loses its champion*

The papers report the death of Spurgeon, that popular preacher, and zealous disciple of John Calvin. Many years ago I listened to him preaching at his Tabernacle in London.

I called at the shire hall for my monthly wage of £4, and then visited the tradesmen to settle all my debts. When I returned to work after dinner, I did not owe 6d to anyone in the Colony.

A woman was killed on the railway near Castlemaine. She had charge of the gates on a railway crossing. She had overslept and had hurried in her dressing-gown to open the gates, but the train cut her in pieces. The jury passed a verdict that death was caused through her own negligence, but censured the engine driver for not having reduced speed in the face of the red light.

I had a visit from Mr Tom Davies. He is lucky in his digging at the moment for he has found a good patch. I hope he will continue to prosper. Gold will do him good for he is a steady man.

Less than one-eighth of an inch of rain has fallen in Victoria this year. This will incur a great financial loss for the state. The atmosphere continues foul with smoke from the Bush fires, and it reminds one of 'Black Thursday' in February 1851 with all its horrors, when only a few sheep were saved through driving them into the dried lakes and water-pools.

I bought a wheelbarrow for myself for £1. It is a common thing and in Wales they would not have the face to ask for more than 7s for it.

A heavy thunderstorm with continuous lightning lasting an hour has just passed, yet it did not bring with it more than an eighth of an inch of rain!

Took my tools to the blacksmith to be sharpened. They soon get blunt because I have strong arms; but not so my legs. Another dust storm, the eighth this year.

March *The short-sighted farmers*

Dreams are beyond my comprehension. Last night I dreamt about the Pope. Why should I dream of him, because I never think about him during the day?

It is the driest and hottest year I have experienced in the Colony. The milk goes sour before I have a chance to drink it.

Returning home late, I found my window broken, and presently an able-bodied man jumped out and ran away. I had a friend with me, otherwise he might have attacked me. Had I been in and even alone, I would have put up a good fight as I have things handy, to defend myself and my little castle. I have tools by me which are more effective than guns and revolvers.

A Mr Beavan from Wales visited Maldon to lecture on his travels, voyages and journeys 'round the world'. People should not use this term if they have only travelled there and back over one side of the globe. They should cross the Sahara Desert before they make the claim.

It is now four months since heavy rain fell. The Colony has sustained losses amounting to one million pounds. Sheep and cattle are starving for the want of care and preparation. As usual there was plenty of food for them in August to October. If this had been preserved in the shape of hay or silage, it would save the animals now. The farmers were too mean to pay wages to the thousands of able-bodied men who are still out of work because of such negligence. Before man and beast survive in comfort in this Colony, the rich land must be properly cultivated and husbanded.

April *The feathered scavengers poisoned*

My spring-water is nearly dry, because the miners use it to wash out the sand when they riddle it for gold. I have to go a distance of 400 yards for water which is unclean. I was up this morning at 5 a.m. and had finished breakfast at 6 a.m. and so to work:

Mae'n dechreu torri'r wawr,	At five o'clock in the morning,
Am bump o'r gloch y boreu.	This is the appointed hour,
I godi tyna'r awr,	To witness the bright dawn breaking,
Ond rhaid cael tân a goleu.	The day is op'ning its door.

Rain and sleet preceded a snow-fall. It is unusual to have snow so early.

The Liberals have gained a substantial majority over the Conservatives at the general election, but in Maldon the standing Conservative member was re-elected.

My first job today was to bury seven fat geese which had been poisoned by someone. They visit the town to graze the young grass that grows in the water-channels, and the owners had received previous notice that they should keep the geese away.

May *The rose by another name*

Two Welsh friends paid me a visit on Sunday. We had a long chat, conversing in Welsh. Indeed, my English speech has not improved since I left Wales.

I have the toothache again, affecting my one remaining stump. I must endure it, because it would cost 10s 6d to have it extracted, which in any case would be painful procedure, while it might result in splitting my jaw, for doctors in Australia are deadly reckless.

A thunderstorm with heavy rain marks the end of the drought which in some parts of the country has lasted for seven months.

Spent the day cleaning the rough drains around the Anglican church. You dare not call it Church of England in these parts.

I get up at 5 a.m. each morning from natural inclination, and finish my domestic duties by 6 a.m. when the whistle is sounded at the railway station by the engine that draws out the first train for Melbourne. I start work at 7 a.m. when the hooter at the Claims calls its miners to go underground. There are nine claims in the immediate district, six of which produce 'payable gold', and two of these pay good dividends to the speculators.

Today (24th of May) being the Queen's birthday is a national holiday, and they hold sporting events at the Reserve Ground. My 'sport' was at the washing tub, where I washed 2 pairs of trousers, 2 shirts, 2 pants, 2 flannel vests, and 2 pairs of socks; I moved to the last, and beat nails into my boots.

June and July
Two friends fall

A Mr Reckets, railway contractor, successful gold prospector, and a philanthropist, died today. Maldon's flags were at half-mast.

One of my best friends in Maldon, Mr Simon Maler, was buried today. He was a sound man.

I learnt from the 'Cambrian News' that my daughter Jane was married on the 7th of May to Daniel, the son of Frithwen.

Received letters from my daughter Nell, and her daughter, Lizzie. Both letters were so interesting that I read them three times.

August
Low blood sugar

Had my finger lanced. I slept well afterwards. It had kept me awake the two previous nights.

John Davies visited me. He wished me to read a letter which he had received from his sister in Melbourne. She had been widowed three times, and once had a capital of £3,000. She is now penniless and seeks assistance. She has lost all her money through speculating in ventures which went bankrupt.

A heavy and prolonged storm of hail and rain has broken out.

I over-slept, which is most unusual for me, and I did not get up till 5.45 a.m. so I had no time for breakfast. At 10 o'clock I became very dizzy. I was never before like this, and I could hardly walk home for the extreme giddiness. Yet, the next day I was at work feeling strong and in good spirit.

September
A tug back home

I replied to a letter from my nephew, Jenkin Jenkins (Aeronian). This same nephew had invited him to return home to Wales in the following verse:

Dychwelwch — deuwch i Walia — Cofiwch
Fod Trecefel yma.
Mae eich anwyliaid — dyaid da
Yn aeddfed am roi'i chwi noddfa.

Friends are anxious to greet you,
Welcome awaits you.
Home and the hearth expect you
Wales remembers you.

He does not mention his reaction to this invitation, but it is likely that he gave the invitation a sympathetic hearing, for about this time there appeared from his pen in a local paper the undermentioned poem:

THE OLD HOME
'Tis many a year from home I've been, but I'd like to try somehow,
To see the old folk once again; but they wouldn't know me now.
But still the thought of dear old home does oft a pleasure bring,
But I have changed and they have changed, and changed has everything.

I'd like to see the old play-ground, and the green lanes where I've strolled,
I think I'd know my way around, though now I'm getting old,
And the grist mill with the water-wheel, the turnstile and the brook,
And the angler sitting by the stream, with his bait upon the hook.

With the blackberries upon the hedge, and the little birds at play,
And the willows and the meadows, do they look as green today?
And the song-birds on the branches, would their music sound as sweet?
And the glow-worms in the bushes, where the lovers used to meet.

And the old churchyard with tombstones thick, some crumbling in decay,
I think I could the old spot find, where they laid a friend away.
And the old school I remember yet, with ink-stained desk of yore,
With the scolds and birching then I got, but the master now's no more.

And by the pathway, near the church, two old graves together;
And the tombstones, sinking in the earth, leant one against the other.
Beneath were friends in life, now in their graves long undisturbed they lie,
It seemed in death a touching thing, for tombstones thus to tie.

What matters it when death does come, and in the grave you're lain?
The friends you knew are very few who'd wish you back again;
And p'haps its well, for when you're old, you're often in the way,
So it's natural-like such things should be, as age to youth gives way.

It is Sunday, and I have twice the amount of work today than usual. In addition to reading, writing, and some resting, I have the 'Cambrian News' which came yesterday, and I shall steal time to read every page of that. John Davies and others also called on me, but I was too busy to take notice of their idle talk about the gold reefs.

The wind has moved to north-north-east. When it rains with the wind blowing from this quarter, it usually rains heavily and lasts for three days; *and so it did on this occasion.*

October *Australia's gold is in its surface soil*

Townships throughout Australia devote too much time to football, cricket, betting and gambling. I feel sure that circumstances will compel the next generation to clear, cultivate, and manure, the glorious, rich, and productive soil. There is more indirect gold in the surface soil of Australia to be collected in a single year, than natural gold taken from its deep recesses.

The crops of barley, oats, wheat, and lucerne are flourishing. In this neighbourhood they mow these as hay, and they do not thrash and winnow the crops for grain, for it is too expensive to employ the threshing team for small quantities.

One-half of the fine gardens in Maldon are foul with dock and other weeds, but the Chinamen are good gardeners, and they grow fresh vegetables for sale.

The circus has come to Maldon; it is a five-yearly event. The show employs sixty attendants and there are fifty-five horses. This a remarkable venture for a town of 2,000 inhabitants, two-thirds of them children under 12 years of age. Dresses and money are borrowed for the occasion. The churches oppose the event.

A moderate hurricane visited the town, and my brick-walled cottage trembled like a gum leaf.

The Colony has borrowed another million pounds from London. Who will be alive to witness its repayment? Certainly, not one of the rising generation. The fine country is being mismanaged, and its rich productive soil is being neglected.

Walking is more tiresome to me than hard toil, my legs are being attracted to mother earth.

I had a visit from my bootmaker. He scolded me for washing and cleaning my boots every Sunday. My boots last far too long for his liking. I am behind with my correspondence; I owe letters to my three married daughters, Nell, Mary and Jane.

The Melbourne Cup was won by a horse called 'Comoola'.

Comoola cel cymalog,	*Comoola, a lusty steed,*
Er gwaitha'r llu, aeth a'r llog.	*Robs the purse through sheer speed.*

November
A homing hint

A popular wedding took place at Maldon. The bride, Miss Colder aged 18, is a local girl, and the groom is a wealthy young doctor aged 23 from Bendigo. He is a cripple and he attended on crutches. The guests numbered 500, and they brought handsome presents for the young pair, which I regard as a foolish custom.

Another Sunday passes without finding time to write to my three married daughters in Cardiganshire, and my friends in Glamorganshire and London.

It is warm and sunny with signs of hot weather to follow. This may go on to Christmas when the long and ripe grass will have withered, and the cattle will starve for lack of fodder, and the carelessness of farmers who do not harvest the hay while it is yet young and plentiful. Farmers simply will not or cannot employ labour to gather and store this precious commodity.

I am greatly upset with the news that my favourite nephew, Jenkin Jenkins (Aeronian) had died on the 17th of October at the age of 46. His wife had predeceased him, so that ten parentless children (nine girls and one boy) are left. I do hope I shall be able to see them before I join their parents.

A man has committed suicide through standing in front of a train travelling at thirty miles an hour. He feared poverty, although he had £457 in the bank. There are more suicides in this Colony than in any other country. Some blame the climate, but I do not think this is the explanation. One-half of the labouring class is unemployed. If the land were properly cleared and inhabitated, some forty million people could find employment here. If this were brought about, it would establish a nation equal to America.

December *His own footwear for ease*

For my dinner today I had toasted-bread and honey with cold tea. It suited my blunt and rotten grinders. It was so cold that my fingers became numb. My feet too were so cold that I was obliged to take off my boots and wear a pair of clogs of my own making twelve years ago.

Searched the gutters for a long time for my lost purse which held money, tobacco, knife, and receipts of payments made yesterday to various tradesmen. Should an honest person pick it up, he or she would know that it belonged to me. I thought that I always took good care of my money.

The newspapers report the death of an American multi-millionaire, Jay Gould. His fortune of (U.S.)$30 million was amassed as a broker when he swindled and made penniless countless innocent and trusting clients.

The corn crop has been gathered. The yield has varied. The farmers complain of the low price, and maintain that 3s 9d a bushel does not cover the expense of producing it. Yet, when the tax is only 1s 6d an acre, a return of twenty-six bushels an acre ought to pay well. Here they can harvest it and take it to market at one-half the expense I incurred in Wales. In fine harvesting weather as now, grain can be collected on the field by 'stripping' the crop, so that farmers avoid paying 4d an hour over a few days while harvesting lasts, for binding, stooking and carting, and later threshing.

I went to the druggist and purchased 2 ounces of hog's lard for 6d, 2 ounces of cayenne pepper for 6d, and some strychnine to kill mice in the cottage for 6d.

Holiday excursions are in full swing, but the complement of passengers is small, because there is no money to spend on pleasure.

Although he makes no reference to the exhibit, there is pinned to his diary for the 24th of December, a press cutting (reprinted below) which confirms the opinion given in the Introduction that he left home because of the acrimony and malevolence directed against him by his wife.

Last week a man asked Mr Bros, a London magistrate, as to what he could do with a disagreeable wife, who was always nagging him and rendering his life unbearable. Mr Bros: why do you live with her? Applicant (shrugging his shoulders): Well, sir, because I am married to her. Mr Bros: If she is as you describe, I advise you to leave her, let her go her own way, and you go yours. Applicant (brightening up): Can I do that, sir? Mr Bros: Certainly you can. This unhappy married man will find that he will have to keep his nagging wife although he cannot be compelled to live with her. Since wives have proved that they cannot be compelled to live with their husbands there has been great rejoicing at the freedom thus opened up for their hen-pecked husbands. How religion is promoted by keeping married people united who hate each other is one of those questions that civilization has not yet answered!

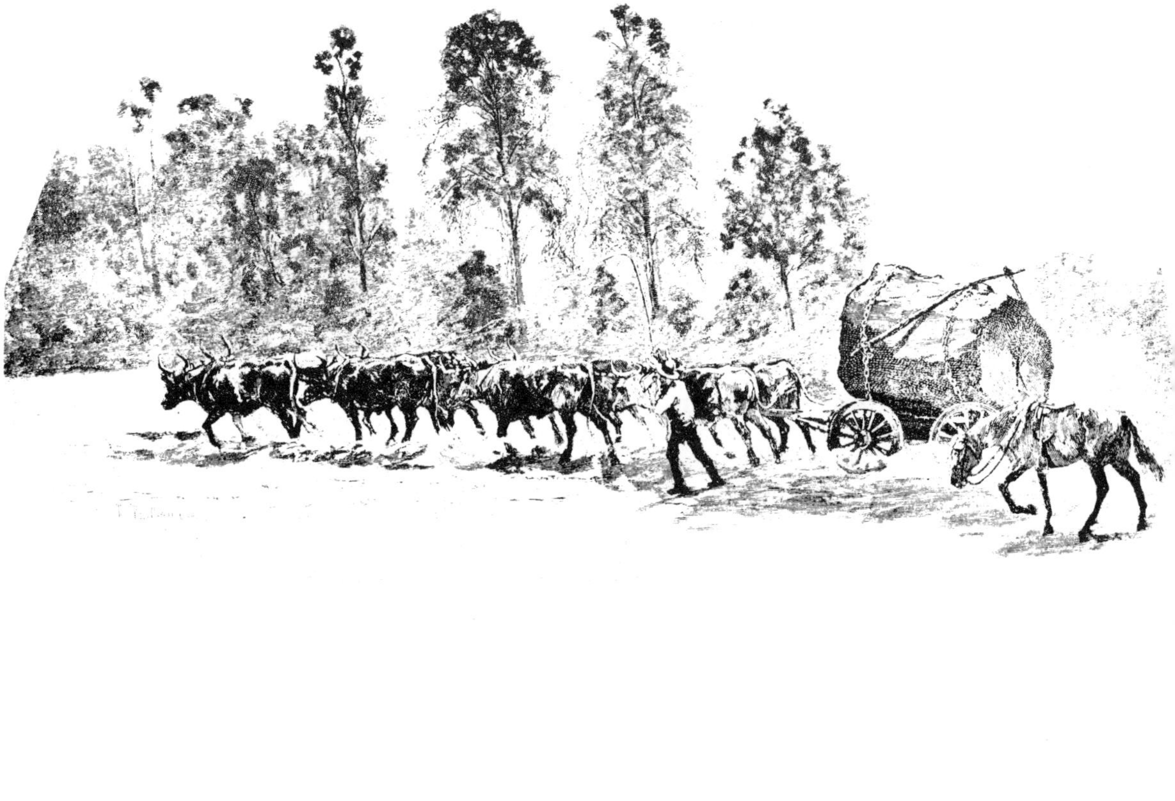

1893

January *The scavenger speaks out again*

I clean the water-channels with my shovel, rake and broom, and carry the stuff away in a barrow, and tip it into a disused gold mine which is seventy feet deep. It is the richest manure that any farmer or gardener could wish for, but in this part of the world they don't believe in manuring the soil. The land will bear an absence of manure for twenty to thirty years, but during that time the farmers blame the seasons when their crops fail. Then, they are obliged to sell their buggies, pianos, and other chattels, and even their land, to the big squatters and land-grabbers. In fact this Colony is going headlong into disaster. It is heavily in debt and to the tune of £50 m, while it craves for still more loans.

I drew my small wage of £4 for the month, and settled with all the tradesmen. I bought a few extra things with my few remaining shillings. I owe fourteen letters to my relatives in Wales, and my friends.

February *Accidental and other fires*

Temperature is $110°$ F in the shade. Many die of sunstroke. The atmosphere is laden with smoke from the Bush. It is so dense that I cannot see the sun. It appears to be in the direction of a big sheep ranch.

A dozen fine geese were poisoned by somebody, and it was given to me to bury them somewhere outside the town.

A big store in Maldon was burnt down. A steam engine, chaff-cutter, and a mill, were saved through the exertions of the fire brigade. The loss was estimated at £400, but it was fully covered by insurance.

A dust storm has filled up all the water channels with gravel.

March *Pancakes for Shrove Tuesday and beyond*

I attended the funeral today of Evan Davies, aged 74, a native of Llanon, Cardiganshire. He had a very good farm at Walmer, but he was too lazy to plant a single cabbage in his fine garden. Nineteen able-bodied children bore his body to its resting place, all from the same mother who is robust and survives him.

An agricultural show held at a place seven miles north-west of Maldon was poorly attended. This is not surprising as two-thirds of the would-be farmers are selling their land to either the graziers or squatters for £5 an acre, having bought it from the Government for £1 an acre. The land is heavily mortgaged at an interest rate of 8 or 9 per cent, and as the farmers had no idea about cultivation, little wonder they have to give up.

Today being Sunday I baked a lot of pancakes, not only for Shrove Tuesday, but also to take with me to eat with cold tea on those days when I am not able to return to the cottage for dinner.

I continue daily to cart excellent manure from the sewers and dispose of it into the old mines. Since coming to Maldon I have discarded that amount which would have been sufficient for Trecefel and Tyndomen land for many years. They will realize its value here in due time.

Very warm and no rain for sometime. The cattle suffer and they eat the horses' droppings. What a pity the farmers do not harvest the grass which was plentiful in the months of August, September and October, and which could be fed to the animals at this time of drought, and save them from starving.

I bought a ticket for a tea-meeting at the Welsh chapel for 1s 6d, and gave it to one who wished to go, but who could not afford the price of the ticket.

April
Banks fail and close

Another bank has failed. Its books showed a deficit of £5 million. It is the twelfth to close lately. When one bank fails it affects another which quickly follows the same fate.

My two friends paid me their usual Sunday visit. Both have worked for the past few months for a wage of 2s 6d a day. That is even lower than my poor wage. They have to go down, 1,000 feet before finding any gold, and only the wealthy firms can afford to dig it at that depth.

I read in the papers that the 'grand old man' Gladstone had a majority of forty-three in the British Parliament in the case of the 'Home Rule for Ireland' bill.

On my way home from work to dinner, my cat came to meet me and rubbed itself against my legs, and seemed happy to see me.

Another bank, the 'London Chartered Bank' has closed its doors. It is short of half a million pounds. The news forms the subject of general conversation.

May *Call to work not prayer*

I get more tired from walking than working. My duties cover a mile square, and I am overseer of forty miles of water channels.

Wrote a long letter to my eldest daughter Nell, and I have not yet finished it. I must write oftener to my children. They used to be very fond of me in Wales.

I have read in the papers that they have decided in the United Kingdom to pray for rain. O how long will they go on mocking the

Author of Nature who will have His way, and knows better than bishops and other ministers of religion how best to provide the need of all? Let the sluggard consider his duty to so provide and prepare for the welfare of man and beast.

June *Libel action*

Two loads of firewood were delivered at my cottage and cost me 14s. Floods affect the whole Colony. Ten inches of rain has fallen in ten hours.

A law suit is pending which is likely to last for a month or longer, when the legal expenses incurred will be in the region of £2,000 a day. The general manager of the railways is bringing a libel action against the proprietor of 'The Age' newspaper which accused the manager of dereliction of duties and of incompetence, which involved the Colony in unwarranted expense to the tune of £2,000,000, through laying unnecessary railway lines, often through useless land, and which was sometimes purchased for several hundreds of pounds. The only traffic carried by the particular railway consists of wool-clip once a year.

On this lovely Sunday morning, the ladies and their men-folk are out walking. The men are clad in bishop-black clothes. Australia has fine factories and finer wool than any other in the world. Yet the woollen tweed of the Colony finds no favour with the inhabitants who prefer to patronize the black cotton clothes and dresses imported at heavy cost from abroad, catering to their pride.

He composes a verse of eight lines in Welsh which he sends to each of his three married daughters. In this he expresses the hope that he will see his grandchildren before he dies. This is the first year, among his twenty-three in Australia, that he admits to a strong tug at the heart-strings to return to Wales.

It is raining heavily, and there are no signs of its abating. Yet, no steps are being taken to use the abundant labour available in the Colony to conserve water for use of man and beast during periods of drought. The capitalists treat the labouring class with less consideration than in the days of the slave-trade in the time of Wilberforce. Civility too is at a premium, and I find the world ten times less civil than when I was a lad of 18 years.

Farmers have again learnt to their cost that they should not sow cereals near the big rivers, so that their crops are again under water as the result of the severe floods. They could also guard against such great losses in crops if they spent a few extra pounds on additional labour to provide field-furrows for drainage.

Reading on Sundays now induces sleep, and as a result I am unable to sleep that night.

Different nationals pass by my cottage on Sundays, the Chinese more than any other. I do not understand a single word of their language. Each letter of their ancient tongue has a meaning and each word is a sentence. They are a persevering people although they are scoffed at here by the other nationals. Their country has never been conquered by any other, nor will it ever!

July
The cottage quakes

Unemployment is rife in the Colony, and many families are starving. I left a new bucket outside my door under the veranda, and it was stolen. Every schoolboy here is a downright thief.

At 1.20 this morning (the 23rd of July) we had an earthquake which lasted two or three seconds. My little cottage trembled like a gum leaf, and plaster fell from the walls. It was not so severe as the one I experienced in 1872 when I was thrown out of bed.

August *News of his two boys*

Some of the roads here are in a very poor state after the heavy rain. The loads taken over them are similarly very heavy. Fourteen bullocks draw strong waggons with narrow tyres carrying a load of about ten tons of timber from the Bush for use of the engines at the gold mines.

I have just read in the 'Cambrian News' that my farmer son Tom was fined for netting trout in the river Teifi. To engage in this innocent sport cost him a pound with costs. There was a dispute over the net. The informer had no right to claim it.

How dare you poor farmers who bear the big flood,
Which spoils your meadows with gravel and mud,
To take from the rivers an eel or a fish
To enjoy your dinner of a nourishing dish.

Two days later he had a letter from his youngest son John saying he had gained the degree of Doctor of Medicine at London University.

Late last night, MacGalliger disturbed me, seeking rest for a few hours because he was 'too far gone' to go home and face his mother. He stayed here for the night. I got up early as usual, cooked my breakfast, and went out to my work, locking the door behind me, and taking the key with me at his request. I returned at noon, and he was glad to see the door opened. He went off directly, and I was not sorry to see him go.

September *Thrift from small earnings*

I managed to deposit £4 in the post office savings bank, where the interest rate has been reduced to 3½ per cent.

Another three weeks of wet weather will spoil the cereal crops in the Colony. The farmers are already talking of rust in the wheat. We always complain of something other than ourselves. In my work on the water-channels, I have to deal with the dust if it is dry, and the mud if it is wet. A beautiful half-circle rainbow appears in the sky between showers.

October *Neglect of meadow hay*

I have never seen the grass grow so quickly as now in Victoria. It grows three or four inches each night and day. The hay paddocks are nearly fit for cutting. The grass stands about four to five feet high. What they term hay here is oats or wheat which they cut while it is still green. They have no use for meadow hay. What a glorious agricultural country this is if it were properly managed, but all are bent on getting direct gold, forgetting that all sorts of comfort for man and beast can be got without it. The prospects of gold mining are again better in Maldon, for they have newly found 'payable gold' at 1,200 feet deep.

The moon over the bright horizon appears larger than when I looked at it in Wales. The 'old man in the moon' appears to be standing on his head with his legs directed upwards. The saying goes that he was transported there because he stole a bundle of thorn bushes. The poor fellow must have stolen something of greater value to be turned upside down.

In the afternoon, I was ordered to help another man to bury a dead cow. It was time too, for millions of fresh lives had sprung up from a single death. So it is with life and death.

November *Vandalism and gambling*

I went to the butcher's shop, and was back within twenty minutes to find my two windows had been broken. They were riddled with stones thrown by schoolboys.

This is Cup Day at Melbourne (the 7th of November). It is the topic of conversation when two men meet in the town. They are all gamblers here, and they risk what they can afford, and even what they cannot. The race was won by half a length by an outside horse, named 'Tarcoola'. The bookmakers gathered in a pile of money. None came to Maldon.

December *Goose and plum pudding in the heat of the day*

Although summer does not begin till the 21st of December, the temperature at midday was 90⁰ F in the shade, which is abnormal so early in the month. Two days later torrential rain accompanied a severe thunderstorm. I got up at 4 a.m. and was out on the streets directly to clear the many clogged foot bridges, and carry away barrowfuls of mud.

On this Hospital Sunday, they only collected £35. The donors are the poor. The richer people do not contribute. As in previous years I dropped in my mite.

It is hot and the flies are troublesome, while their bites are poisonous. On Christmas eve a band played three airs in front of my cottage. They and their instruments departed after I gave them 1s, and I got from them a promise not to return before New Year's eve.

A friend and neighbour brought me my Christmas dinner of young goose, plum pudding, etc. In the afternoon I went to see Melbourne play Maldon at cricket. Maldon were the victors.

1894

January *Hooligans and vandals*

The children of Maldon (the larrikins) are the reckless governors of the place when removed from the influence of their parents and teachers. They will steal and break up anything they see, and molest undefended people.

I owe a number of letters to the folk in Wales, and on Sundays when there is time, I am too tired to write. I go to bed early, but I cannot sleep till the morning hours because of the intense heat. Day temperature is 105° F in the shade, while the corrugated iron roofing to my cottage retains the heat through the night hours.

No visitors this Sunday so I was able to read much of the Bible. I read the 'Sermon on the Mount' most Sundays.

The hooligan children molest me, so I took out my gun, and when they saw me loading it, they soon ran away.

Sand fleas are a great nuisance when they settle in garments. Insect powders won't kill them. They won't drown in cold water even when immersed for a week. I boil my garments for an hour and I fancy they will not survive that treatment.

February *The poisoner abroad again*

I had to bury twenty fine geese that had been poisoned, some say by butchers in order to save their own trade. The geese do no harm. On the contrary, they clean the streets through devouring the garbage, and picking up the spilt grain.

The harvest is almost over. No sign of rain. The cattle begin to suffer. The grass is plentiful, but it is withered and contains no nourishment. No water has been stored, and no fodder prepared for the pining creatures.

I do not feel well, nor fancy any breakfast, so I drank half a pint of water to which I added a tablespoon of sugar:

Dwr a siwgwr yn y boreu	Sugared water in the morning
Sydd well imi na'r ddiod oreu.	Suits me more than wine excelling
Dwywedai mam pan o'wn yn fabi	From Mother's lips I learnt it first,
Mai tyna wnai fy nisychedu.	That it was best to quench my thirst.

I dream a lot of Wales. When one dreams I do not believe one is really asleep.

This is my 76th birthday. I was born on Friday the 27th of February 1818, at 20 minutes past 6 in the evening.

I made a mistake yesterday over the precise hour of my birth. Here we are 9 hours and 20 minutes ahead of British mean time. Thus, I completed my 76 years at 20 minutes to 3 this morning; so I will take another half-day's holiday. *He then composes the following verse:*

Os byw a fyddaf foru,	Should I live to see tomorrow,
'Rwyn addaw bod yn well.	I do promise to be better.
Daw dranoeth i amlygu	When it dawns, I note with sorrow
Fod foru etto'n mhell.	Tomorrow is no nearer.

March *Corresponds with a shipping line*

I am still unwell. I have the hiccough. This is a bad sign in an old man, but a healthy sign in children. I have been in the doctor's hands for sometime, and I am no better, so I am going to dispense with the consultations and live in accord with my own feelings, and take only a child's natural food.

Gladstone, aged 84, has resigned from the British Premiership. *Up to now he has not made any definite pronouncement that he intends to return before long to Wales. There have been two hints, namely about his grandchildren and his favourite nephew's bereaved ten children, he has said, 'I hope to see them before I die'. Now, however, the flap of an envelope is found inside his diary which bears the stamp 'Orient Line of Royal Mail Steamers'. This indicates that he has been in communication with the Orient Shipping Line concerning the booking of a passage home.*

I am in great discomfort from chronic dysentery. I took fifty drops of laudanum to ease the pain and enable me to go to work.

I intend writing a letter to my youngest son, David John who is now 25 years of age and a doctor in London.

I called on Mr Smith who is headmaster at the school to complain that the children hinder me in my work. He told me to go and see the police as he was not responsible for them outside the school. I wanted him to give them a talk on how to behave when out of school, believing that it would do no harm. Their language is foul, and forty per cent of them do not know which end of a cabbage plant to put into the earth in their parents' rich gardens which are overrun with weeds and brambles.

I have just read the 'Cambrian News'. It is a grand paper, and Mr Gibson, its editor, is a splendid philosopher. *Previously, he has named him Wilson.*

April *Sorrow and joy*

Many old people are ailing here, and quite a number have died. Not many of my age are left. I am not fit to work, although it continues to be my delight.

I have just drawn my month's wages, and have been round to settle my accounts at the shops. I was able to spend £1 on underclothing. The leaves of the beech trees are falling and filling up the water channels. The rain has come and the cattle are beginning to improve in their condition. The bare hills are green after the acceptable heavy rain.

I attend the funeral of my friend Mr Nantkevil who was a land surveyor. He was 83 years old and had twenty-four children. He had survived four wives. There were forty-five carriages at the funeral, for he was greatly respected.

Numerous flags are flying, and street arches are being erected in preparation for the visit of the State's Governor, who is a popular good-looking young man of 35. (*He refers to Governor John Hope, Earl of Hopetoun.*) The occasion will cost the ratepayers £60.

May
He gives notice

A letter from a friend informs me that my brother John (Cerngoch) died on the 24th of March. It has upset me greatly because I was very fond of him, and we always agreed on current problems.

I had hoped that I would have no callers this Sunday because I had so many letters to answer, but alas it was not to be, and I was disturbed by many visitors.

I gave a month's notice to the council today, for I hope to start for Wales in a few months. There are many things to see to before I leave, and I have yet to get the Mail boat to accept me as a passenger. A young man has brought me another load of firewood which cost me 12s 6d.

June and July
Lack of occupation breeds loneliness

I read in the 'Cardiff Daily News' that the House of Commons are debating a bill for the disestablishment of the English church in Wales.

John Davies promised to repay me £1 2s 4d which he borrowed from me seven months ago, within a fortnight. I don't suppose I shall ever get it back.

Rwy'n eistedd wrth y tan	Deep in thought the evening long
Heb neb yn agos attaf.	I sit before the fire.
Pe bawn' in llinio can	If I should now compose a song,
Does neb i wrando arnaf.	There's no one by to hear.

I went for a spade which I had lent to a man some time ago. It was a useful tool, but it is now useless and broken in two places.

It is a warm and sunny day, so I put out my mouldy diaries and other things to air. I hope the good weather continues so that I can complete this work.

I bought some timber to build a new ladder, so that I can mend the roof of my cottage. I look over my diaries. I have nothing to do except attend to the fire and cook meals. I am sorry now that I resigned my job, for it may be another two months before I commence the voyage. Half of my belongings will have to be left behind for no one will buy them. My cottage is very cold, but when in bed I am as warm as a piece of toast from the cook's hands. The rain hinders me in the repair work, and yet I cannot leave before I complete this work. I feel unhappy and sorry that I resigned. I am entrapped, and must spend the few pounds I had saved to pay for my voyage to Wales, in order to exist here. If I do not start my journey soon, I will have spent all my money. I do so want to see my grandchildren.

I have applied to the council for wages owing to me in respect of work done outside the terms of my contract, work carried out on directions from the clerk of works. In addition to this, the council reduced my wages when I was absent because of a scalded foot, and again during my stay of three weeks in hospital. A rebuttal of my application would mean a great injustice, and a case of taking an unfair advantage of the services of an old man.

I went to be measured for a new pair of boots. When I came back I found that thieves had broken in and robbed me of many things. One of my diaries had been thrown outside. The cottage was set on fire, but I was able to put it out. I boarded up the broken windows, but failed to keep out the cold.

August
The unbeliever's soliloquy

I had nothing to do today because the bad weather prevented me from going outside, so I opened my box and parcels, and found that £5 was missing. Someone must have got hold of the key. It is time I left here and Maldon.

I am preparing for my long voyage, but it will take me some weeks yet, and I shall have to leave behind me more than half of my small possessions.

At my advanced age, I brood continuously over diverse subjects, and am reminded of words by the poet Clough, who was considered to be an infidel:

And almost every man when age,
Disease, and sorrow, strike him,
Inclines to think there is a God,
Or something very like Him.

The heavy rain prevents the repair of the cottage. I continue to wonder whether the brokers will accept me as a passenger on board the mail boat. I engage myself in reading and mending my clothes.

September
Fortune eluded him

I lifted £10 from the post office savings bank, and spent £5 on a new suit of clothes. The moths had played havoc with those I had stored. I should not have bought so many, and just do with the ones I wore daily. The mice too have been at my manuscripts.

Cooking, eating, and cutting firewood to keep myself warm, are my present activities. My headache has eased after taking mutton broth. Mutton agrees with me better than any other kind of meat.

The Paterson Government has resigned and Turner of St Kilda was called to form a new Government. He is leader of the Liberal Party which has a majority of sixty.

They have discovered a new source of gold at Tarnagula which is some twenty-six miles north-west of Maldon. I had walked over the lucky spot several times, and had no idea that the precious metal was right under my feet.

Three years ago I did join three prospectors in the neighbourhood, and paid out scores of pounds in miners' wages. Later, I opted out of the venture, and within three weeks they struck a patch that yielded them £1,800 each in a single week. Luck has never come my way, but I don't envy other men's luck.

A Mrs Needle has been found guilty of poisoning her husband, a second man, and her three children. Another mother is on trial at Maryborough for murdering three of her own children. Both mothers were not in need of this world's goods.

October *Money is running out*

I will lose over £90 in wages due to the clerk of works' stratagem, and more through forfeiting my land, house, and its contents. I must take care, otherwise I will not be able to embark for home.

I acquired another load of firewood, and hope that this will be the last I shall need here, and that it will suffice to keep me warm for another two weeks.

Heavy rain has caused severe flooding. The flood may spread for a distance of 500 miles on each side of some of the big rivers. People back in Wales do not realize the expanse of this Colony. There are many in the county I come from, who think that Cardiganshire is nearly half the globe. Don't believe them!

Since coming to Australia I have never gone hungry, but the families of those who strike are often half-starved when the men refuse to work for less than £2 10s a week. Whenever I was out of work, and that was often, I would find a place to put down my swag for the night, and wake to a good breakfast in the morning in exchange for cutting up firewood. I would then take up my swag, and walk on in search of work so as to buy some clothes and provender, making inroad into pastures new, perhaps 100 miles before resting.

I went to the town to buy two pocket handkerchiefs, and to get my watch mended and cleaned before I start on my intended voyage. I wonder if I ever will start because I cannot get half the money owing me, and nothing for my premises. This fine country is glorious, but too many of its inhabitants are so ready to rob one another. Attention to my watch cost me 9s, a cap for night-wear, 3s 3d, and 7s 7d for cheese. My money is running out for I earn nothing now.

Interleaved in the diary is a price list of goods from the general stores of Mr E. D. Williams: tea, 1s a lb; best sugar, 3d a lb; soap, 3d a bar; baking soda, 2d a lb; clothes' pegs, 1d a dozen; spades, 2s 3d; nails, 2s 2d a lb; houses furnished throughout, £18.

John Williams has called on me. He is in the last stages of consumption, yet he is daily digging for gold, and hopes to make a fortune before his dissolution. Such is the way of the world.

My health too is declining, and I fear I shall not be able to stand the homeward voyage over the southern sea, but I do want to see my grandchildren before I die.

I have just received another copy of the 'Cambrian News' from Wales. I usually read it twice or even three times, because its wise editorials are among the best I have ever read. Cardiganshire would do well if they adopted Mr Gibson, the editor, as their member of Parliament.

An agricultural show is held at Maldon, but there are few competent farmers within eight miles of this place. The butchers have gone far afield and bought fine stock which they have exhibited under their own names, and as many of them act as judges, they make certain of the prizes. There were many new farm implements on view, but few were sold, because there is very little money about.

November
Sets sail for Home

I have told my friends in Wales that I shall be with them before Christmas. To accomplish this I should sail by the mail boat on the 10th of this month, but I do not think I can manage this.

I walked all round the township to collect the loans I had made to different people. The oustanding debts amount to nearly £200, but not a single person repaid me. I can only pass judgment on them now, and regard them as swindlers and complete rogues.

It looks as if I shall have to leave behind me my cottage, land, and furniture, for I am unable to sell anything.

A severe dust storm has just passed. I hope that my diaries and manuscripts will reach their destination at Pont Llanio railway station for the care of my children, Ebenezer and Elinor Evans of Tyndomen.

On the 23rd of November two of my neighbours assisted me to take my luggage to the railway station where I entrained at 6.15 a.m. and arrived at Melbourne at 9.30 a.m. I went to the Orient Shipping Office to inquire whether they would take an aged man like me as a passenger. I was offered a cabin to myself for £26 15s 6d. I proceeded to the post office savings bank to withdraw my money. Returning to the Orient Office, I procured my ticket without any question being asked regarding my age or health. Having collected my luggage from the railway station, and partaken of a meal at a restaurant, I proceeded down to the Ship at Port Melbourne, and took possession of my cabin on the 'Ophir', where ended my labour for the day.

I visited Cole's Book Arcade where I bought a pair of spectacles for 6d, which suited my vision better than the ones I bought at Maldon for 3s 6d. I returned to the ship which weighs 10,000 tons, and is driven by 10,000 H.P. engine (sic).

I wrote a letter to Mrs Catherine Rees whose late husband I had befriended. She mothered me when I was unwell, and she had wished that I should be buried in her husband's vault, but my wish was, and is, to be buried in Welsh soil.

On the *25th of November* we set sail. This afternoon I placed in the hands of the steward a postal order for £32 and three sovereigns to be locked up during the voyage. The postal order is drawn on Tregaron post office. I hope that on this occasion I shall not be duped as has happened to me so often in the past.

The next day, in a temperature of 105° F, we called at Adelaide.

December
Nearly there

On the 12th we anchored off Colombo where tea and coal were taken aboard.

Sailing in the Indian Ocean on the 16th, and heading for Aden and the Red Sea, which we reached three days later.

Although it is very hot, the climate is tempered by a fair breeze, and my health keeps better than I expected.

On the 23rd we arrived at the gate to Suez, and the following day we dropped anchor at Port Said where the ship took on 2,000 tons of Welsh coal.

On Christmas day we are in a storm in the Mediterranean Sea (not a storm in a teacup as described by Barnard), but a real grim one, through which the 'Ophir' steers steadily, with no discomfort to the passengers, apart from the cold wind when walking on the deck. The ship's double-screw propellers, and twin keels keep her steady.

We have passed some fine ships on the voyage, but none better than the 'Ophir', especially in regard to speed.

On the 30th of December we pass through the straits of Gibraltar, and turn northwards in high expectation of viewing the white cliffs of Dover.

Rwy'n mynd tua Chymru gyda brys,	*(I sail for Wales, proceed apace,*
Heb graig nag awel groes;	*The ship rides smoothly on the wave;*
Ond cyflymach yw fy mrys	*But swifter still, another race,*
Tua'm taith i ddiwedd oes.	*My journey to an early grave).*

On the 5th of January 1895, and the 41st day out of Melbourne, the

'Ophir' docked at Tilbury, London. The voyage out, twenty-five years before, had taken 103 days!

He was met by his two sons, Tom and John, his brother Jenkin, and two friends. His brother inquired of him, 'are you indeed, Joseph?' because the years had wrought a great change in him, from one, sturdy and strong, to a feeble and tired old man. He returned to his home at Trecefel two days later, where he continued to keep his diary until his death on the 26th of September, 1898, at the age of 80.

During those declining years, he found that his old friends in the village had predeceased him, and he gained greatest comfort and solace from quiet walks over the fields he had once so fondly and efficiently husbanded, while he paid frequent visits to his eldest surviving daughter Nell at Tyndomen, and often to his favourite niece (daughter of his sister Jane), Mrs Hugh Williams, of Derigaron.

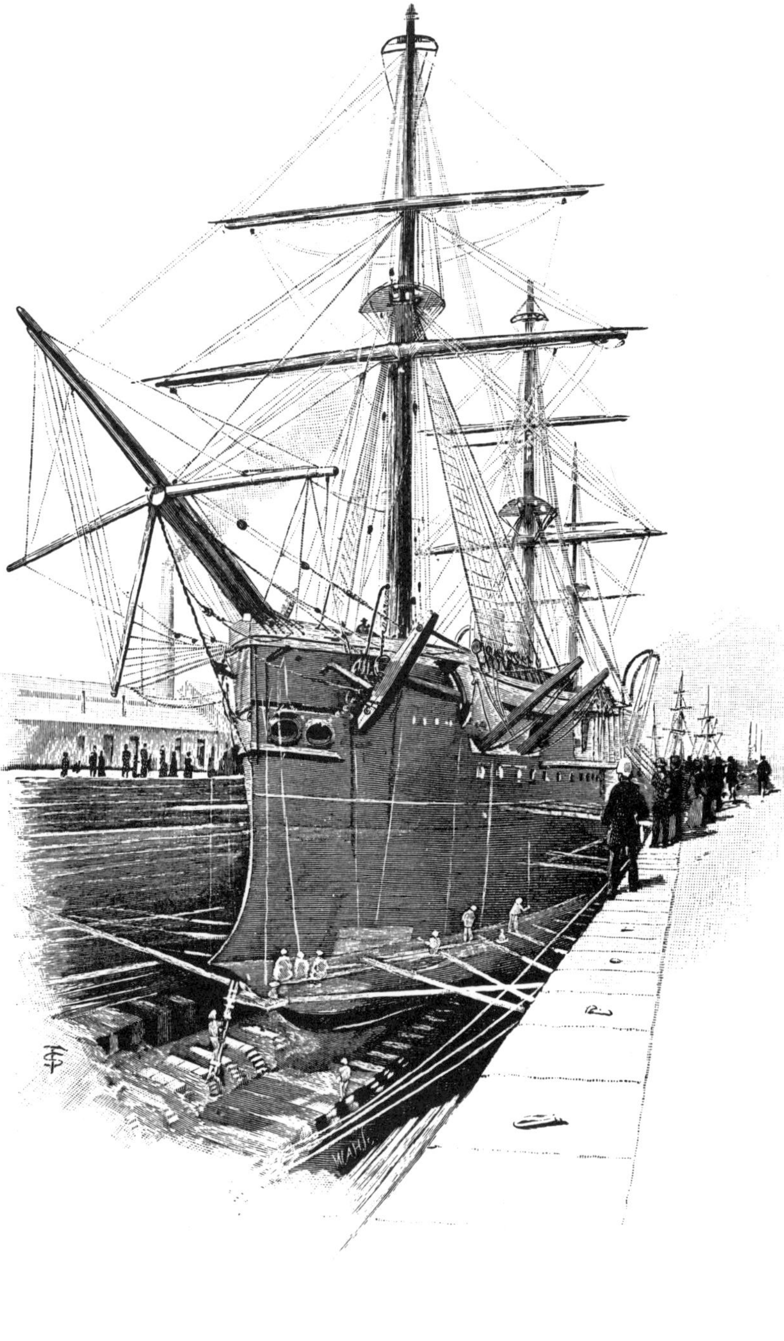